The treatment of indigenous and tribal peoples, the world's largest minority, is a major humanitarian issue. It shapes world history and raises profound questions about what it really means to be human. This book explains who these peoples are, how they live, why governments hate them, and why their disappearance is far from inevitable.

It proposes new definitions of 'indigenous' and 'tribal', and looks at many aspects of their lives, including their attitudes to sex, religion, and money. Concepts such as 'culture' and 'the noble savage' are examined, as well as the impact of big business, globalization, backpackers and the internet.

Easily accessible, the book is a distillation of a life's work. It argues passionately, and controversially, that hunting and nomadism are neither backward nor primitive, but intelligent and conscious choices — and that upholding the law and understanding racist prejudice solves most tribal peoples' problems. It shines a light on the ground-breaking, but entirely unrecognized, contributions they have already made to the world, and exposes the inconvenient truth that their survival is in everyone's interest.

TRIBAL
PEOPLES
for tomorrow's world

A guide by Stephen Corry

A Freeman Press publication

ISBN 9781447424130

Published by Freeman Press
Freeman Press is an imprint of Read Books

Read Books
Home Farm
44 Evesham Road
Cookhill
Alcester
B49 5LJ

All profits & royalties go to Survival International
Survival International (USA) is a 501(c)(3) non-profit organization
Survival International Charitable Trust,
Registered charity no. 267444, London
www.survivalinternational.org

Design: Honor Jolliffe

Cover photos
(top): © Stephen Corry/Survival, 1999. Bushman rock painting, Tsodilo Hills, Botswana. The government removed the Bushman community nearby to stop them begging from tourists.

(in screen): © Survival, 2004. From a Survival film, showing Xoroxloo Duxee, a Bushman woman from Botswana, who died the following year because the government banned the Bushmen from accessing their water.

Contents

Preface

On the same day in 2006 that I accepted the challenge of writing this book, the United Nations General Assembly rejected a 'Declaration for Indigenous Peoples' Rights', sending back to the drawing board a statement that had taken hundreds of indigenous people about twenty years to assemble. (It was approved nearly a year later with four countries voting against it – Canada and the USA, Australia and New Zealand.) The following week the Seminole tribe from Florida paid nearly one billion dollars to buy the Hard Rock Café chain and its unique collection of rock memorabilia. Less than another week later, some five hundred years since its first invasion of South American Indians, Spain agreed to adopt ILO 169, the international law on indigenous peoples, a much tougher instrument than the United Nations declaration.

Probably most significant of all, on the same day the news broke of Spain's new legal stance, judges ruled in the longest and most expensive case ever to appear in Botswana's courts. A few hundred Gana and Gwi Bushmen had fought for four long years to oppose eviction from their ancestral land. To everyone's astonishment, they won against the government, in what was probably the most widely publicized case there has ever been for any specific tribal people. The landmark judgement will affect how tribal peoples' rights are viewed throughout Africa for decades to come.

No one would claim that this was an ordinary month for indigenous peoples: very important things were happening and they increasingly drew the attention of headline writers. What is going on? Why does the world care about the fate of a few hundred Bushmen? How can an Indian tribe, which history books say was defeated by General (later President) Jackson in 1818, buy one of the world's most hip restaurant chains nearly two hundred years later? What do governments fear so much about indigenous peoples' rights that they reject a UN declaration in their support (which is not even legally enforceable) whilst at the same time Spain is happy to sign up to a much tougher law which – at the time of writing – Britain and the United States still reject?

This book sets out to answer these questions and many others about an issue which is at last being recognized as one of world importance. Indigenous people number about three hundred and seventy million individuals and so constitute the largest minority on the globe. About forty percent of them can also be defined as tribal. Although the terms 'indigenous' and 'tribal' are often used interchangeably, including sometimes in this book, there are also important differences. Who are these people? How are they different to 'us', and how are they the same? Where do they come from? What has 'culture' got to do with it? What are their problems? What do they want? Are they likely to get it?

The misconceptions and controversies surrounding them are much better known than the facts. Are they primitive savages, or noble environmentalists? Is their life nasty, brutish and short, or a better one than 'civilization' has in store? Do they threaten the future of the nation-state, or show us the way to save our planet? Are they amongst the most important human rights issues of the twenty-first century, or merely an invention of white people satisfying their romantic longings? How is it possible that in Canada, one of the world's most moderate and law-abiding nations, people get so angry about them that they daub graffiti such as 'Die Indians' on walls? Incidentally, this 'liberal' state, with the mad hatter's logic, imposes a breathtaking condition before negotiating with Indians about land claims: the tribe must agree to abandon its fundamental right to land titles before talks can even start.

Indigenous peoples have international attention, are negotiating with governments and are even taking them to court and winning. However, there is an interesting development at one end of the very wide spectrum which these peoples cover: we know about the existence of far more 'uncontacted' peoples today than we did a generation ago. Almost as fast as some are being wiped out, others are being 'discovered'.

We tend to view our time as one of extraordinary technological achievement and progress. For those of us, usually 'Western' and urbanized people, who enjoy the fruits – as well as the poisons – of this, it is extraordinary to realize that there are about a hundred tribes in the world who have no peaceful contact with anyone else. We tend to make far-reaching and often highly debatable assumptions about the state of the world. For example, we think we live in a digital age of supposed global interconnectivity, but until very recently most human beings would never have made a telephone call. The vast majority of people have still never been in an aeroplane. That is nothing: there are tribes who have never heard of the country they inhabit, let alone the United Nations, who have never seen a banknote, and have no concept whatsoever of homelessness, paid work or prison. Most of what we see as the inventions of the last two thousand years have passed them by, though in fact tribal peoples have been responsible for some key innovations of their own, principally the development of foods and medicines which have changed the course of history and saved millions of lives. So do they need to 'catch up', or is their way of life and view of the world nothing at all to do with being 'backward'?

The book takes a fresh look at indigenous peoples. It touches on myriad aspects of the issue, confronting several sensitive topics along the way which many want to remain buried. It presents the conflicting opinions about the most contentious issues. It is not rooted in distant study, but rather in the real world of indigenous peoples today. Initially commissioned by Oneworld Books, Oxford, as a 'beginner's guide', the work is intended as an introduction, and has no references, footnotes or jargon. I hope that some readers will have their interest fanned, and go on to seek further knowledge of, and so sympathy for, these peoples. After all, some tribes undoubtedly face destruction over the next few years. They need understanding, respect, and help.

Ironically, although tribal peoples' problems are often thought to be intractable – a sort of inevitable, historical imperative driven by 'progress' – in fact they are easily solved. Simple enforcement of their land rights, as well as changing the opinions of ordinary people is really all it takes. This book is an ambitious one and should declare its bias at the start: it is based on the surprising, though easily provable, fact that the more indigenous and tribal peoples are simply properly understood, the less they will be mistreated, and the more they will be respected as both our very close relatives and a vitally important sector of our great human family.

Acknowledgements

This book is in many ways a personal one, and a distillation of forty years supporting tribal peoples. It is based on my own experiences, as well as conversations with many others, principally indigenous and tribal people of course, but also anthropologists, missionaries, government agents, development workers, and so forth. They must number well into four figures, far too many to list or even remember. I have had the immense privilege to work with many talented and dedicated colleagues at Survival International. It is invidious to pick any by name, but without the particular support given to me by Jane Rosenberg, Lucy Howen, Honor Jolliffe, Caroline Pearce, Lucy Arnot, and Kate Holberton I could have done nothing. I would certainly not have written this book, and doubtless another author would have taken a different approach.

I am indebted to many people who commented on and corrected drafts or facts, including Thomas Acton, Alice Bayer, Gordon Bennett, David Beresford-Jones, Clara Braggio, Alastair Burns, Natalie Coates, Chloe Corbin, Joanna Eede, Phillip Endicott, Raquel García, Sophie Grig, Utsa Hazarika, Jerome Lewis, Stafford Lightman, Rupert Manners, Jonathan Mazower, William Milliken, Linda Poppe, Richard Solly, Rebecca Spooner, Chris Stringer, Tess Thakara, Ingrid Turner, Terence Turner, Paloma Varela, Fiona Watson, Phoebe Weston, Miranda White, James Wood, and Jo Woodman. In particular, I would like to thank Hugh Brody and Stephen Hugh-Jones who made numerous helpful suggestions – and especially Kate Holberton who shepherded the book into its final form, improving it a great deal.

I would also like to thank the photographers who waived payment, as well as Clare Brookman for managing the images. I am grateful to Marsha Filion and Robin Dennis at Oneworld Books for, respectively, asking me to write the book in the first place and editing some sections. Although this guide is intended for 'beginners' to the subject, it is hard to imagine anyone will gain more from reading it than I did from writing it. It forced me to examine afresh ideas that have dominated my life, but trying to turn them into effective action has meant there has never been enough time to write them down. I would not have attempted it without Marsha's initial encouragement.

A significant part of what I feel and know comes from the intelligence, companionship and humour of many tribal people. Indeed without their care, on more than one occasion I would not have survived at all. Again, they are too numerous to list but I would nevertheless like to mention Pemba Rinzing Sherpa Lama who, decades ago, accompanied an eighteen-year-old to where neither of us had been before. One of several Damascene moments on that iconoclastic and beautiful journey was sparked by the natural friendliness and cheerfulness of a grubby little herdgirl, high near the glacial moraines. In a way, it was she who triggered the notion that tribal peoples are not children waiting in dumb ignorance to 'catch up' with 'us', but that each has their own unique version of that enchanting genius which is all our birthrights. She was both deaf and mute, and my prayer is that this book will help give a little voice and understanding to the predicament faced by her people and those like them; whether or not it achieves that aim, it can certainly never begin to repay what I owe them.

I could not have done anything at all without the love and support of my late mother, Sonia, my wife, Jenny, and our daughters, Maya, Amie and Tara.

Obviously, I do not speak on behalf of any tribal people, or anyone else for that matter, and, as ever, all mistakes are mine alone. Although all revenue from the book goes to Survival International, it is written in a personal capacity and does not necessarily represent Survival's views.

It is of course up to the reader to judge to what extent the book achieves its aim. The arguments used to defend tribal peoples must be rigorous and convincing, and I would be grateful if those who take issue with any or all, as well as those with factual corrections, would take the trouble to let me know (stephen.corry@survivalinternational.org).

photo credits

Savages
© Victor Englebert 1980 / Survival

Disease
© Antonio Ribeiro

Image
Edward Curtis

Uncontacted
© Gleison Miranda / FUNAI

Killing
unknown

Finished
© Alok Das / Survival

North
© Livia Monami / Survival

Land
© Bob Bartel / Survival

Law
© Louise Gubb / Survival

Hunters
© Andy & Nick Rain / Survival

Nomad
© Stephen Corry / Survival

Language
© Grenville Charles / Survival

War
© Kate Eshelby / Survival

Protest
© Survival

Naked?
© Stephen Corry / Survival

Lobbying
© Craig Ritchie / Survival

Drugs
© Dominick Tyler / Survival

Roads
© Salomé / Survival

Symbol
© David Callow / Sport, The Library

Support
© Stephen Corry / Survival

Who are indigenous & tribal peoples?

Our breathing is the same breath which springs from the world: the air, the winds, and the breeze. All the races of people are equal.

Arhuaco, Colombia

I have never been with anyone who likes to party quite as hard or long as Amazon Indians. All their ingredients are, of course, both organic and homemade: drink; powerful snuff; stuffing your cheeks with fine green coca powder; pulling on cigars as thick as a chair leg. All contribute to a surprisingly clear-headed sense of belonging, of community. Though the drugs are for the men only, everyone is caught up in the party spirit, from infants to the ancient. There are no shy 'wallflowers': unalloyed self-confidence reigns. During such fiestas, it is easy to be moved by the unquestioned importance of the community over the individual, and to realize this was once the common experience of humankind.

A few days before one such party I attended, two Tanimuca Indians in Colombia had decided not to take their pubescent daughter back to the missionary boarding school for the start of term. The students had been having a rough time. The priest was beating them, and much worse. The Indians' decision was quickly challenged: the priest turned up in person to collect the girl, by order, with the local policeman as his backup. The father asked the men to wait by their boat, then quickly returned to the riverbank with both his small daughter and his large sabre-like machete. He stood between the priest and the child and softly said, 'Now, try and take her and see what happens!' The priest left empty-handed. (About a year later he was removed from his mission.)

The few hundred Tanimuca Indians of the Amazon seem to epitomize the idea of a fragile, disappearing tribe. Yet here they were wilfully confronting the power of both state and church. Actually, theirs is an even deeper challenge: it questions the most basic history lesson – the presumed betterment that comes with 'civilization'. It even flies in the face of the much lauded Universal Declaration of Human Rights adopted by the United Nations shortly after the devastation of World War II. This hastily-chiselled tablet concerns itself exclusively with individuals, not communities, and has almost no relevance to those living separately from the state. It even includes a demand which would destroy most intact tribes in a generation or two: that elementary education be compulsory. In fact, enforced schooling is the most powerful weapon used by governments and missionaries to instil in tribal children values which are different, often contradictory, to those held by their own societies.

When it comes to tribal and indigenous peoples, not many issues are universal or straightforward. And amongst the first of these that must be tackled is the question of who they actually are, what makes them different from other peoples, and what makes them the same.

When I have given talks on the issue, questioners who ask, 'What do you mean by tribal peoples?' often turn out to be social scientists. Perhaps only a smart aleck would retort, 'Everyone knows who tribal peoples are. That is… everyone

2

except anthropologists!' But it remains an important question: words are not people, but they can determine what we think about those we have not met. This makes it very important to work through the definitions with some care.

What is a people?

Forget 'indigenous' and 'tribal' for the moment; the first thing is to understand what a 'people' is. Understanding all peoples – where they come from and how they change – can lead to an appreciation of indigenous and tribal peoples. This does, however, require rooting out some prejudices about how and why human beings adapt.

The word 'people' has two superficially similar meanings. The most common is the plural of 'person'. The other, which is our focus here, is 'a people' meaning an identifiable society. This could be used to refer to a nation, for example, so we can distinguish between the Scottish and the Moroccans. This does not just indicate that Scottish individuals are different from those in Morocco, though of course they are: it signifies that the one nationality is distinct from the other. In this sense, 'people' is a singular, not plural, word.

There are usually several different peoples within one country: in Great Britain for instance, there are the English, Scottish, Welsh, and Manx (some would add the Cornish), as well as many relative newcomers from around the globe. Some argue that highlanders and those from the northern islands are sufficiently different from other Scots to make them distinct. Some go further, asserting that those from each individual Scottish island can claim to be a different people.

The arguments presented here depend on accepting that we can all be characterized in this way. Not everyone does believe that, at least not all the time. When Margaret Thatcher famously declared that there was no such thing as society, she meant that the population should be looked at only as individuals, that there was no underlying social fabric which bound them into something which extended beyond themselves. She was talking about Britain, not about indigenous peoples, of course. (Paradoxically though, she was also a proponent of the British as distinct from, say, the French. She certainly did believe there was a distinctive British people, and that is really no different from acknowledging the reality of society.)

Though Thatcher was articulating a perspective shared by some on the political right, a similar view can also be seen on the far left where, for example, solidarity amongst the working class can be considered more important than identification among a people. In this view, a factory worker from Peru shares the most important characteristic – exploitation by capitalists – with a factory worker from Italy, despite their different backgrounds. In the most extreme versions of this belief, their differences might be viewed as just a ploy by capitalists to prevent workers uniting. Similar attempts to deny the real differences between tribal, indigenous, and other peoples crop up repeatedly, contributing to the specific problems that bedevil them.

Extremist views aside, it is obvious that the world's population is divided into countless different peoples. Each has many characteristics – or 'markers' – which both allow the members to identify with each other and act as a signal to others that they are 'outsiders', that is, not from the same society. Most categories of markers are evident across all peoples, and it is necessary to have a clear understanding of how they work and, importantly, where their limitations lie.

One of the most obvious markers is a shared common language, what is articulated through it, and the mediums of expression used. This can range from a written heritage to the telling of stories verbally; nowadays this includes radio, television (often viewed in bars and shops), film and the internet. It is easy to forget that quite a few people in the world who watch television and films cannot read, but this is not unusual. More than eleven percent of the world is illiterate; in some areas, which include some Arab states, much of sub-Saharan Africa, and large areas of Asia, most people cannot read. This is not confined to poorer countries: about one million working adults in London are unable to read with confidence.

Whose Bible?

A consideration of language and stories is a good starting point for exposing a common prejudice and important lesson: we think things belong to us when in fact we have taken them from elsewhere. All peoples, tribal peoples as well as us, do this all the time.

Consider, for example, the Shuar Indians in Ecuador who have stories in their language which they see as their heritage. In the same way, Norwegians have their own literature. Very few, if any, Norwegians know the Shuar language or oral histories; similarly, no Shuar know Norwegian literature. Each people has its own distinctive marker of language and stories.

However, there are also areas of considerable overlap. For example, many Shuar and Norwegians now both know the same Bible stories, certain features of major world news, and something about the same celebrity footballers, film stars, and musicians.

Bible stories are a very good illustration of the fact that both peoples, Norwegians and Shuar, have taken things from outside which they now consider their own. Of course, the Bible originated in neither Norway nor Ecuador and was unknown to the ancestors of both peoples. Religious beliefs are one of several markers which cross many boundaries. Other international crossovers are Hollywood films, pop music and top sport: all are familiar to individuals from many different peoples around the world. Language and stories provide both highly distinctive markers to a people, as well as much which is shared across peoples.

A place of origin

Another key marker defining a people is descent: who an individual's parents and relatives are, and where he or she was born and raised. Some of this marker is based on the town or place of a person's origin. But it arises just as much from a person's 'peer group', because those whom the person spends time with reinforce a particular view of the world, and often lead him or her to find a spouse from the same group.

A person's sense of origin is closely tied to his or her people's story of its origins, and always mixes history with mythology or religion. For example, the American people celebrate Thanksgiving with a ritual feast to commemorate the first hard winter of colonization, though the stories are as much fable as documented fact. Many newcomers to the United States also embrace the ritual, confirming another story of the nation's origins: the 'melting pot' that welcomes immigrants into the country.

As this might indicate, mythology and religion extend into ritual, music and dance and other matters. How people treat their dead is, perhaps surprisingly, one of the most variable of all rituals. There are numerous options: burning them, chopping them up, leaving them to rot, burying them in a special place, or interring them inside the house to keep them close to the living. Amongst the most touching is a New Guinea custom of placing children's bodies in a living tree trunk, 'so they can keep growing'.

Geography and religion can also shape a people's diet, another extremely important marker of peoples. A common refrain in parts of Amazonia is, 'White people eat bread but Indians eat manioc (a root vegetable).' Some African tribes do not eat fish, which are thought to be like snakes. Hindus rarely eat meat. The method of slaughter is crucial for Muslims and Jews but not for Christians. Jews and Muslims do not eat pig; the French eat horse; the British do not; the Chinese, but not Europeans, eat dog. One only has to look at the categories of restaurants in cities all over the world to see the degree to which food is used as an indelible marker of peoples.

Another marker of a place of origin can be body decoration, clothing and, in extreme cases, surgically invasive manipulation such as genital mutilation, or cutting the face or body to produce identifiable scars. This can be as simple as a particular haircut, type of jewellery or dress. Both the Shuar and nearby Waorani Indians in Ecuador wear their hair long at the back. However, until recently a distinctive Waorani haircut was instantly recognizable: it was cut short from well behind each ear around to the front, leaving both the face and ears exposed.

The limitations of 'markers'

The boundaries which define different peoples, separating one from another, are at the same time extremely porous. A good analogy is an individual's skin, which is constantly letting water and chemicals pass through. It is the thinnest of the body's organs – only skin deep! It is elastic, and constantly being renewed as new cells replace dead ones, but it is crucial to the individual's survival. If it is badly torn, it must be repaired or the person will die. So it is with the invisible membrane which defines a people. Ideas, things and even individuals can cross in both directions, but however porous and elastic the boundary is – and both are major components in its strength – it must retain its integrity if the group is to survive as a definable people.

A middle-class Kenyan might read English literature, drive a Japanese car, eat Indian food, wear a Swiss watch, watch American films, drink South African wine, and buy Chinese toys for his children, but none of that brings him any closer to belonging to any of those nationalities, nor does it make him any the less Kenyan. That should be obvious, but the same common sense is rarely applied to tribal individuals. If a Penan hunter-gatherer from Borneo listens to a portable radio, many think it makes him less Penan. This is neither true nor reasonable: every people on Earth takes and uses things from outside its boundaries and always has.

The capacity to adopt and adapt markers from others is so great that a people often falsely claim ownership to maintain their sense of identity. A powerful illustration can be found with the Andoke Indians in Colombian Amazonia. Before their first contact with whites, the Andoke made the best stone axes in the region. So much so that their tribal neighbours did not make their own, but simply traded goods in exchange for a fine Andoke axe. The Andoke thought of themselves as 'the people of the axe', the creators of the very first axes in the world.

In the late nineteenth century, white people brought steel machetes into the Caquetá basin where the Andoke live for the first time. Anyone who has used a stone axe to chop down a tree and then had a go with a steel instrument will throw away the stone one. It is true that flint tools, even from hundreds of thousands of years ago, can be as sharp as a surgeon's scalpel, but the Andoke did not have flint, and cutting down a tree is very different to skinning a deer. Practically overnight, the Andokes' expertise, their very definition of themselves, was rendered futile. The tool they had created and used to define themselves as a people was now worthless. This did not present the Andoke with any economic threat: they did not trade their axes to get anything in particular. However, it did risk shaking their view of themselves.

The Andoke soon found a solution to this incipient identity crisis. The 'people of the axe' had not only created the world's first stone axe, they decided they had also originally invented the steel machete, but that in primordial times the ancestor of the white man had stolen it away. The machete was now simply being returned to those who first created it.

All peoples, from Amazon Indians to Norwegians, are taking things and ideas from other peoples all of the time. Sometimes these are even the markers they consider to be central to their existence, but it doesn't diminish their view of themselves as distinct peoples.

Peoples within peoples

As well as being elastic and porous, the boundaries around different peoples are also like Russian dolls, with one nesting inside a bigger one, in turn lying inside a still larger one, and so on.

The fact that peoples exist within peoples can easily be seen by looking at peer groups defined by age, often called 'age sets'. These include such groups as children, teenagers, and adolescents, parents/adults, and grandparents/elders. Age sets can be distinct in many, and even most, of the markers which identify a people – their language, beliefs, diet, and behaviour. A Parisian teenager, for instance, behaves and speaks very differently when at home with her grandparents, as compared to when she is out clubbing with friends. The differences might be so great that were the grandparents bravely to visit the club, they would be unlikely even to understand the vocabulary in use. The French teenager and her French grandparents would appear to belong to distinct peoples. But such a divergence is not unique to urbanized societies: it is found in many peoples all over the world, and has been for a very long time.

The separation of a people into age sets can sometimes be seen in the 'rites of passage' that serve as a marker of the larger people. Some of these seem to be a simple product of the clash of generations. Older people can find teenagers more than tedious, even dangerous, because they 'break the rules' and appear 'out of control'. Teenagers of course *are* out of control as they seek to detach from parental care. They want to escape what they see as the claustrophobic conformity of the old, as their brain chemistry and bodies undergo the changes leading to adulthood.

Many peoples, though not all, acknowledge this, and institutionalize some separation from teens. Take the Maasai, a cattle-herding people of East Africa. Their male youths, or 'moran', go as far as building their own separate villages, and living according to their own riotous rules, until their age set graduates into married life. They try to flout almost all conventions: they eat hunted meat; they have sex with 'uncircumcised' girls; they even steal cattle. So extreme is their divergence from what the Maasai regard as normal, that the older people sometimes try and get the practice of 'moran' outlawed, despite the fact that it has existed for centuries. Youth will wildly sow its oats, often to the despair of elders. Though it is also true that teenage rebellion is not visible at all in many other societies.

Peoples are also subdivided along gender lines. With regard to women, there is considerable evidence that the weight of childrearing and home-keeping falling on their gender is ubiquitous, and has been so for thousands of years. Conversely, no one has ever come across a people who practice big-game hunting where this was not a preponderantly male pursuit. Such distinct roles create another sense of a people within a people. So much so that it should not be surprising that women – especially – from different peoples can readily find an affinity with each other which leaps frontiers.

This 'division of labour' within a people does not necessarily mean that women are subservient to men. In thousands of societies women possess a forceful voice, and in many they control daily life at least as much as the men do, though it is true that men might not always think so.

In the 1970s, a Peruvian Indian leader travelled to Europe on his first trip overseas. He was protesting against the invasion of his lands by oil companies and was asked at a public meeting what political role the women played in his society. Insensitive to liberal Western sentiments he answered, 'None, they raise the children and tend the garden plots.' His translator was embarrassed by the chauvinism and fudged his interpretation in an attempt to keep the audience's sympathy for the land question. The same point was raised a few days later, but by now the Indian was aware of the sensitivities at stake and he assured listeners that the women were fully consulted.

The speed with which speakers adapt their message to suit the listener is not the point here. The paradox is that the Indian came from a society where the women did actively participate in making decisions; they were probably as powerful as the men. However, the leader was initially not prepared to admit that – even to himself! None of this is to claim that there are only a few societies in which men oppress women: there are clearly many.

No people is uniformly homogeneous. Individuals walk through life with their peers, from one age set to the next, changing their behaviour and language as they grow older. Men and women are often divided, based in part on women's unique ability to give birth, though the divide between them is crossable. Other internal differences arising, for example, from job specialization, class division and disability, are aspects I will touch on later.

One individual, several peoples

Most of us are equally at home in more than one group, putting on identities rather like changing clothes. We do this within the people we belong to: teenagers have one identity in the club and another at home. We also do it by crossing the boundary from one people to another. For example, those with some fluency in another language can sometimes adopt the mannerisms of the people who speak each language when they speak it themselves. The same is true of those who reside in a community or country other than their own, or marry someone from outside.

Indigenous people can be extremely accomplished at the crossing of boundaries between peoples, especially when visiting the wider society. When they venture outside their group they are frequently looked down on as somehow 'inferior', and may defend themselves by merging with those around them, adopting the language and behaviour of others and even going so far as to deny they are indigenous. An Inuit ('Eskimo') woman from Arctic Quebec visiting Montreal or Ottawa might try to cast off all her visible Inuit 'markers'. You might conclude that she is not an Inuit, or had given up her Inuit heritage. Yet on returning to her village on the Hudson's Bay coast, she would immediately resume speaking her language and re-adopt the other characteristics of her people.

One group of tribes around the Brazil-Colombia border, known collectively as the Tucano, enjoy a feature of belonging to several peoples at once which apparently is unique in the world. They consist of more than a dozen different tribes, each one speaking its own language. Each tribe is exogamous, which means that a man cannot marry within his own people: that would be like marrying one's own sister. So he must marry a woman from a different Tucano tribe, speaking a different language to his. The rule seems straightforward, but it means that every married woman is from a different tribe to her husband, as is everyone's mother, and every girl knows she must leave her people to find a husband. In practice it works fine, and everyone can communicate because they all speak several languages as a matter of course.

While we may not all be as good at crossing boundaries as the Tucano, many of us belong to more than one people. Unfortunately, the ease with which a person can adapt behaviour to fit in with another people, even seeming to deny his or her identity when interacting with the wider society, may make it seem as though an indigenous or tribal group is on the wane. But we all want to belong and to be treated well, or at least fairly, by those around us. The fact that indigenous individuals can appear in certain contexts as if they were not indigenous at all should not surprise anyone who has ever been a Western teenager.

All the problems and exceptions of trying to define 'a people' have roundly defeated lawmakers. Although 'peoples' feature in some of the most important international laws, there is no attempt to define them. Instead, the United Nations Covenant on Civil and Political Rights captures the key principle when it begins, 'All peoples have the right of self-determination.' In other words, no people should be subjugated by another. Unfortunately, the text makes no attempt at saying what 'peoples' actually are.

They are one of the most fundamental categories of human beings: everyone can recognize a people in real life, and everyone is a member of one or more. Yet no one can actually say exactly what a people really is without resorting to numerous generalizations which are riven with exceptions.

What is 'indigenous'?

Things are thankfully a little easier when it comes to describing indigenous peoples. As a start, it can be said they are those peoples who were there before others arrived. 'Indigenous' is from a Latin root which gives the words 'gender', 'genitals', 'generation' and 'Genesis'. In other words, it is connected with birth, reproduction, and descent. It means the same as 'native', but in many places that word is not used now because it carries too many negative colonial associations. As a nineteenth century dramatic hero might declaim, 'The natives are restless, better ready the troops!' (An exception, by the way, is in the USA, where 'Native American' became an accepted term for United States Indians in the 1970s.)

The idea of 'before someone else arriving' is easy enough when dealing with the Americas, Australia and the Pacific islands where there were no Europeans, no 'non-natives', until the European colonial expansion began five hundred years ago. So, for the moment I will restrict my definition to such places: indigenous peoples are those who were there before the arrival of European colonists.

That is simple, but immediately throws up a problem. It applies to the past, not the present. European colonization happened many generations ago, and although there is still an expanding colonial frontier, particularly in South America, which is only now coming into contact with some indigenous peoples, most of them have been interacting with the descendants of colonists for several generations, and much has changed in that time.

Referring to indigenous peoples in the twenty-first century is not the same as describing them a hundred years ago, and it will be different a hundred years into the future: neither they nor their situation will be the same.

Regardless of how we define 'indigenous' in a book, everyone experiences our existence as now, not as something in the past. None of us, whether we are the highest-tech of urban entrepreneurs or the most nomadic of hunter-gatherers, live the life that our ancestors did a hundred, let alone a thousand, years ago. Similarly, all societies will live a different life in a hundred or a thousand years from now. Time is like a train never stopping or even slowing, and everyone on earth is in the same carriage. We will always journey together at a constant speed into the future, regardless of the technology and the markers we adapt and adopt (that is, assuming time-travel is not invented!).

When Europeans first arrived in the Caribbean, they were greeted by peoples they mistakenly called 'Indians', since these explorers thought they had arrived in Asia, in the 'Indies'. But, to state the obvious, there are no individuals alive today who were in the Americas before Columbus, or in Australia before Captain Cook. This calls for a refinement of my definition: indigenous peoples are not exactly those who were there before the arrival of European colonists, they are their descendants. And this throws up another problem: to be 'indigenous' must one be entirely descended from the original people? Obviously not. If you are an Australian Aboriginal today, living in an Aboriginal community, speaking an Aboriginal language, and one of your eight great-grandparents was born in nineteenth century Ireland, this does not make you any the less Aboriginal. This is not in fact an unlikely scenario, and the Aboriginal in question may well not even know about his Irish great-grandfather. In fact, in Australia today some define themselves as Aboriginal if they have a single Aboriginal great-great-grandparent – that is just one out of sixteen.

In 1988, an organization of Australian Aboriginals sent an ambassador to Europe to ensure – successfully as it turned out – an Aboriginal perspective in the two-hundredth anniversary of the British 'founding' of Australia. He claimed to include an Afghan camel driver amongst his forebears. Bizarre as this sounds, it is not unlikely: the British had taken both Afghan camels and their handlers to Australia in the nineteenth century to provide desert transport. The camels had reverted to the wild and some of their handlers, ostracized by the racist British, married Aboriginals.

In fact, a significant proportion of indigenous people, particularly in the Americas, are descended from the colonists who took over indigenous lands, or from the Africans taken there as slaves.

Such ancestral mixing means that being indigenous is only partly about descent. It also depends a great deal on one's own self-perception: believing oneself to be indigenous is a significant part of being indigenous. There are even some instances of individuals who are *entirely* descended from colonists and yet they have 'become' indigenous people. In the Americas, for example, there are cases of children of white colonists who have been brought up by Indians and have been assimilated into the tribe. Sometimes the Indians killed the parents who were encroaching on their lands, sparing and adopting the children.

The converse is also true, but this time on a massive scale: for example, in much of Central and South America practically the entire population is descended largely – and visibly – from the indigenous peoples who were there before the Europeans. Many part-Indian Peruvians and Mexicans speak no Indian language, have never lived in an indigenous community and look down on 'the natives', though they are, themselves, part Indian.

In other words, genetic descent is an important feature in defining today's indigenous peoples, but it is far from being the only factor and there are always exceptions. The fact that no categorizations of indigenous peoples are absolute should not be surprising: the same is true for attempts to define any human group, whether Arab, Chinese, African or anything else.

Indigenous peoples – a definition

Indigenous peoples are the descendants of those who were there before others who now constitute the mainstream and dominant society. They are defined partly by descent, partly by the particular features that indicate their distinctiveness from those who arrived later, and partly by their own view of themselves.

No categorizations of indigenous peoples are absolute, except perhaps when it comes to the issue of control. For the most part, the term 'indigenous peoples' is used today to describe a group which has had ultimate control of their lands taken by later arrivals: they are subject to the domination of others. Used in this sense, descent is less important than political perception.

For example, genetic analysis of a nine thousand-year-old skeleton in England called 'Cheddar Man' amazingly found his direct descendants living nearby today. That is a longer period than some American Indian tribes have been on their lands. However, Cheddar Man's descendants are as much a part of English society as anyone. Indeed, prior to the genetic testing they did not even know that a direct ancestor from thousands of years ago came from down the road. They do not see themselves as an indigenous people in the midst of others, because they are part of mainstream society, not under its domination.

This political dimension to what it means to be indigenous is why these peoples are now an important factor in identity movements, the United Nations system and world affairs. But it is a wilful misreading of the idea of indigenous rights to claim, as some contemporary 'nationalists' do, that defending these rights means expelling or refusing entry to immigrants or refugees from elsewhere. The two are not connected. So-called nationalists may argue that their countries are being taken over by newcomers, but this is an irrational fear stoked by racism, since none of the relevant governments, such as those in Europe for example, are dominated by recent immigrants.

It is worth looking at how the law copes with defining indigenous peoples. Law-writers must pay particular attention to the words they choose, knowing that lawyers will spend years arguing about what they mean. There is only one international piece of legislation exclusively about indigenous and tribal peoples, the International Labour Organization's Convention 169.

Its definition of indigenous peoples is a good one: *Peoples in independent countries who are regarded as indigenous on account of their descent from the populations which inhabited the country, or a geographical region to which the country belongs, at the time of conquest or colonization or the establishment of present State boundaries and who, irrespective of their legal status, retain some or all of their own social, economic, cultural and political institutions.*

It goes on: *Self-identification as indigenous or tribal shall be regarded as a fundamental criterion for determining the groups to which the provisions of this Convention apply.*

To count as an indigenous people under this law, the group must retain some of its own 'institutions': it is not sufficient to be an indigenous individual by descent. So even a 'full-blood' Mohawk Indian in the United States who lives like any other American, might still be an indigenous person but that does not necessarily make her a member of an indigenous people. If she participates, for example, in Mohawk gatherings, and is perceived by other Mohawks to be one of them – and if she accepts that categorization – then she would be part of an indigenous people according to this legal definition.

Although the political and legal status of indigenous peoples is usually characterized as a minority issue, these peoples today number about three hundred and seventy million individuals in total – about the same as the total population of the United States and UK combined. Furthermore, through general population growth, ancestral mixing, and self-identification, their numbers are now increasing.

The 'Amish error'

Taking a trip today from New York City to an Amish community in rural Ohio, we can easily trick ourselves into thinking it is like going back in time. The Amish, originally a seventeenth century Anabaptist Christian sect, believe in separating themselves from the 'things of the world'. Many refuse to have cars or electricity, and they dress in styles popular a century ago. Nevertheless, they live in the same year as everyone else and are just as aware of the history of current events as anyone. Some teenage Amish are encouraged to join the mainstream for a few years before choosing if they want to live as Amish adults, or leave the sect. They might remind us of our supposed past, but they are not from it and, if you have no Amish ancestors, they were not part of it either. Apart from some similar technologies, such as using horses instead of cars, any notion that the Amish live as our forebears did is false.

The mistake of assuming that certain peoples live in the past simply because they use different technologies is also applied to many indigenous peoples, particularly those who have a 'tribal' lifestyle. This is so common that it is useful to give it a shorthand name: I call it the 'Amish error', and it will crop up repeatedly in the course of this book.

What is 'tribal'?

Whilst 'tribal' is a more common English word than 'indigenous', it is just as impossible to arrive at any definition of it which is remotely watertight. The etymology of the word does not help: *tribus* is Latin for the three original peoples that comprised the Roman state. That is why it begins 'tri', like tripod or tricycle.

'Tribal peoples' are usually understood as those who have a mainly self-sufficient way of life, largely outside the mainstream of urban nation-states. For example, these peoples – and they are peoples, not simply individuals coming together by choice – hunt, collect, grow or herd most, if not all, their own food, and build their dwellings themselves of local materials.

Tribal peoples – a definition

Tribal peoples are those which have followed ways of life for many generations that are largely self-sufficient, and are clearly different from the mainstream and dominant society.

It is simple prejudice which makes us think that some peoples are 'modern' whilst others are 'backward'. Everyone, everywhere, everyday, is facing choices about what they adopt and how they adapt. Of course some individuals, notably the rich, may be more in control of those decisions than others. Many people do not have the resources to realize the changes they seek, and of course no one has total control: all of us are prey to the vagaries of accident and disease as well as to the inevitability of decaying age and death. Nevertheless, even if everyone had the same resources and abilities, they would still make different choices.

Most people in the Western world, and probably many readers of this book, do make rather similar choices to each other in many highly visible areas – cars, electricity, television – and that can be deceptive because it leads to a belief that there is only one 'right' way forward: the path we ourselves have chosen. Indeed many, probably most, of us are primed by generations of Western education and thinking to believe that non-Western peoples are backward.

When considering these issues, it is vital to keep in mind that this assertion – that there are peoples who choose a different path – must not be taken to mean that poverty itself is a matter of choice. Most people today live with terrible impoverishment and rightly strive to better their lot. This is a very different issue to tribes living as they do because they want to.

It is a crucial point. Critics of tribal peoples' rights often assert that those who support them want the people to remain poor. But that is not what is at stake at all: it is rather a case of trying to prevent people being driven away from self-sufficiency and towards impoverishment by others taking their land and resources. People who are largely self-sufficient may not have much, or any, money, but they have food and housing which they do not have to buy, and this puts them in a much better position than most. This is not confined to tribal peoples: a great deal of impoverishment today is a direct result of powerful, profit-driven markets taking over land, homes and resources.

Returning to the question of who is 'tribal': in the past, all indigenous peoples were also tribal. Of course, everyone was once tribal, though it is just an 'Amish error' to think that this means tribal peoples today are like our ancestors were yesterday.

Some indigenous peoples consider themselves tribal peoples today as well, but would not be so under my definition. This raises the question: if self-identification is a key to the definition of indigenous peoples, why not for tribal peoples as well?

Consider, for example, a group of hippies who live off the land, pursuing a way of life different from mainstream society. This gets them part of the way towards being 'tribal', and they might even adopt the term for themselves. But they are not a people that has been pursuing a separate and identifiable way of life, with its own clear markers, for generations. Perhaps if they maintain their way of life for centuries, growing increasingly apart, they could legitimately argue to be a tribal people if they so wished.

Could those who dwell near the western seaboard of the British Isles and who often think of themselves as 'Celts' claim to be a tribal people under my definition? No, they are not significantly different from anyone else in Britain. They are not members of a tribal people, or an indigenous one for that matter. The Amish do however fit the definition of 'tribal', though not 'indigenous', rather better, but they do not see themselves as tribal people. In this way, self-identification does matter: if a group rejects the categorization for itself, others have no right to press it upon them. A group can choose not to be seen as 'tribal', but must fulfil certain criteria, as described, to fall within the definition. Otherwise, the term ends up meaning nothing.

It is especially in Australia and North America that definitions of tribal peoples can run into problems with indigenous people. The indigenous Aboriginal (the two words mean exactly the same) population in Australia can be seen as comprising two main sectors – 'tribal' Aboriginals, who live in their own rural settlements, and 'urban' Aboriginals, who live around towns and cities. Those who refer to themselves as 'tribal' are likely to speak their own language and follow many of their own beliefs and rituals. There is also usually a significant state presence in their communities: government employees administer development projects, run schools, handle welfare grants, and so forth. Many Aboriginals receive a state income and appear dependent on its provisions. They therefore do not comply with part of the definition because they cannot be considered largely self-sufficient, or 'tribal' in the sense I am using the term. Many share the same problems of 'urban' Aboriginals, such as diseases associated with poverty and high levels of imprisonment. A similar situation exists in the United States, where many indigenous people live somewhat separately from mainstream society, on 'reservations', which are lands reserved for them by the American government.

The fact that, at first sight, 'tribal' Aboriginals or United States Indians do not seem very self-sufficient takes them outside my definition of tribal peoples. We should however be wary of assuming they are necessarily as dependent on outside assistance as they appear. They take the handouts, but many also hunt and fish and come together for rituals and story telling, often more than observers think. If some unimaginable catastrophe severed their contact with the outside world, they would doubtless fare better than non-Aboriginals, and readily find their living in their surroundings.

Of course, to categorize individuals in such a rigid way, as either 'tribal' or not, is an enormous over-simplification: there are countless gradations. But if neither Western hippies nor many North American or Australian 'tribes' fully fit the definition, who does? The answer is an estimated one hundred and fifty million individuals worldwide, about forty percent of indigenous individuals, as well as a few thousand others who are not indigenous to the areas where they now live.

The International Labour Organization Convention 169 also makes a distinction between 'indigenous' and 'tribal', though it defines 'tribal' peoples much more broadly than I have.

According to the convention, tribal peoples are: *Peoples… whose social, cultural and economic conditions distinguish them from other sections of the national community, and whose status is regulated wholly or partially by their own customs or traditions or by special laws or regulations.*

As you can see, this makes no mention of the need for any degree of self-sufficiency, nor necessarily any historical basis for the people. Both of course are unquantifiable: how 'self-sufficient' does a group need to be, to be 'tribal'? One hundred percent? Sixty percent? And who decides? For this reason, it can be argued that the legal definition fails to have much meaning, as it is so broad that almost any group which lives differently could fit it. For example, the urban poor in Western cities have 'conditions (which) distinguish them from other sections of the national community', and many could be said to have their own customs, though obviously, they do not identify themselves as tribal, or indeed as a distinct people at all. Because my purpose is to understand rather than merely to define, I believe the proposed description I have provided, which insists on 'tribal' involving both historical basis and some self-sufficiency, is the more useful one.

Mistaking 'tribal' and 'indigenous'

Before going on to look at how indigenous and tribal peoples overlap, we should defuse two irrelevant uses of these terms: the way 'tribal' has been used in Africa, and the way 'indigenous' has been used recently in North America and Europe.

At the time of colonial expansion, Europeans used 'tribe' to describe all the thousands of distinct African peoples, including those which were largely urbanized and reliant on trading and markets as extensive and complex as any found in Europe. Some of these peoples were very powerful and dominated their weaker neighbours. They made up the mainstream society in their region and several still have populations running into tens of millions. Describing such peoples as 'tribes' is now viewed as a pejorative legacy of colonialism, and it is true that Europeans did reserve the term for those they thought 'primitive'.

On the other hand, many Africans believe themselves to belong to a 'tribe', a people to which they are tied more strongly than they are to their nation state. This is a similar, though often stronger, sentiment than that held, for example, by those Scots who see themselves as Scottish rather than British. This is not surprising: when they arrived, the Europeans imposed borders on the continent in order to claim ownership and simplify their rule. These borders ignored the real frontiers between peoples, and so made little sense to the indigenous peoples. Hundreds of ethnic groups were thrown together in a number of vast countries, or divided between two or more. The largest country drawn in this way, Nigeria, incorporates at least two hundred and fifty different peoples and, with its one hundred and fifty million souls, has a population far larger than any European nation. As the colonial empires were forced out in the twentieth century, their imposed frontiers sowed catastrophe, with several so-called 'tribes' striving for either domination or survival, and pitting themselves against their neighbours.

This high level of ethnic diversity in African countries creates problems for those trying to promote patriotism towards the nation over and above allegience to these 'tribes', which we might more properly call 'ethnic groups'. Those keenest on national unity are, not surprisingly, national governments, which are often controlled by members of the dominant 'tribes'. They may be powerful elites who already enjoy the support of their own people, a loyalty commonly nourished by their conferring favours on their kin. They do not want their power challenged by other ethnic groups, and so identify their own group as the nation to which all must vow allegiance. The government of Botswana, for example, regards criticism of it as 'unpatriotic'. In this ideology, patriotism is promoted as love for the government and the elite, rather than for the country and its peoples.

Governments everywhere downplay the fact that almost all countries are inhabited by several different peoples. At the same time, they emphasize and exaggerate the distinctiveness of their nation as opposed to others. In this way, governments try to control the 'right' to be different. The Kenya government, for example, promotes the distinctiveness of Kenyans as opposed to Tanzanians, but rejects the distinctiveness of the Maasai and other different peoples within its frontiers.

In Africa, favouring one's own 'tribe' over and above the nation is called 'tribalism' and is viewed with extreme hostility by rulers, although they commonly practise it themselves. A president of Kenya was not alone in describing it as a 'cancer'.

This is a complex and controversial issue affecting hundreds of millions of people and generations of history; it remains a catalyst for many bloody conflicts. However, it is not the subject of this book. In spite of the indistinguishable names, African 'tribalism' is nothing at all to do with tribal peoples as defined here: those which are largely separate from the mainstream of national society and are invariably minorities. The thirty million or more Yoruba, who form much of the dominant society and ruling class in Nigeria for example, cannot possibly be described as a tribal people in this sense.

A separate issue, already touched on, concerns those in America and Europe who try to claim 'indigenous rights' for themselves. In this, 'indigenous' is often code for 'white skinned'. Recent immigrants – many 'non-white' – are said to be a threat to the jobs and security of the 'indigenous' population. This of course has nothing in common with the lives of true indigenous peoples, who are ruled and dominated by others.

There is one people in continental Europe, the Sami, who fit the definition of indigenous, and I will turn to their situation later.

Indigenous, tribal, both?

There are two reasons why it is important to grasp the definitions and distinction between indigenous and tribal, which is why I have gone into it at some length. One is simply to help understand the issues. As a 'minority', the three hundred and seventy million indigenous individuals amount to six percent of the world's population, and they are made up of a very broad spectrum of groups and individuals. There is little that an uncontacted tribe in New Guinea has in common with millionaire casino-owning Indians in New England, although both are indigenous. The second is that tribal peoples face a different raft of problems. While the number of indigenous individuals on the planet is growing, that of tribal individuals is shrinking and some peoples today face total disappearance.

It is impossible even to guess at how many different indigenous and tribal peoples, as opposed to individuals, there are. The question, 'Are the Scots one people or more – highlanders, lowlanders, islanders, and so on?' can be applied to practically every people on Earth. It may be impossible to answer, but it is still a good question. One way of approaching it is to ask how many indigenous or tribal languages there are, for this is of course a central marker of a people. This only helps a little though, as many tongues have lots of variations and so numbers here are rather arbitrary as well. It is reckoned that about half of humanity's remaining six thousand five hundred languages are each spoken by fewer than three thousand individuals. Most of these minority languages can be safely assumed to be indigenous, as are a further one thousand five hundred languages used by a larger number of speakers. Equating languages and peoples is far from exact, but these numbers indicate that whilst fewer than six percent of the world's individuals are indigenous, it is probable that fifty to seventy percent of the planet's peoples (based on their tongues) are. Many of these peoples are also tribal.

So however difficult to prove with numbers it may be, it is likely that of all the various lifestyles on the planet a majority, even today, are different to the dominant industrialized society. This flies in the face of the deeply ingrained assumption, held by many, that there is only one way to live. In fact, once away from the 'beaten track', different ways of life are common, though most travellers may not experience them because the infrastructure which caters for their needs is very similar all over the world. The many different lifestyles found away from the tourist routes and sites should be a clear challenge to those who think that it is not only desirable for everyone to live like industrialized Westerners, but that everyone really does want to. The truth is simply that not all do.

The problem of culture

You may have noticed that, apart from one unavoidable reference when quoting the law, the words 'traditional' and 'culture' have not yet appeared in this book, despite the fact that both figure very large in the popular view of indigenous and tribal peoples. This is deliberate: both terms are loaded with prejudice. They are often assumed to mean something that is static and unchanging, and so point to the past. This is wrong: culture is simply the pattern thrown up by the characteristics which indicate that one people is distinct from another – our markers. Culture is changing all the time; sometimes visibly and fast, sometimes and in some places the differences are more hidden or slow. Every people is constantly changing, just as they always have, and just as they always will.

The desire to characterize culture as something backward-looking and superficial is commonly used by governments seeking to dominate and control. For example, theatrical displays of folkloric music and dance might legitimately have their place in a community's sense of its history, but they are also heavily promoted by governments trying to confine culture to formulaic stage acts rather than daily life. This is a sensible strategy for the bureaucrats and politicians because culture's ever-changing nature makes it innately subversive to government control. By pretending culture is a theatrical mask, rather than a living face, governments try to render it lifeless.

Real culture is not a dead mask. It is alive, but not like an organism which is born, grows old, and then dies: it is more like the weather, which is always there and never disappears and can show a thousand different aspects in the course of a day or a year. None appear from nowhere: each derives from the last, and each leads to the next. No two 'weather moments' are alike.

To take the metaphor further, the relationship between a people and its culture is rather like that between a large mountain and the weather it creates. As the great mass of the mountain changes the airflow around it, it can provoke rain and wind, or drought, which would not otherwise be the case if the land were flat. The western seaboard of the British Isles is wet because the hills push the Atlantic Ocean winds upwards. The Tibetan plateau is dry because the Himalaya forces the monsoon clouds to drop their rain to the south. If the mountains and hills were not there, these weather patterns would not appear. Similarly, if a people is not there, the culture is gone. The mountains are never without their own weather which changes every day; no people is without its culture which also changes with time. The mountain weather depends on and interacts with distant weather, so too a people and their culture interact with others with which they come into contact.

The effect is also reciprocal. The southern slopes of the Himalaya are furrowed by the rain the mountains draw from the clouds; the northern watershed is dry and eroded only by the wind and cold. The mountain makes the weather which, in turn, shapes the mountain. A child is born into his parents' culture and is subject to its norms, though he will also begin to adapt and change those norms, especially when parenthood arrives. Thus, the weather shapes the mountain, carving the rock with rain and wind, and the culture shapes the people, guiding their behaviour and expectations. In this way, it can also be seen that culture may be always changing, but it does not necessarily evolve into something better, any more than the weather does; not all cultures are equally beneficial or kind to human beings, any more than the weather is.

No open-minded student of history could possibly conclude that the passing of time leads inevitably to an improvement over what has gone before, yet that is the belief which underpins, at least in part, the assertion that industrial society is more advanced than others.

In summary, we all belong to one or more distinct peoples which give us our identity. We can often change this identity, but cannot escape having one. It is as important for our wellbeing as our health or intelligence. Indigenous peoples were there before others arrived. Defining them is difficult, like defining most human categories. With a very few exceptions, all tribal people are indigenous, but the category of 'indigenous' also includes many who are no longer tribal.

So why are there so many peoples, living and thinking in so many different ways? This question can be approached from many angles – environmental, genetic, psychological, and so on – and there is no simple answer. But even the sketchiest view of prehistory, and how human beings come to be where they are now, is a good place to start looking.

Genesis and exodus

Yes, from beginning to end, every tribe has a different knowledge and there is a story about how we become involved with each, become relatives.

Wandjuk Marika, Aboriginal artist & actor, Australia

By tracing human prehistory we can begin to understand the origins of today's indigenous peoples, as well as all peoples on the planet, because in many ways we are – or at least once were – one family. However, it is not without dangers, because referring to 'ancestors' and indigenous peoples in the same breath risks thinking that today's tribal peoples are more backward than those of us who live in industrialized society. In fact, whatever our way of life or view of the world might be, we are all exactly the same number of generations removed from our Stone Age forebears. The fact that tribal peoples travelled a different path does not make them inferior, less intelligent, or backward.

So where did we all start? If we step back some six million years we would encounter a species of ape, now disappeared, which was the ancestor of chimpanzees and bonobos as well as – probably – all the several different humanlike creatures the world has seen. Running time forward again, a number of distinct creatures evolved from that animal, some becoming increasingly humanlike as time passed, others remaining apes. Of the latter, two have survived, evolving into our nearest animal cousins, the chimpanzee and bonobo. No one knows how many humanlike species, called 'hominids', evolved. We have found remains of at least fifteen; there were certainly others, but most eventually disappeared. One hundred thousand years ago, which is not long in evolutionary terms, it is likely there were still at least four humanlike species in existence, and we know that at least three survived until the recent past, some twenty to thirty thousand years ago. At that time two of them died out, leaving just one – us – to walk into the present. To distinguish our own species from all these others, anthropologists use the technical term 'modern humans'.

One of the best known hominid species to die out has a bearing on indigenous peoples only inasmuch as their popular image, as primitive dimwits, is close to many racist views of tribal peoples. The Neanderthals or *Homo neanderthalensis*, inhabited Europe and parts of Asia for about four hundred thousand years, far longer than modern humans have been in existence. After our modern human ancestors arrived in Europe, the two species shared the continent for thousands of years until the last Neanderthal died, and no clearly Neanderthal remains found so far date more recently than around thirty thousand years ago (which does not of course mean that they disappeared then). No one knows why they died out – although there are several theories, none seem particularly convincing.

In 2010, when scientists were able to analyze Neanderthal genetic material, or genome, for the first time, the results were sensational: a small percentage of everyone of Eurasian descent is Neanderthal. This means that on one level Neanderthals did not become completely extinct after all, as they may well have interbred with our modern human ancestors. Their tools were about as efficient as ours, their brains were roughly the same size, and there is no compelling evidence that they were any dimmer than we are. They were hardly unsuccessful as a species, surviving a great deal longer than we have so far. (Though, if we go back far enough, remember we share the same origin as Neanderthals.) If we are still around in the year 300000 AD and then die out, Neanderthals, not us, will have been the most successful human species on the planet – though there will presumably be no one around to care.

The other recently extinct species of humanlike 'people' was discovered in 2003 on the Indonesian island of Flores. The remains of just a handful of these one metre-high, half-size creatures have been found. Called *Homo floresiensis*, and nicknamed 'Hobbits', the remains seem to date from around seventeen thousand years ago – more recent than Neanderthals – but there is no evidence that this hominid interbred with modern humans.

The Hobbit discovery shocked evolutionists so much that it would be wise to allow for the possibility that there were other human species in the recent past. In 2010, for example, a finger bone and tooth from Siberia pointed to yet another human species, nicknamed 'Denisovans', living there alongside Neanderthals and modern humans within the last fifty thousand years. It even appears that this hominid also contributed genes to living humans – this time to the people of Australasia.

Scientific analysis doubled the number of known recent human species, from two to four, in the space of just six years, making it much more likely that there were others, perhaps many others, as yet undiscovered.

Our own species, which we grandly call *Homo sapiens* (wise man!), is generally reckoned to have originated in Africa. At one time, perhaps one hundred and fifty thousand years ago, the total number of individuals was probably only a few tens of thousands, the population of a town today. Amongst these thousands was one woman who is a direct matrilineal ancestor of everyone on the planet. She was my, and your, mother's mother's mother's – and so on, for thousands of generations – mother. Everyone alive today is descended from those few first modern humans. As I said, we are from one family, at least in this sense.

On many occasions, bands of these people crossed out of Africa into the Middle East and then either returned home or died out. Then, sometime around sixty thousand years ago, a group left Africa, perhaps to the north of the Red Sea, or over the Bab el-Mandeb strait at its southern end, and settled on the Arabian-Asian side. Amongst this band of a few thousand was one woman who, by chance, is the direct matrilineal ancestor of everyone in the world who is not African. Every Australian Aboriginal, Amazonian Indian, Papuan, Chinese, and European is related to her – and to me – by a shared maternal descent. This line also appears in Africa, where it is most common in the east and north.

This successful exodus from Africa, which led eventually to the first colonization of the planet, would not have seemed momentous at the time. Even if the southern route were taken, the sea crossing of the Bab el-Mandeb, the 'gate of tears', would not have been difficult. There is an island halfway across the strait, and water levels were much lower then than they are now; even today, the widest sea passage is a mere fifteen kilometres.

It may seem surprising that the descendants of these few bands of humans simply walked all the way to Southeast Asia, as well as through Siberia, into Alaska, and on down to the southernmost tip of South America, but it is not really that extraordinary: they had a great deal of time. They probably largely followed the coastline with its never-ending supply of fish, shellfish, and edible sea plants, and if they advanced at even only a mile a year their descendants would have arrived in Australia some twelve thousand years later. It is not unlikely that this was indeed their average pace, as it is now reckoned that the Aboriginals' ancestors may have first turned up there about fifty thousand years ago. From examining gene mutations it has been calculated that the journey from India to Australia probably took around five thousand years, again about what one would expect at one mile per year.

There is no need to invoke any yearning for adventure or exploration in this creeping migration. A twenty-minute stroll, or paddle, each year along a safe coastline, where dangerous animals can easily be avoided, is hardly striding into the unknown. Nor is there any need to wonder at the difficulties of sea crossings, most of which were short. The longest was probably the last, to Australia, but even this was only about one hundred and fifty kilometres. Trees could have coped – particularly the very buoyant bamboo lashed into rafts, or dugout canoes, though the first people to step onto an Australian beach would doubtless have been more than relieved to touch dry land. It is not unlikely that they were really heading for a closer, known destination but found themselves swept off course.

These first colonists spread over the Eurasian landmass, inhabiting almost every corner, from the tropics to the icy north. Much later, perhaps as recently as fifteen thousand years ago, though some anthropologists believe it was earlier, another great crossing took place: people walked over the exposed land bridge across the frozen Bering Strait from Siberia to Alaska and set foot in the Americas for the first time. The isthmus would have been only some eighty kilometres long and, as with the Red Sea exodus from Africa, no one would have had any sense of going somewhere 'new'. They would not have even been aware which was the footfall which took them into the Americas, but it was the first step of a long walk, probably mixed with journeys by canoe. It led the ancestors of the thousands of tribes of American Indians all the way south, from the Arctic tundra through the forests of Canada and the United States, the deserts of Central America, the rainforests of Panama and Amazonia, all the way to the frozen tip of Tierra del Fuego. Where they chose to settle in this extraordinary variety of environments was to shape their way of life over the following generations.

Between one and three thousand years ago, seafaring tribes perhaps from around Korea and Taiwan spread across the Pacific, inhabiting many hundreds of its islands. On the other side of the world the Vikings sailed to North America around a thousand years ago, and rowed up countless rivers into the heart of Europe and Russia. When their longships landed in Greenland in the tenth century, the island had already been settled by humans from the Americas for at least three thousand years, and Inuit tribes arrived on the island at around the same time as the Vikings. Their meeting could be seen as the first encirclement of the globe by humans – the 'completion' of our sixty-thousand-year journey out of Africa. These latter sea crossings were extraordinary odysseys: they must have implied really adventurous commitment, leaving only Antarctica and some islands free to the animals and birds.

This sketch is the outline of human prehistory as it is currently known. The new sciences involving extracting genetic material from humans – both the living and prehistoric remains – and comparing similarities and differences, are largely confirming the story. It would be foolish to think that there will be no surprises as further evidence is uncovered – such as the recent discoveries of 'Denisovans' in Siberia, and 'Hobbits' in Indonesia. In fact, there are already some tantalizing anomalies. For example, a few palaeontologists think that a jawbone with modern human features found in southern China could date from before the presumed exodus out of Africa. Would that mean our species originated in Asia, not Africa, after all? Or could we have originated in both? Discoveries of ancient remains in North America are often inconclusive, unsuitable for genetic analysis and sometimes appear to be more European than Asian in origin. Could that mean 'white Europeans' arrived first? A very ancient discovery in South America might look more like an Australian Aboriginal than a Siberian. A problem is that such 'evidence' is based on very scant remains. Scientists chasing research funds are not always shy of media attention, and journalists can be eager to grab headlines and trumpet sound bites as definitive results. The combination can sometimes lead to extrapolations and press reports that stretch beyond sober reason.

Questions about where our ancestors come from, and who was where first, run much deeper than mere science, and play an important role in the human need to belong, which seems as necessary to us as food and shelter. Religious and political beliefs are often underpinned by these questions, and notions of race, often unfortunate ones, are usually not far behind.

The problem of 'race'

The word 'race' may derive from the Latin for 'root', though this is not certain. It is commonly used to refer to people in two different ways. One is simply as an alternative to the human species: in this, we are all members of the same 'human race'. The second is to describe the various physical types by which we can all, fairly obviously if also problematically, be divided. These categorizations depend largely on skin colour, hair colour and texture, and eye shape. For example, most peoples of Southeast Asia, including the Chinese and Japanese, have distinctive, almond-shaped eyes. They are produced by a piece of skin, called the epicanthic fold, which may be a means of protecting the eye from intense light or – probably more likely – could simply be a result of preference in sexual attraction. The epicanthic fold is also shared with the Bushmen of Africa.

The names of different 'races', such as 'Caucasian', Asian, African, American Indian, and so forth, continue to be used today, but in fact, when their genetic background is examined, many people are surprised to find they have 'mixed' ancestry, and science can now prove that there is no such thing as a 'pure' race.

As well as being tied to ideas of belonging, the concept of race is also crucial to notions of one group's assumed superiority over another, which is, of course, the definition of 'racism' or 'racialism'. For example, the Chinese authorities go to some lengths to deny any suggestion that ancient human remains discovered in their country may show more 'Caucasian' characteristics than Chinese ones: they want China to have always been 'Chinese'. Similarly, Indians in the United States are hostile to any idea that ancient remains might be of people who looked different to themselves.

Indigenous and tribal peoples are not the only ones who see themselves as originating in their homeland, the idea is very common indeed. The prehistoric migration from Africa, the fact that all were once colonists – with the sole exception of our original ancestors in Africa – is ignored.

This rejection of a scientific view is widespread of course. A significant minority of Americans believe in their literal interpretation of the Old Testament's Genesis story: according to them, God created Adam and Eve one day about six thousand years ago. These are beliefs and myths, like any creation story. They are unquestionably powerful and real, and can even ring true, but they belong to a different level of reality and truth than science. How tribal peoples treat myth, and realize that several apparently conflicting realities can all be valid, is a topic I will touch on later. For the moment it is worth noting that most of the apparent conundrums of human settlement can find answers in scientific prehistory, even if some do not like the conclusions.

We are all descended from a small number of humans. Our species was clearly in Africa one hundred and fifty thousand years ago, and probably evolved there. Over the last sixty thousand years it spread throughout the world, perhaps occasionally interbreeding with other human species, forming thousands upon thousands of peoples, or tribes, which grew to view themselves as distinct from their neighbours. These migrations left a pattern that remains today, as some stayed close to lands they settled a very long time ago. Their descendants form today's indigenous peoples, though the term is only used now for those who are no longer the dominant force in their homelands, as I have explained.

As these small tribes moved through Asia, some settled in India, the Andaman Islands in the Bay of Bengal,

Thailand, Malaysia, the Philippines, Indonesia, New Guinea, Australia, and probably elsewhere. Most of these have long disappeared, merging into one another as the population grew, but the few black tribes which remain in those countries – as well as the Papuans and the Australian Aboriginals – may well be largely descended from these first colonists. So are all of us who are not Africans of course, but the difference is that the black tribes have probably remained separate from others, whilst the rest of us have become much more mixed up.

Some anthropologists use the word 'negrito' ('little negro') to differentiate these black tribes (apart from those in and near New Guinea and Australia), but it is surely time to consign that term to the dustbin. I will coin 'black Asians' in its stead, though with some misgivings as it too unfortunately emphasizes skin colour as the defining characteristic, with many of the problems of race I have described. However, as this is the most obvious difference between them and others, particularly those with copper-coloured skin who spread from the Middle East into Asia and the Americas, I can think of no sensible alternative.

Sometimes black Asians remained separate because of geographical isolation. As sea levels rose, island hopping became harder. The Andaman Islands, for example, became cut off and remote, and the peoples who had settled there stayed put. At their peak, they probably numbered only a few thousand. The descendants of those who survived British and Indian attempts to 'civilize' them over the course of the nineteenth and twentieth centuries are still there today, a population of a few hundred. No one knows, or is ever likely to know, why the Semang of Malaysia, the Mani of Thailand, and the twenty-nine or so black tribes of the Philippines, retained their separate identities. As the millennia passed, many individuals undoubtedly left these groups to be absorbed into other peoples, to the point where their distinct genes were effectively lost. Some individuals from outside the tribes would have joined them too. But even today, these black tribes may well be largely made up of direct descendants of some of the first people out of Africa.

Perhaps they live in a fairly similar way to the first colonists. The Andaman tribespeople thrive on fish, turtles, dugongs or sea cows, from the sea, and boar, small mammals and birds, and vegetables and fruits which are plentiful in their forests. As their environment has probably not changed much in millennia, it might well follow that neither has their way of life.

This poses an apparent dilemma for those, like me, who argue that tribal peoples today should not be equated with our ancestors: they are not backward but have simply developed in a different way. The Andaman way of life, based on fishing, hunting and gathering probably *would* be at least partly recognizable by our joint ancestors of, say, fifty thousand years ago, whereas that of city dwellers today would seem very alien. All this is, however, just a further manifestation of the 'Amish error'. These tribal peoples use their intelligence and skills, honed and passed down over generations, to gather everything they need in order to live well. It is impossible to know how much the way they live now is similar to the way their ancestors lived. All we can say is that this is the way they choose to live today – and that they, like other tribal peoples by my definition, are largely self-sufficient. How they achieve this comprises the largest part of how they define themselves.

Life-giving land

Why does the government think they are more important than the people? The government just wants to take all our good things, like a poor fellow who sees a rich man, and is jealous and wants to take what he has.

Mogetse Kaboikanyo, Kgalagadi, Botswana

We need few things to live: water and food; some shelter; and the sense of purpose and fulfilment from relationships. So it should not be too surprising to learn that the most important characteristic by which tribal peoples, as well as social scientists, define their differences is in how they get food. Tribes are categorized into a handful of food-getting baskets. There are hunter-gatherers, pastoralists, and agriculturalists. The rather oddly named 'shifting cultivators' are peoples who move their vegetable plots every few years; they are often hunters as well.

Although these terms are a necessary shorthand, and are usually determined through conversations with the people actually acquiring food in these ways, they are also loaded with prejudice and misconceptions which need to be stripped away. One is that although a people may see themselves as 'hunters', 'herders' or 'crop growers' – designations they take very seriously indeed – the terms are, in reality, far from absolute. The activities involved vary widely, from extreme mobility and reliance on wild game, to seasonal perambulations and dependence on herd animals, to permanent settlement supported by farmed crops and herds. But there is also a good deal of overlap: Bushman hunters might also keep goats; Amazon hunters also grow crops; East African herders also hunt at certain times.

It is widely thought that everyone was a 'pure' hunter-gatherer until agriculture was developed in the Middle East. This is said to have revolutionized the way people lived, greatly improving living standards for those who adopted it, and eventually giving birth to 'civilization'. Such a simplistic rendition of the human experience is integral to the notion that tribal hunters are 'backward'. In reality, it is the idea itself which is out of date: it is simply wrong and in need of urgent demolition.

Whilst it is true that once upon a time everyone relied on hunting and foraging, there was certainly no 'discovery' of agriculture. Hunter-gatherers do not just gather edible vegetation they happen to come across, they also encourage useful plants to grow near where they live and are likely to have done so for a very long time indeed. The first plants cultivated near habitations were probably not for food at all. The bottle gourd vine is a prime candidate; there is simply no easier way of obtaining a fine waterproof receptacle, and you can even eat its flesh. It is possible that the plant originated in Africa. If so, early humans may have taken it with them more or less everywhere it could survive as they spread across the globe.

Encouraging the growth of plant foods would have occurred in one form or another many times in prehistory, repeatedly adopted, dropped and re-adopted with changing environmental conditions. This was far from confined to the Middle East: it happened in many places, perhaps almost everywhere humans settled. The 'full' domestication of plants – which involved crossing their seeds to get crops which were more plentiful or nutritious – also occurred in many other parts of the world that we now know about, and almost certainly others as well. Finally, what we fundamentally think of as agriculture – a reliance on the major staples (maize, rice, wheat and barley, potatoes, sweet potatoes, manioc/cassava and taro) – came much later than the first cultivation of these plants and it coincided with what seems to have been a deterioration in the quality of life, exactly the opposite of what is usually thought.

The evidence found in bones and teeth points to an increase in child deaths and a decrease in average longevity where farming gradually supplanted hunting and led to a population expansion. A sedentary life, with soft foods to wean babies, and youngsters able to work in the fields, meant women produced more children, even if they were smaller, weaker, and died younger. People suffered more from dental disease and osteoporosis, and also began falling ill from the bacteria and viruses carried by farm animals. As many tens of thousands started living close to each other, these illnesses turned into deadly epidemics. For the first time, people caught measles from their cows and influenza from their ducks and chickens, originally bred from Asian jungle fowl. Their crops, herds and flocks were also susceptible to disease and people were less able to evade this by moving and adapting. In addition, they needed to store larger quantities of food and so risk it rotting or being stolen. They had to guard their resources much more seriously than before. Paradoxically, their food supply may have been *less* reliable than that enjoyed by most hunters.

Over the millennia, some hunting peoples may also have fared badly of course, perhaps failing to survive changes in their environment, such as lower temperatures or rainfall. Nevertheless, the idea of a hierarchy, with 'backward' hunters and 'advanced' farmers, is largely a colonial myth, used to justify the theft of tribal territories. The colonists claimed to know how to use the land 'better' than the 'primitive' hunters who had always lived there. With all this in mind, it is time to examine what each of these lifestyles entails.

Hunter-gatherers

By the simplest definition, a hunter-gatherer tribe gets its food by hunting wild game, including fish, and collecting plants that have largely grown 'naturally', without being cultivated. Some tribes from the far north of the Americas, the Inuit, are classic examples. Their men hunt for seals, walrus, whales and caribou, as well as catch fish. Because it has not been possible to cultivate crops in the Arctic, the women supplement this animal stockpile by gathering a wide variety of berries and other wild plants, including seaweed. These once provided all their food, fuel and almost everything else they needed. (Nowadays, of course, they also eat shop-bought provisions, but I will confine my descriptions largely to the time before such stores were widespread.)

At the other temperature extreme, in hot and dry climates, live hunter-gatherers such as the Kalahari Bushmen, Australian Aboriginals, and Indians of the South American Chaco. Their men hunt the largest animals they can because, as is obvious, they provide the most meat. These might be giraffe and antelope in Africa, kangaroo and emu in Australia, and deer and armadillo in the Chaco. The tribeswomen collect seeds, wild berries and fruits, and dig for underground tubers.

Hunter-gatherers are also found where it is warm and wet, in the forests and grasslands of Amazonia, the Orinoco, the Caribbean and Pacific coasts, Central America, North America, Southeast Asia, and West and Central Africa. The men hunt for birds, animals and fish in the sea or rivers, and the women collect the forest fruits, nuts and tubers. Many there are shifting-cultivators as well as hunters, growing a wide variety of plant foods. Amazonia contains many examples of how different societies can rely on hunting but still vary from small, highly mobile peoples with no permanent dwellings at all, through to those who live in large – sometimes huge – houses or settlements which remain in place for generations.

These are the broadest distinctions, but there are hundreds of exceptions. For instance, many Australian Aboriginals are likely to have lived near the coast before being pushed inland by colonists; they relied heavily on seafood and some still do. Parts of Australia are covered in rainforest, and tribes would have lived there too. Similarly, some southern African Bushmen are river dwellers, relying largely on fish rather than desert game.

The hunt

What is universal to hunters is the importance of the hunt itself; it is about far more than merely finding food. When anthropologists have calculated the amount of time different peoples take to complete all the productive activity needed for life, the total for hunting and gathering came to only about twenty hours per week for hunter-gatherers, far fewer than for other ways of life. However, a good hunter does not view it as work which must be done, but as one of life's supreme accomplishments. Hunters love hunting.

Mostly highly skilled, the hunt consists of moving close enough with sufficient speed and silence to ensure the strike is deadly or, alternatively, patiently lying in wait in the right spot. Inuit hunters need immense patience; having found a breathing hole in the ice, they can expect to wait there barely moving for hours. They then strike immediately and with great speed before the emerging seal realizes the danger and dives to safety.

Hunting weapons include the spear or harpoon, often with spear-thrower, bow and arrow, blowgun, club, or, nowadays, shotgun or rifle. The blow itself might be aimed as much by sound as sight. To do this successfully means the hunter must have an extraordinarily well-tuned understanding of the game animal. He has to predict accurately its movements and habits. He needs to know where to start looking, and to recognize the subtlest of signs, whether tracks in the ground or its smell on a leaf or in the air. He has to hear and interpret an animal's sounds from a distance, recognizing what they mean. A hunter may mimic a predator to frighten it towards a fellow hunter or copy the call of a female animal in heat, to attract males. Some Amazon Indians can imitate a hurt monkey, drawing others who approach to see what is wrong.

Great ingenuity is usually required. In many cases, the weapons used lack the force to kill on their own: they rely on poisons. The invention of the blowgun, for example, shows a remarkable leap of imagination.

The blowgun projects a sliver of a dart, thinner than a knitting needle, towards its target. The idea originates, obviously enough, with a hollow reed which can shoot a projectile a metre or two with fair accuracy. However, to turn this child's toy into a device for killing birds and monkeys high in the rainforest canopy requires several steps, each more impressive than the last. Firstly, the weapon needs to be long enough to project the dart with precision. Amazonian blowguns can be longer than two-and-a-half metres, and are made from two pieces of the hardest wood found. The bore is chiselled out of each half, firstly and roughly with a stone knife, or nowadays steel machete, and then polished down with sand so that it is as straight and smooth as the world's most expensive shotgun. If it is not straight, it will not be accurate. Once bored, the two halves are bound together. The hardwood dart is sharpened and fletched with natural cotton wool. When placed in the mouth end of the gun, a sudden, explosive breath will project it an easy ten metres or so – enough to reach the tops of the trees.

So far so good, but by itself the dart is unlikely to kill. It is too light to have momentum, and can pass straight through an animal without inflicting significant damage. To render it lethal, the dart's tip is coated with the famous 'curare', a favourite poison of crime novelists. Unfortunately for their plots, but not for the hunter, it is not particularly fast acting. A mix of different plants is boiled down to thick glue, smeared on the darts and left to dry. As it enters the blood of the smitten bird or animal, it relaxes their muscles. Monkeys can no longer hold branches and birds can no longer fly. They must be tracked as they move off, but eventually they drop to the ground where they can be collected and killed. You might think that a quicker-acting poison, saving the effort of the final chase, would be an improvement. But curare's weakness is an asset: the darts, which are silent, can be shot at several monkeys before the troupe notices the effects and realizes it is under attack. Tribesmen hunting with a noisy shotgun can only fire once before everything flees. Most importantly, meat killed with curare is not poisonous.

Many Amazon tribes also fish by crushing plant poisons, commonly called 'barbasco', in the water and then following the cloudy residue downstream. Barbasco stuns the fish, preventing their gills from working. They are not killed by the toxin, and will recover and swim away as it dissipates. The Indians simply pick the fish out of the water as they succumb and float to the surface. It is a communal activity, involving women and children as well as men, and is enormous fun, providing an opportunity for much joking and gossip. Streams can be fished periodically without exhausting the food stock and the Indians are well aware when it is time to stop and wait for full recovery. The Yanomami in Brazil recognize over twenty different plants that may be used in this manner.

Poison is not only found in Amazonia. It is crucial to many other hunters, including the Bushman in the Kalahari. The desert provides only short and weak staves of wood for bows which have little power and only a short range. When used on an antelope, let alone a towering giraffe, the arrow will penetrate just a few centimetres. It acts really only as a carrier for a poison, in this case usually made from beetle larvae. Although this is stronger than Amazonian curare, a struck Kalahari antelope is still capable of running many kilometres before becoming too weak to escape. The Bushman must follow with sufficient haste, sometimes for hours, even days, to prevent other predators stealing the meal.

Hunting involves creativity and innovation, but it also has its rules. For example, Bushman bands in the Kalahari have strictly defined territories. If they find themselves pursuing stricken prey into another's land, they should seek permission before proceeding, even though this would never be denied and might be a rule observed more in theory than in reality. One of the most elegant regulations is found in some parts of the rainforest where everyone must give away his catch, only eating what others provide. From an economic viewpoint this makes no sense: why bother to be a good hunter if you never benefit from your own skill? But of course you do gain, through enhanced prestige. The excellent hunter, who provides the community with the most food, may eat only the paltry catch of his less competent friends, but that is a small price for everyone's respect. He is not the only one to gain. The health, wellbeing – and consequently security and confidence – of all society's members are enhanced. Nothing goes to waste: when there is a lot of food it is, in a way, 'invested', not only in the stomachs of each man, woman and child, but most importantly in their appreciation of each other. (Not all men are equally good hunters and those who are rotten may be subject to mild ridicule, especially from the women. If it is hoped this will make them improve, it does not always work!)

A hunting tribesman combines the skills of master craftsman, consummate athlete and astute strategist. Learning how to do this can take more than a lifetime. Boys accompany their fathers from an early age and spend many hours listening to the men transmit knowledge built up over generations. In my experience no outsider has even begun to approach the hunting skill of a tribesman. In Colombian Amazonia, an anthropologist colleague spent years learning to hunt. He tried, but he knew he would always remain out of his depth and he failed to bring home a single kill.

Animal-lovers who find hunting unpleasant will be heartened by the intimacy that hunting tribes display towards animals, both through their knowledge of animal behaviour and through their belief. The attitude of many tribes to pets is a good example. Rainforest peoples in particular keep hundreds; monkeys and birds are the most common. When animals are killed, leaving live babies, the creatures are often brought home, raised as companions, and never eaten. I once came across an adult tapir, the size of a Shetland pony, kept by an elderly Amazonian woman. It was so attached to its mistress that it would follow her everywhere, even swimming behind her canoe. Some tribal women suckle baby animals if they are too young to eat by themselves.

The hunt itself is often conceived as happening on a 'spiritual' as well as a physical level. Game animals are highly respected as the sustainers of human life and a common feature is the notion that the hunter comes to a kind of 'agreement' with the hunted animal. It is a sort of trade, rather than simply making a kill. I describe this idea in more detail later.

The hunting environment is not without its dangers, both physical and spiritual. Even for a previously competent hunter, the expedition can become a source of fear. Some Inuit in Greenland recognize a state, 'kayak angst', which can affect even the bravest. Attacking a large sea creature, such as a whale, from a flimsy kayak is dangerous, and after some years even the experienced can find their 'store' of courage beginning to run dry. Kayak angst is recognized as a spiritual ailment, one that can render a man shore-bound forever.

Hunting is not only the pursuit of an animal with a weapon. There is evidence that large mammals, such as North American bison, were once caught by driving herds over cliffs. This of course would have resulted in a huge amount of food and, even though many tribal peoples know how to preserve meat by smoking, drying, salting, or freezing, it is obvious that such practices were intrinsically wasteful, except of course that the Indians would have believed the huge bison herds to be inexhaustible.

It is possible that the largest mammals in many places were hunted to extinction thousands of years ago, perhaps sometimes using the same cliff-fall method. Herds of mammoths used to roam Europe, North Asia and America, until they became extinct, largely about twelve thousand years ago. Australia and South America were also once home to much larger mammals than survive today. The cave paintings in France and Spain – some of the oldest representational art yet found, as well as amongst the most exquisite – are clearly linked with hunting, and depict mainly mammoth, bison, deer, horse, ibex and the extinct European ox, called auroch. This creature was much more massive and dangerous than its probable descendant, the farmyard cow. Perhaps it is not surprising that prehistoric Europeans were happy to hunt it to extinction. (They did not quite succeed: the last auroch died in a Polish forest in the seventeenth century.)

Gathering

Although lacking some of the danger and adrenalin of the hunt, gathering requires no less skill. It often involves larger numbers of people and, as with much communal activity except war and politics, is more the domain of women rather than men. Men are hunters and women are gatherers.

As part of the common rivalry between the sexes, men believe hunting is much more important than gathering. A hunter may even restrict the definition of 'eating' to mean eating meat. I have been with unsuccessful hunting parties of Amazon Indians, when all the men were devouring copious amounts of manioc whilst at the same time repeatedly and morosely claiming they had 'eaten nothing' for days. In fact, it is not unusual to find separate words for 'eating' in the languages of hunter-gatherers – one for meat, another for everything else. In Inuktitut, the principal language of the Arctic, the word 'niqi', means 'meat' and with additional suffixes means 'food' in general, as well as 'eating'. Eating implies meat.

Nevertheless, most of the hunter-gatherers' diet actually comes from gathering, not hunting – which has prompted some scientists to invert the name to 'gatherer-hunters'. The Ka'apor Indians in Brazil are known to collect at least one hundred and seventy-nine wild food plants, as well as cultivating more than thirty species. Such large numbers are not unusual.

The variety of foodstuffs supplementing the hunt is not restricted to plants. Gatherers also forage for honey, insects, larvae and shellfish, whilst smaller animals, such as lizards, frogs, small rodents and birds, are trapped or dug out of their lairs. This is just as well, for in some parts of the world, including much rainforest, plants contain little protein: vegetarian Amazonians would be lucky to survive. Women's gathering, in other words, is the most vital source of food – despite what the hunter, himself, might claim.

It is perhaps in the 'gathering' part that the 'discovery' of agriculture is most clearly revealed not to be the great leap that is usually portrayed. A hunter-gatherer tribe also manipulates the landscape and builds up an immense knowledge of the vegetation in its territory. The tribe knows exactly where it can find fruits in season, and will revisit these sites repeatedly, often for generations. New growth is encouraged, perhaps casually, but no less effectively. Young fruit trees are carefully left to mature, for example. Some Kalahari Bushmen make a point of putting the seeds of the 'wild' melons they eat in places where germination and growth are likely. They may not then tend the seedlings as they sprout, but the Bushmen are perfectly aware that by not throwing seeds on the fire, they are assisting a natural process from which they will benefit. Who is to say that the melon is really wild and found by foraging, rather than consciously grown?

Herders and nomads

Herders, or 'pastoralists', usually live largely from the milk-products and meat provided by their animals. Cows, goats, and sheep are the most common stock, but there are others: camels in Africa and the Middle East; horses in Central Asia; reindeer in northern Europe and Asia; and llamas and their relatives in South America. Many such animals have the useful feature of being able to be ridden, or draw carts or sleighs, so extending the geographical spread of the tribes which use them. In fact, the spread of nomadic peoples turns another assumption on its head: although we think of great empires as essentially a Western creation, the largest land empire ever seen was forged in the thirteenth century by the horse-based tribes of Mongolia. This was so vast that genetic evidence suggests that one in every two hundred men now living on Earth is directly descended from its famous founder, Temüjin or Genghis Khan.

Herders are often called 'nomadic' or 'semi-nomadic'. These are terms which aim to define the amount of time the tribe spends in one place before moving: semi-nomadic peoples up sticks less often than nomadic ones. Incidentally, when I use the word 'nomad' it is with some misgiving. Like 'hunter-gatherer', it too is loaded with assumptions, conjuring up a vision of random wandering which is entirely wrong. A better term might be 'mobile'. The levels of mobility are particularly apparent when describing herding peoples, who usually travel a seasonal circuit, going to where the pasture is best. They revisit the same locations annually and may keep dwellings at each, to await their arrival. They are likely to spend months in each place – far from a wandering existence. Most hunter-gatherers are more mobile, often spending only a week or so in a camp before moving on. Their peregrinations are also often weather-dependent, going to where the game or food gathering is likely to be better.

These movements may appear random to outsiders, especially in the tropics where there is little or no difference between summer and winter. But nomadic peoples do not generally travel without knowing where they are going. They revisit old campsites and know exactly where they are in relation to rivers, stands of trees and other features of the environment. Bushmen, for example, move over a large area, but do not wander about aimlessly. As discussed above, each clan has a precise territory which may be unmarked but is nonetheless respected by neighbours. Territorial knowledge is incredibly detailed: Bushmen know, and often have names for, individual trees and bushes, as well as undulations in the terrain; they know exactly where their individual ancestors are buried, and consider their whole territory to be their home.

Westerners, including many social scientists, still commonly think of a hierarchy, with 'backward' hunters and 'advanced' farmers. Hunters and herders do not agree. African pastoralists like the Maasai of Kenya and Tanzania look with disdain on 'mere' growers of crops, even those who provide the maize flour the Maasai buy and depend on (a plant developed, incidentally, by Central American Indians). A commonly held fiction, usually intended to shock, is that the Maasai also live off blood drained from living animals. It is true that cattle blood is occasionally used in this way, mixed with milk and maize porridge, but it is usually only resorted to in times of scarcity. Maasai cows and goats are considered too valuable to weaken in this manner; even slaughter is relatively rare, usually taking place only when there is a good excuse, such as the arrival of an important visitor or a festival.

Herds not only provide food: bones are used to make artefacts; skins are turned into clothes, bags, and housing; guts are stretched into rope and stringed onto musical instruments; hooves are boiled for glue, and so on. Even dung can make both an excellent fuel and building material. North American Indian hunters famously used every part of the bison, and Inuit use every bit of their seal catch. Many African herders today similarly make use of every part of their cows.

Animals and plants for the human condition

The argument that humans discovered a more 'advanced' way of life by learning how to domesticate animals and plants some eleven thousand years ago in the Middle East, leaving today's hunters behind and backward, can easily be proved false, beyond the general principles already outlined, by looking at when and where the domestication of animals and plants developed.

Hunters domesticated animals. The first species to live alongside man was almost certainly the wolf. Its descendant, the dog, claimed its place at the hearth well before agriculture; and it remains the best hunting assistant today. Hunting dogs can track, sometimes make the kill unaided, and protect against dangerous predators. American Indians can become as affectionately close to a good dog as can any Briton. I was once in an Indian house in Amazonia when it was flattened by a freak storm; the only fatality was a favourite dog. The death was greeted with a long and repetitive lament which recounted the animal's skills with heartfelt affection, acknowledging the tragedy for what it was.

If hunters domesticate animals, from dogs to pet birds and monkeys, then is the difference between them and farmers one of impact on an environment, where hunters leave their places 'wild' when farmers change the land to their will? Stone Age farmers certainly felled forever the forests of northern England about five thousand years ago; the 'natural' beauty of England's moors and hills actually results from man-made deforestation. In the Philippines, astonishingly complex and extensive ancient terracing was built by indigenous farmers in order to grow crops on slopes too steep to support agriculture. All around the world farmers have dramatically changed their landscapes.

The evidence reveals, however, that this, too, is a false dichotomy: many hunting tribes also change the land, sometimes radically, to suit their needs. For example, an emerging theory is that Australian Aboriginal hunters cleared parts of the continent by burning undergrowth and grassland; a practice that is routinely used all over the world to improve productivity. Regular burning encourages new growth which attracts much game (and, incidentally, prevents catastrophic forest fires).

Fire is also used to clear tropical vegetable gardens in 'slash-and-burn' cultivation. It is the most efficient way and, in spite of the hostility it engenders amongst some conservationists, is not environmentally damaging at all, at least not when carried out by indigenous peoples who know how long to leave the land between clearings, and who have been cultivating like this for generations. Smaller trees are felled and left to dry before they are put to the torch; this clears the bigger trees and bushy vegetation, returning many nutrients to the soil at the same time. Vegetables, fruits and root crops are then planted in the clearing. The ubiquitous tropical manioc, also known as cassava or yuca (which is nothing to do with the cactus-like plant, yucca), is the easiest to grow; a piece of stem is cut from a living plant and simply pressed into the earth and ashes; it roots in a few days and starts producing edible tubers only a couple of months later.

Planting can be highly sophisticated. The Jumma peoples in Bangladesh, for example, put a mix of seeds in each hole so they can collect different crops in different seasons. Scientists used to think that slash-and-burn plots were abandoned for new ones when the soil became too poor to support further growth, but in many places the primary reason is actually because it becomes easier to fell a new plot than to weed an old one.

Most tribal vegetable gardens are small, perhaps a hectare or less, and can appear so natural that untrained eyes can miss the fact that they are man-made, seeing only less dense patches of native forest. Botanists can distinguish between zones where vegetation has grown back over abandoned plots, differentiating this 'secondary forest' from places untouched by human intervention. To a trained eye, secondary forest does not begin to resemble wild primary forest for decades. To the most trained eyes of all – tribal people themselves – plots which were abandoned generations ago are still easily discernible in the midst of the forest. Experts are now suggesting that even huge tropical forests, such as Amazonia, have been inhabited for so long that every bit of them has been cleared at least once. If they are right, almost none might be totally 'natural' at all.

Few of the world's landscapes have not been altered by the food-producing activities of peoples – hunter-gatherers, herders and farmers alike. All have applied a range of complex strategies to ensure the land provides food and shelter. Agriculture does not hold any unique status in this.

Further proof that hunters were not 'left behind' by the 'discovery of agriculture' is to be found in many places. Hunter-gatherers and agriculturalists often live in close proximity, and pursue their different ways of life not out of ignorance but out of choice. One of the most beautiful examples comes from northwest Amazonia where two 'types' of tribes reside. The multilingual Tucano live by the rivers, are expert canoeists, build large communal houses, and have a rich 'material culture' – an anthropologist's term meaning they have a lot of things. The Tucano hunt and gather wild plants, but also cultivate, clearing the forest and growing many kinds of vegetables which form the bulk of their diet. The other distinct group of tribes nearby consists of numerous bands of nomadic peoples, loosely called Maku. These do not build houses at all, but live in small temporary shelters before moving every few days. The Maku have no canoes, preferring to live away from rivers in the forest interior, and are true hunter-gatherers. If the Tucano vegetable gardens mean they enjoy a 'more advanced' way of life than the hunting nomads, as prejudice might dictate, why have the nomadic tribes not simply copied them and 'caught up'?

This would be very easy to do because the nomads know exactly how the Tucano grow crops, and how they build houses and canoes for that matter. In some places, individual Maku join the longhouse-dwellers as long-term guests, living with them for months at a time. Both types of Indians know that neither is interested in permanently adopting the alternative way of life. They simply prefer their own. They exchange things with each other on a constant basis, though not out of necessity: the Maku provide meat and the Tucano give crops. This does not stop the Tucano from thinking the Maku are 'uncivilized', though they respect their neighbours' superior knowledge of the forest. The Maku, on the other hand, have no sense of inferiority, they think Tucano ways are fine for a few months 'cultural exchange', but decidedly limiting and not the best way to live. This mutual lack of appreciation, even in those cases where a people depends on another, is not unusual. Many who live today without intensively cultivating crops, like the Maku, know how to do so, but choose not to.

In Borneo, most of the nomadic Penan people have, since the 1950s, been settled by the state government and Christian missionaries, a process accompanied by the introduction of large-scale commercial logging of the island's forest. As thousands have been shifted from a mobile life to one based in villages, most have seen their self-sufficiency eroded. Those few hundred who have successfully resisted and remained on their lands as mobile hunters think themselves far better off as a result. They are not alone: settled Penan also lament the loss of their nomadic way of life and the forests which sustained them. They continue to hunt as best they can, and also grow a few crops but without much enthusiasm; they claim they do not really know how, but demonstrate little inclination to find out.

The disparagement of hunting and the elevation of agriculture are rooted in the idea that all of our ancestors were once hunters and then some adopted a supposedly 'more civilized' life – agriculture. Yet, over the millennia, hunting tribes have adapted to changing climates and developed a repertoire of tactics and tools, from the technology of poison to the control of plants and animals, that probably bear little resemblance to the way prehistoric peoples lived ten thousand years ago. Prehistoric peoples left very little behind for us to find, but a Stone Age hunter, chasing large mammals in the icy forests and plains of northern Europe for example, would find very little in common with today's Amazonian or Southeast Asian hunter, picking off birds and monkeys from the rainforest canopy with poisoned dart or arrow. So, the fact that Europeans are descended from Stone Age hunters does not imply that the Amazonian Indians or Kalahari Bushmen can be meaningfully likened to our ancestors.

The crop-growers

As we have seen, the divide among hunting, herding, and farming is not as clear-cut as is usually presented. Many farmers hunt to some extent, and many people gather wild foods. In parts of Europe today, wild mushroom picking remains a vital part of the economy, for both the family dinner plate and commercial exploitation. In Botswana, when the government asserts that herding is more civilized than hunting, the Bushmen retort that the wild antelopes are not so different from the farmers' cows, just more reliable, much less susceptible to illness, and no work to manage.

There is, however, one obvious difference between

hunters and agriculturalists that will be familiar to anyone who has lived with both. Hunters are often capable of consuming huge amounts at a single sitting, and then happily go for days eating very little. This is just one of several tribal practices which would offend nutritionists. A more dramatic example is the consumption of inherently poisonous foods. One of the most important of these is manioc, which, like the potato, was developed by South American Indians – one of these peoples' most valuable, but generally unrecognized, contributions to the world economy.

Manioc grows in poor soil and is little bothered by drought, making it an ideal crop. The hundreds of different varieties eaten are cultivars, which means they were developed over many generations through deliberate and selective crossbreeding. This human intervention went so far that some varieties cannot now reproduce naturally: they must be planted by man – or, more likely, woman. The root is broadly divisible into sweet and bitter types, but both are poisonous. Sweet manioc can be carefully peeled to remove the toxins, but the bitter varieties must be subjected to a longer preparation to ensure that their cyanide content is extracted. The root is soaked for hours, after which the juice must be carefully squeezed out, and the residue cooked into a form of flour or flat bread. Get any step wrong, and the food can kill. Many Amazonian tribes eat either the bitter or the sweet manioc, but rarely both. Most grow dozens of different varieties of their preferred type; the Tucano alone cultivate over fifty.

So, if both sorts of manioc are cultivars and have been deliberately bred since antiquity, why didn't the early Amazonian farmers simply breed out the poison? Some scientists think that the reverse may have actually happened: the bitter type was selectively bred to make it more, not less, toxic. If true, this shows remarkable foresight. Properly prepared bitter manioc provides more starch than the sweet type, but it carries another advantage: the root is less vulnerable to being eaten by pests and animals. The processed food is also easier to store and transport because the dried flour will keep for months longer than sweet manioc. Hunters travelling with just a bag of manioc flour and their weapons can survive for weeks, even if they find no game at all, and these are indeed the only things a hunting party normally takes with them on their expeditions.

Another important cultivar is maize, which also brings nutritional problems if not prepared with indigenous knowledge. Horrific and deadly pellagra epidemics swept through large parts of the Americas and Europe when it was first eaten outside its Central American homeland. The disease, caused by a vitamin deficiency, was first described in Europe in 1735, but it took two centuries for Western medicine to identify its cause. The Indians who first developed maize soaked their crop in an alkaline solution of ashes or mineral lime, releasing the vitamin and an amino acid in a form which can be absorbed by the body. Untreated, maize's essential nutrients remain locked up and inaccessible. If the colonists had learnt how the Indians prepared their maize, who knows how much suffering would have been averted?

Manioc and maize were developed in hot climates, but the potato was domesticated in the colder weather of the Andes at least five thousand years ago. There is even some disputed evidence of its cultivation stretching back nearly as far as the 'discovery' of agriculture in the Middle East. Thousands of varieties of potato exist, and over one hundred cultivars may be grown in a single Andean valley. The Indians also invented a means of storing potatoes through freeze-drying, creating what are called *ch'uñu*. This can be preserved for months or even years. Unless properly cooked, many potatoes too are poisonous, though not as toxic as manioc, and it was not until the late nineteenth century that they began to be more widely accepted as a food outside South America. Despite their relatively recent arrival in the West, potatoes are now so routinely eaten that their provenance has mostly been forgotten.

The two root crops developed by peoples indigenous to South America are great sources of carbohydrates, and their cultivation has saved countless people throughout the world from starvation. Manioc and potato each provide the staple diet for about a billion people, and potatoes are now the fourth most important crop in the world, after maize, rice, and wheat.

Most hunter-gatherers have a diet far more varied than any agriculturalist, or any European or North American for that matter. About eighty percent of the world's population relies on just a dozen plants for food, but it is reckoned that no less than an astonishing thirty thousand species are consumed in total, mostly by tribal peoples. A single hunter-gatherer tribe routinely consumes hundreds of different foodstuffs. One, however, is often absent: non-human milk.

In parts of Amazonia, the Indians copy the colonists and keep some cows. These can be sold for cash, but are otherwise not much use. The livestock tend to wreck vegetable gardens and often fall sick. It would be more rational in economic terms if the Indians at least drank the milk, but they do not like it. Some peoples lack the enzymes needed to digest dairy produce – a condition called lactose intolerance – and it could be that the facility to process lactose developed only in populations which have raised dairy animals for generations.

This begs the question: why did anyone bother to keep cows or other herd animals in the first place? There are two other factors, already noted, which make this an especially interesting occurrence: early farmers contracted a whole raft of diseases from their livestock, and they spent much more time working for their food than hunters did. Yet there is one significant thing which agriculture *did* permit that hunting and nomadic herding did not: it enabled the growth of larger and more permanent populations. The development of irrigated crops and domesticated livestock lay behind the origin of towns and cities, as well as the armies needed to defend and expand them. Cities need agriculture, though their citizens may not actually perform the hard work: prior to mechanized harvesting, food was usually provided by an exploited underclass of slaves, serfs, or peasants.

Humankind's genius is found everywhere, but everywhere it is different. The Arabs preserved the mathematical knowledge uncovered by the Ancient Greeks, and then refined it further, so enabling the much later development of electronics; the British built steam engines which gave rise to the complex machines of the industrial age and radically shaped how most of us live today; and Indians in the Americas created foods that today feed much of the world's population. If the prospect of life without computers or engines seems bleak, then what about one without potatoes or tomatoes?

Electronics and complex machines are, of course, inconceivable without numbers, yet some tribes live perfectly well without them. In fact, the least mathematically inclined peoples of the world – many hunter-gatherers in Africa, Asia, Australia, and the Americas – find a counting system of 'one, two, many' perfectly adequate. Others might go as far as five. The tone used to express 'many', and the word's repetition, can indicate variations between 'just a few' to 'a lot'. They might not be able to count, and can find the notion hilarious when they first encounter it (I have often lain in my hammock listening to Amazonian Indians count endlessly in newly-learned Spanish, accompanied by much laughter), but few visitors have been left in any doubt as to their intelligence.

Tribal peoples have technology; it is just not machine-based. Nevertheless, it is sophisticated, and has served and supported them almost everywhere on earth, enabling them to thrive in an enormous variety of environments. These include many now characterized as 'hostile' by those dependent on industrial goods or services, but which are, or were until recently, the comfortable, life-giving homelands of countless tribal peoples. Almost no one thinks his own place is hostile.

Before looking at who they are geographically, it is important first to note the complications surrounding the names given both to particular tribes as well as to peoples in a wider sense.

What's in a name?

We were the first people of this Apoh area. The waters did not have a name then, not until we gave it a name in our language.

Ayan Jelawing, Penan, Malaysia

Tribal and indigenous peoples' names, even the ones they use for themselves, are never straightforward. They are subject to varied spellings: for example, the Waorani and 'Huaorani' in Ecuador are the same people. Names are often altered after contact: the Panará in Brazil were commonly called 'Kreen-Akrore' before their first encounters with other Brazilians in the 1980s. The name 'Mohawk' for an Indian people of North America bears no relation to the several names they use for themselves, and its origin can only be guessed at.

More often than not, indigenous peoples do not have any word to describe themselves, or have only adopted one recently. Most originally just called themselves 'people' or 'those who speak our language', using a different term for their neighbours. These were often derogatory.

For example, until recently, the Waorani called everyone else *cowode*, meaning 'cannibal'. They included in this insult their Indian neighbours, such as the Kichwa. Waorani wrongly thought that all non-Waorani were cannibals, but the insult was also reciprocated. Outsiders called the Waorani tribe 'Auca', a word meaning 'naked savage', which was once used for any little-contacted Indians in that part of Amazonia. It could have originated with an Andean Indian term, meaning 'enemy'. The word is still employed in parts of Ecuador to refer to anyone, particularly children, who are thought to be a bit wild, including one of the capital's football teams, the Aucas!

The neighbouring Kichwa Indians do not call themselves Kichwa at all. They commonly take the name of their village, and add the word 'runa', meaning 'people'. For example, Canelos-runa are the Kichwa-speaking Indians who live in and near the village of Canelos.

A name change, as in 'Auca' to Waorani, following increasing contact with a tribe and its growing ability to articulate its own feelings to outsiders, is common. So are changes introduced by anthropologists who might be unhappy with the names or spelling used by previous visitors. Perhaps the best known example of this is Inuit, the most usual term nowadays for the peoples formerly called 'Eskimo'. Inuit is employed as their own name for themselves throughout most of the Arctic, though is not used as much in Alaska and Siberia, partly because a more technical definition of Inuit excludes some Alaskan natives. At the root of the original rejection of 'Eskimo' was the idea that the name was derogatory and meant 'raw meat eater'. Although still widely believed, it is in fact more likely that it means simply, 'those with a different language' and was never really insulting at all.

A larger problem hangs over what to call the indigenous peoples of the Americas, as practically every term is thought objectionable by someone. Some US Indians adopted 'Native American' in the 1970s, but it is rather less used now. Similarly, some Canadian Indians favour 'First Nations'. But, in reality, most Indians in North America see no problem calling themselves 'Indians', referring to themselves both as 'nations' as well as 'tribes'.

Interestingly, both words in 'American Indian' derive from mistaken identity. 'America' was probably named after a Florentine, Amerigo Vespucci, who sailed a few years after Columbus and who was once wrongly credited with having 'discovered' the continent. 'Indians', as I have already explained, was used by the fifteenth century Europeans who thought they had arrived in the 'Indies'. To add to the labyrinth, the first known publication of 'America', was by a German cartographer, writing in Latin, and working in what is now France. Vespucci probably never knew his name had been co-opted (if indeed it had; there are other theories). By the way, Columbus, or 'Colón' in Spanish (who was from Genoa in what is now Italy) never realized his role in history: he always wrongly believed he had sailed to Asia.

'Indians' is generally used without problem in English, but the Spanish equivalent, *indio*, is now considered derogatory in much of Latin America where the polite form is *indígena* meaning 'indigenous person'.

Names are often powerful, as well as complicated. For example, many Australian native peoples prefer to be called 'Aboriginals', rather than 'Aborigines', though the two words mean the same thing. A Waorani nowadays would be insulted to be called 'Auca'. This is not surprising; for example, the 'n-word' once applied to African Americans is now so potent it is considered insulting even to spell it out. Many names are believed to be too strong to be spoken. If you want to know the name of a Waorani man, you should never ask him directly but can put the question to his friend or relative. A person should not speak his own name out loud: he could attract bad luck. Some Gond peoples in central India name their children after things of no value –

such as 'Cowdung' – in order to avoid malevolent ghosts taking a fancy to them. When government officials first appeared in their area, names as curious as 'Dfo' (District Forest Officer) began to be adopted, for these hapless colonial administrators were also thought to be worthless by the tribe!

'Bushman', the term for the indigenous tribes of southern Africa, presents another problem. It may be derived from a Dutch word meaning 'outlaw' and so is insulting, though not because it means someone who lives in 'the bush', which it probably never did. In the 1970s, American anthropologists invented the word 'San', to avoid the implied contempt and sexism of 'Bushman'. Unfortunately, this turns out also to be pejorative, and is not from a Bushman language either. In Botswana, home to about half the remaining Bushmen, they are called *Basarwa*; but this too is an insult. There is in fact no accepted term referring to all Bushman tribes which is not pejorative. Some Bushmen themselves have tried to get around this by using *Khwe* which means 'people' in some of their languages, but the word does not appear in dictionaries and is only recognized by a few. I use 'Bushman' and 'Bushmen' in this book, including when referring to women, as it is the most readily understood by readers of English, and when I have asked Bushmen what they think themselves, they generally reply that, if speaking English, they prefer 'Bushmen' to names like *Basarwa* or San.

There are very few sizeable countries where an indigenous word has achieved an acceptance in parallel with the colonists' name for it. One is 'Aotearoa', used for New Zealand, and meaning 'land of long white cloud' in some Maori languages. The early Maori explorers would certainly have seen the clouds hanging above the landmass well before they became the first humans to step onto the New Zealand beaches, but they probably had no name for the archipelago at that time. Since the 1970s, through repetition and a desire to accommodate Maori feelings, Aotearoa has become fairly accepted as an alternative name, and now appears in some dictionaries. The same cannot be said for 'Turtle Island', a name that some radical United States Indians tried to apply to North America, but which seems unlikely ever to catch on. Canada, on the other hand, reflected its indigenous heritage from the beginning. The name is an Indian word from the St Lawrence River meaning 'settlement'.

Names may be arbitrary, and are often problematic, but they are an essential shorthand and, unless there is a very good reason not to, I favour using those most likely to be understood by a wide spectrum of readers. I apologize if I offend anyone in doing so.

I turn now to sketching the situation of different tribal and indigenous peoples around the world.

Africa

Brothers and sisters: do not let your persecutors
make you forget who you are. No matter how far
away from it you have been taken, the land and life
your forefathers gave you belong to you. Be strong!
You will see your land again.

Kiplangat Cheruyot, Ogiek, Kenya (addressed to Botswana Bushmen)

Africa has had a close connection to both Europe and
Arabia for thousands of years. The most recent European
colonization began in the fifteenth century with the
Portuguese exploration of the west coast, and ended in 1975
with Angola's independence from Portugal. Beginning and
ending with this same country was coincidence: the main
protagonists in taking over the continent were actually
France and Britain, with Germany and others playing lesser
roles. The colonization was certainly underpinned by terrible
suffering and death, but Africa was not invaded as
irrevocably and with such genocidal intent as the Americas
and Australia were. Africans govern Africa today, whereas
indigenous Americans and Australians hold almost no power
in their countries. This calls for further explanation to define
which peoples might be properly called 'tribal' in the way I
am using the term.

If tribal peoples in Africa are not connected to the
colonial concept of all Africans belonging to 'tribes', as in the
'tribalism' I have already described, then who are they? There
are hundreds of peoples throughout the continent who live

somewhat apart from national society, and who remain largely reliant on their own resources. They also share an additional trait: they are looked down on and threatened by their more mainstream neighbours in exactly the same way as tribal peoples are on other continents.

The Africans who most obviously fit this definition are: the so-called 'Pygmy' peoples of West and Central Africa; the hunter-gatherers of East Africa; and, most famously, the 'Bushman' peoples of southern Africa. Most are predominantly hunter-gatherers, rather than farmers or herders, or were until recently. All of them are also indigenous – pre-dating the arrival of other peoples into their areas.

'Bushmen'

Most Africans are indigenous in the sense of originating in the continent. As I have explained, their ancestors were in Africa probably before anyone else was anywhere in the world, though they did not occupy every part of the continent equally. For example, as far as we know, the ancestors of today's 'Bushman' tribes in southern Africa were in the region tens of thousands of years before anyone else. They can uniquely claim to be the 'most indigenous' peoples in the world; having been there longer than anyone else has been anywhere. Although the scant tangible evidence of their occupation can only be traced back twenty thousand years ago or so, there is no reason to think that they have not been there for seventy thousand years, or more. Indeed, our species may have originally evolved in the region a few hundreds of thousands of years before that. Academic guesses oscillate between favouring southern and eastern Africa as the likely original 'cradle' of humankind where we all started, but it seems unlikely we will ever be certain. Recent studies also suggest that earlier guesses about origins were substantially correct: today's Bushman tribes are genetically closer to the ancestors of all of us than anyone else is. In one way of looking at it, all of us were once Bushmen!

'Bushman' is really just a collective term to describe the hundreds, probably thousands, of tribes which were the only inhabitants of southern Africa until the arrival of more numerous, largely herding, peoples from further north. Bushmen were mainly hunter-gatherers, but not exclusively so. Some were fisherfolk, and there seems little reason to suppose that some may not have herded animals as well. About three thousand years ago, the Nama and similar peoples, who are not themselves Bushmen, started spreading down the west coast of Africa, bringing sheep and goats, and probably eventually reaching the southern tip of the continent. Other small groups of newcomers from the north and east entered the region from the fifth century onwards. However, the main immigration into southern Africa is much more recent and is thought to have begun only about five or six hundred years ago, roughly the same time as Columbus. The incoming peoples were distinct from those who were already there.

The Bushman tribes spoke their own languages, characterized by several click sounds in addition to the consonants and vowels we all use; the new immigrants largely spoke Bantu languages, such as Shona and Zulu. The Bushmen were physically small, with copper-coloured skin, and the 'almond-shaped' eyes similar to many Asians and American Indians. The Bantu-speakers were larger, black-skinned, and had rounded eyes, like other Africans and Europeans. It is thought that they pushed many Bushman tribes further and further south as they moved in, eventually to occupy the southern cape, taking over the best lands for grazing, and often clashing with the Bushmen or exploiting them as herdsmen, servants, or labourers. However, the Bantu peoples looked to the Bushmen for more than this: they depended on Bushman knowledge to survive in a climate which seemed to them particularly hostile and life-threatening. The Bushmen taught them how to find water in the desert. As time passed, many Bushman women married into the more powerful Bantu tribes, and there are plenty of southern Africans today who have some Bushman ancestry. Such fraternization did not stop many Bushmen being killed by the Bantu newcomers.

The Bushmen then got it from both sides. Europeans landed at the fertile southern tip of Africa, and then pushed north two hundred years ago, to settle what are now South Africa, Zimbabwe, and Namibia. Like the Bantu, they brought cattle and wanted to clear the Bushmen out of the way of their farms. As the Europeans moved in, the Bushmen saw their hunting disappear and often resorted to eating the farmers' livestock, which the Bushmen took to be fat and dozy game; in their view, almost all animals were potential lunch. Retaliation was fierce and Europeans and Africans soon began organizing parties to hunt and kill Bushmen. The ensuing genocide is much less acknowledged than those to which the American Indians or Australian Aboriginals were subjected, but it was equally unforgiving. It is likely that hundreds of entire peoples, hundreds of thousands of individuals, were eradicated without trace.

Today, about a hundred thousand Bushmen survive out of an original population which may have numbered around one or two million. About half are in Botswana, with nearly forty thousand in Namibia, and others in Angola, Zimbabwe and South Africa. Many now live on the fringes of mainstream society, and work as cattle hands or domestic servants, often for little or no wages. Others are slum dwellers, begging and scrounging, and repeatedly booted out of the towns they try and settle near. Few still live mainly by hunting, though many still hunt when they can. Most Bushman tribes have seen their lands stolen for farming, mining, or for conservation zones such as national parks.

Considering the disdain in which Bushmen are now held by mainstream society, it is paradoxical that two of the early twenty-first century's most revered Nobel prize-winners, Desmond Tutu and Nelson Mandela, are both part-descended from Bushmen.

Hunter-gatherers of East Africa

East African hunter-gatherers are now reduced to less than a thousand Kwegu in Ethiopia, some twenty thousand Ogiek and thirty thousand Sengwer in Kenya, and the Hadzabe, numbering only about a thousand in Tanzania. Like the Bushmen, they are largely surrounded by herders and farmers. Also like the Bushmen, most have been pushed into the least hospitable areas and all are routinely denigrated as 'primitive' and 'backward' by their neighbours. They are survivors: there were several other hunting tribes in the region but, apart from a few small remnant groups, they have largely disappeared over the last century.

The creation of animal conservation zones in the 1940s and 50s cleared numerous peoples off their traditional lands and spelt the end of many. For example, the Waliangulu people once lived in the area of the Tsavo Park in Kenya but have now effectively ceased to exist following their eviction and attacks by anti-hunting patrols. At one stage, one in every three Waliangulu men was imprisoned for 'poaching', which for them just meant hunting as usual of course.

A recent threat shows an even greater irony. In 2006, the Hadzabe were confronted by a project to create a hunting reserve for wealthy, mainly Arabian, clients. This was expected to result in tourists shooting game, even using automatic weapons, as happened on nearby Maasai land. Foreigners paying to kill for sport threatened the Hadzabe right to hunt for food. Luckily, the proposal was ditched following its exposure in the press.

Eviction from their lands, usually for tourism or conservation, remains the main threat to these peoples throughout East Africa. The Ogiek, for example, have been repeatedly told to get out of their lands in Kenya's Mau Forest. This is supposedly to protect it as the authorities now pretend the tribe constitutes a threat to the forest's conservation.

'Pygmies'

There are nearly half a million 'Pygmy' people in dozens of tribes in the Congo Basin countries, particularly the Democratic Republic of Congo. They are generally recognized as the indigenous peoples of the area and some scientists believe they were once a single people.

About sixty thousand still live largely by hunting and gathering, and the rest now grow some crops as well. All of them interact with their farming neighbours. Sometimes this takes the form of mutually beneficial trading, but often the

Pygmies are exploited as they hand over their forest produce for outside goods and foods. The settled farmers often consider the Pygmies to be barely human, though they still recognize their superior knowledge about the forest, especially its plant medicines.

The Pygmies' biggest problem comes from their eviction to make way for both settlement projects and conservation zones. The World Bank-funded Chad-Cameroon oil pipeline destroyed the forests of one tribe, the Bagyeli, in Cameroon, and the Batwa people of several countries now eke out a living as labourers and beggars, seeing most of their forest felled for pasture and farms.

To add to these problems, which are common to forest-dwellers everywhere, is the extremely violent history of the area. Armed militias, both anti- and pro-government, have roamed there for years; they have tortured, killed and raped Pygmies and there are even credible accounts that they have resorted to cannibalism, killing and ritually eating parts of their victims.

The Republic of Congo (which is, confusingly, not the same as the Democratic Republic of Congo) passed a law in 2011 supposedly to support the rights of the Pygmies. Although it included several worthy provisions, it also outlawed the use of the term 'Pygmies' altogether. Although this might at first be seen as an anti-racist gesture, in fact it made it much harder for the country's one or two hundred thousand Pygmies to define themselves as a sector with their own special problems and needs. Pygmies themselves were no longer allowed to call themselves 'Pygmies' without risking fines they could never afford.

This was a powerful tool to try and make these peoples invisible as a group – which was its intention. In Rwanda, this has gone even further. As a response to the civil war and genocide of the early 1990s (in which nearly a third of Twa Pygmies died), no organization is allowed to represent any ethnic group, so the Pygmy association was forced to drop the word 'indigenous' from its title and re-invent itself as an organization of potters.

Pastoralists

As well as these hunting peoples, there are several million herders in Africa who live largely self-sufficiently and independently, mainly in East Africa from Ethiopia down to Tanzania. The Mursi, for example, have faced many problems in recent decades with state-owned farms, hunting concessions, and conservation initiatives taking their land in Ethiopia.

Perhaps the most famous herders are the Maasai in Kenya and Tanzania. Numbering nearly a million, they include a majority who live largely off their cattle and goats, and maize meal traded from local farmers, as well as others who are partly integrated into mainstream society. They include businessmen, politicians, security guards, and so forth, and, although they might appear indistinguishable from other East Africans, many still own herds which are kept for them in their home villages. When they return to visit or to retire, they are likely to speak their own language and fall back easily into the family and peer group networks they grew up with.

The Maasai acquired much fame during the early days of colonial rule when they resisted European attempts to push them off their territory. Their fight-back, with spears against rifles, was a hopeless but brave endeavour. The coastal Arabs helped create an image that the Maasai were very dangerous, largely to keep trade routes out of European hands. Although generations have passed since the Maasai fought in this way, it is an image which has endured. Many people still believe Maasai 'warriors' have to prove their manhood by killing a lion, an idea many Maasai themselves foment, but which is hardly ever realized. Once, I found myself with a dozen Maasai men, squashed in a car only a few metres away from a large lioness. The men loudly registered their disappointment at not having spears to hand, and daringly described how they were itching to leap to the chase, but none actually budged from the vehicle's protection.

The Maasai have had routine contact with European society only since the late nineteenth century – much more recently than many Amazon Indians – yet surprisingly the University of Oxford reportedly welcomed a Maasai student to its quadrangles just a few years after these first contacts.

The degree to which the Maasai and other herders are indigenous to their region is largely conjectural. They probably moved progressively south over many generations and may be relative newcomers to where they live now, arriving perhaps around the eighteenth century. They sometimes clashed with the more settled agricultural peoples, and this, exacerbated first by colonial rule and then by independent nations whose governments denigrate herding, has left a legacy of land disputes which are similar to those faced by other tribal peoples.

Although they largely fall within my definition of tribal, and have participated a little in the development of indigenous rights in Africa, this has been a smaller movement than elsewhere, and it would be fair to describe the Maasai and others like them as being on the margins of those peoples I am focussing on in this book. If the thirty million or more West African Yoruba, the dominant 'tribe' in Nigeria, are not my subject, and the hundred thousand individuals comprising the Bushmen tribes are, then the one million Maasai lie somewhere in between.

They have a tradition of strong political leadership, partly expressed through the 'age-sets' already described, and these make them considerably less vulnerable than hunters like the Pygmies or Bushmen. Maasai have met outside society with a cohesive resilience which makes it unlikely that their future, as Maasai, is in much doubt. However, there are some numerically smaller herding peoples, such as the thirty thousand Barabaig of Tanzania, or the similarly-sized Himba of Namibia, who are significantly more threatened. The former because they were thrown off their lands in favour of large wheat farms, the latter because of dam-building proposals which, if they go ahead, will flood their land.

The Maasai are fiercely proud of their herding way of life and are fully aware that migration to the city slums, which are never far away, is a step towards hopeless poverty. Much the same goes for peoples of North Africa, including nomadic herders such as the famous Tuareg of the Sahara. They too live largely self-sufficiently, but they have played no role in the indigenous or tribal peoples' movement and, like the Maasai, are unlikely to face disappearance.

African tribal peoples, in the way I am using the term, come from either a hunter-gathering or a herding way of life. Elsewhere in the world, tribal peoples include settled agriculturalists as well, but those who live mainly by growing crops in Africa are largely integrated into much larger, often very old, trading networks, and are firmly embedded within national life: as such, they do not fit my definition of tribal peoples.

Just as hunting is the most important thing to a hunter-gatherer, so stock animals dominate the lives of pastoralists. The first question a Maasai is likely to ask any visitor is, 'Do you have cattle?' The Maasai provide a rather good example of how ways of life very different to the industrialized norm are enjoyed by many people who do not want to become city-dwellers. Blankets have largely replaced skins as 'traditional' dress, but many Maasai men and boys see no paradox at all in watching over the cattle herds armed with both spear and mobile phone.

Africa may be a fantastically varied environment, home to an extraordinary number of different peoples, but if we follow our ancestors' journey to its east, we come to the most diverse continent of all.

Asia

The Earth is shaking as the tree falls with a great thud.

Boa Sr, last member of the Bo tribe, Andamans (died 2010)

Asia has the world's highest mountain range, coldest steppes, great deserts, and vast areas of tropical forest. The most varied of all continents geographically, it also contains the most populous nations. Most people in the world are Asian, with nearly half of humankind living in just two places, the Indian subcontinent and China. Asia is also home to the largest number and greatest diversity of tribal and indigenous peoples.

As populations moved throughout the continent for thousands of years, they left a historical map more complex, and less understood, than elsewhere. Recent genetic studies are largely confirming what scientists had previously guessed: the 'black Asians', as I call them, were almost certainly there before anyone else, whereas lighter-skinned peoples with almond-shaped eyes, and possibly some even lighter-coloured, who looked much like Europeans, began to move across the continent thousands of years ago. On the islands of Japan, for example, the indigenous tribes were almost entirely displaced or absorbed by incomers from the mainland about two thousand years ago; their descendants are today's Japanese. Only one indigenous people remains, the physically larger Ainu.

A handful of black Asian tribes remain on the continent's mainland; principally, the Semang who live in the hills of the Malaysian forest, and the Mani, from over the Thai border. Some south Indian tribes are also partly descended from the same peoples. All other black tribes now live on islands, and this has helped keep them largely separate from others; most can be found in the Philippine archipelago, and I will look at the situation there shortly. Before doing so, I will describe one unique area in more detail.

Andamans

The Andaman Islands in the Indian Ocean have long been home to several black tribes. One, called the Sentinelese after the tiny island they have entirely to themselves, retain almost total isolation from everyone else. Probably numbering less than a couple of hundred – just one big extended family – their ancestors were almost certainly there around fifteen thousand years ago and may well have arrived an astounding forty thousand years earlier. As sea levels rose over the millennia, any contact they had with neighbouring islands became progressively less frequent.

However, their isolation was not total. Ships from Egypt, Arabia and China as well as Europe would have seen them gazing out from their beaches. The Andaman tribes are mentioned in Marco Polo's thirteenth century chronicles; his informants told him they had dog, instead of human, heads. It is probable that some explorers landed to have a closer look, and that an unlucky shipwreck survivor occasionally crawled up their sands. If so, they were probably killed. The Sentinelese certainly made better use of other things that washed up, including fashioning metal blades from bits of wrecks and jetsam.

When India fell to imperial Britain in the nineteenth century, a prison was built on a nearby island. In 1879, soldiers captured two adults and some children 'in the interests of science'. The adults quickly died and the children fell ill. According to their captors, they were like, 'the average lower class English country schoolboy'. In World War II, the Japanese occupied some of the archipelago; and after the China-India war in 1962, a Russian naval base was built nearby. All these events will have been noticed by the Sentinelese, and may have provoked some undocumented meetings. Then, in the 1970s and 80s, the authorities conducted an extremely dangerous contact programme. In one of the first encounters, they left a doll and live pig on the beach. The Sentinelese promptly speared and buried both. As the months passed, small boatloads of officials regularly approached the shore to look at the tribespeople, who stared back. Gradually, confidence grew. The officials left more presents on the beach, such as balls, mirrors and fruits. Finally, in 1991, some Sentinelese swam to the boats to collect coconuts.

During these encounters, some extraordinary photographs and film were taken. They show a proud and healthy people who had clearly adapted brilliantly to tens of thousands of years of presumed near-total isolation, and all on an island less than ten kilometres across. This is an area slightly larger than Manhattan or, to look at it another way, only fifteen times bigger than Robben Island, where Nelson Mandela was imprisoned.

It is possible that some Sentinelese left their island in past generations but, as far as we know, they do not regard their isolation as in any way imprisoning and have not shown any desire to go. They did, however, clearly appreciate some of the new things they were brought, especially bananas, and began to view the meetings as fun, though they stopped short of a joke which another Andaman tribe found particularly entertaining – urinating on visitors' feet, and squirting them with breast milk. In any event, the officials seem to have retained their sense of humour too, and remained well behaved, in spite of being occasionally threatened with drawn bows; both sides remained ever ready to beat a hasty retreat. No one knows whether any Sentinelese later died of disease resulting from these encounters, or whether any have been killed by outsiders, but they have themselves killed fishermen who encroached on their territory. The contact expeditions were halted in 1996. Some had met clear hostility, and international pressure bolstered the views of a few local officials that the tribe was better left in peace.

Isolated peoples such as the Sentinelese have not encountered the raft of viruses and bacteria which outsiders have lived with for generations and consequently developed a strong natural immunity against. Mild illnesses for most of the rest of us, especially ailments like colds and influenza, often rage through peoples who have never known these microbes, leaving many dead in their wake. Of course, it is quite possible that this has also happened on North Sentinel Island. If one day we can understand them, and if they have retained a memory of such events, perhaps we will know more, though it is also likely that any increasing contact will destroy them.

There were about thirteen Andaman tribes until a century ago; most have now been annihilated or reduced to a few dozen individuals. The 'Great Andamanese', for example, are the remnants of ten different tribes; the fifty-five survivors are kept by the authorities in what critics call a 'breeding station'. They are given food but otherwise largely left to themselves. Most of the men are alcoholics.

Another tribe, the Jarawa, live in forests on two of the larger islands, where there are also thousands of settlers. A road runs right through their land, and some have had many encounters with outsiders; they hitch rides on passing buses, and visit settler villages, where they take whatever they want. The settlers are advised to let them help themselves and not to try and stop them, as it could result in fights. Jarawa even go to the local hospital when they are ill. Some have begun to learn Hindi. They remain, however, both largely isolated and extremely vulnerable.

Interestingly, none of the Andaman tribes seem to have suffered from the massive 2004 tsunami. It is reckoned that, when they saw the sea recede as the waters gathered before the killer wave struck, the tribespeople acted in the opposite way to many of the victims: instead of going out to look, they immediately retreated to higher ground. It is possible that they had such foresight because they remembered accounts of previous tsunamis. Over tens of thousands of years, their ancestors clearly survived many. It is a curious paradox that there are some situations when a reliance on literacy might not be as practical as the prodigious memories, stories, and sheer self-sufficiency of tribes that remain illiterate.

They might well know how to survive a tsunami, but all the Andaman tribes remain in a precarious situation. In 1999, a local lawyer tried to force the authorities to 'civilize' the Jarawa by making them settle in villages. Exactly the same happened in 1976 to another tribe, the Onge, reducing this formerly proud people to a state of total dependency, and going some way towards finishing them off altogether – although the British army had already gone some way to massacring them a couple of generations previously. Had the Jarawa also been settled, it is unlikely the outcome would have been any different. Luckily, a legal opposition prevailed as the judges heeded international testimony from experts who explained the likelihood of catastrophe.

In 2002, the Supreme Court ordered the road though their land closed. Local officials promptly ignored the ruling, and kept the road open, but at least the threat of enforced settlement had been abated. Today, poachers give out alcohol and tobacco as they steal Jarawa game. Until an international campaign put a stop to it, tourist resorts encroached ever closer to the Jarawa reserve, greatly increasing the risk of infection, and some highly irresponsible companies advertised tours to see Jarawa, treating their forest like a human safari park.

Researchers have begun to build a sketchy picture of the Jarawa way of life. Not surprisingly, they live much like many other tropical forest dwelling hunter-gatherers the world over. They make dwellings of logs and leaves, as well as small lean-tos which take only minutes to construct. They clearly see no need for larger, more permanent buildings.

Houses or 'tents'

Elsewhere, there is another way to live in tropical forests: one which echoes most of the food gathering activities of the black Asian hunter-gatherer tribes, but with a very different attitude to housing. A good example can be seen with the Iban of Malaysian Borneo who, unlike the Andaman tribes, favour grand and complex houses which are home to dozens of people and which last for years, and even generations. These 'longhouses', with facilities to host visitors, hold feasts, and store smoked meat and other provisions and possessions, are crucial to the Iban way of life and to how they see themselves. Their neighbours, the nomadic Penan, have a different self-image.

The Penan are an extraordinarily accommodating and peaceable people who, since the 1980s, have been pushed to opposing the destruction of their forests by regularly blockading the loggers' roads and stopping their trucks getting through. Some Penan have paid a heavy price for this, suffering much violent intimidation and even killings. In spite of this, a few hundred Penan remain defiantly mobile, living in a similar way to the Andaman tribes, and relying on hunter-gathering, and especially on their main staple, flour made from the sago palm tree. Their dwellings are temporary: effectively 'tents' made of branches and, nowadays, old tarpaulins salvaged from the loggers. One way of looking at it is that the Iban live in houses but both the Penan as well as many black Asian tribes spend most of their lives 'camping'.

The Penan and Iban of Malaysia and Indonesia are not themselves black Asian: they are brown-skinned, with the same (epicanthic) shaped eyes of most eastern Asians. Less than a generation ago, there were many tribes throughout Southeast Asia living in a way broadly similar to either the longhouse-dwelling Iban or the nomadic Penan. Most have now disappeared or been forced to abandon much of their way of life as their forests have been taken from them. However, there are still millions of Asians who live largely off their own food, keeping livestock, doing some hunting and fishing, growing fruit, and eating a staple such as sweet potato, rice or sago palm. Many are also linked to their country's mainstream economy, selling produce at village markets, which in some places includes drugs such as opium.

War

In addition to the litany of problems which tribal peoples face the world over, many East Asian tribes have also seen a tragic amount of open warfare. In some places, such as Malaysia during the 1950s, and Vietnam and Cambodia in the following decade, they were largely caught up in the disputes of others, but elsewhere they have been the victims of deliberate and sustained military assaults, sometimes lasting for more than a generation, designed to get them out of the way and to take their land.

This has produced some curiosities amid the horror. For example, some tribes became refugees to avoid reprisals after the Vietnam War and were offered immigration into places as far away as North America and Europe. Thousands of individuals accepted and went on to establish communities on the other side of the world. For example, there is a community of Hmong, an indigenous people of Southeast Asia, living in the Amazon region of French Guyana.

In the Chittagong Hills of Bangladesh, several tribes, collectively known as the Jummas, have suffered both military occupation and the theft of their land by Bengali settlers since the 1970s. The Bangladeshi government has even been accused of genocide there. The Jummas reacted by forming a poorly-armed, and vastly-outnumbered, resistance group. They finally signed a peace agreement with the government in 1997, but even today conflicts still flare up, tribal people are still killed and attacks on their villages remain common.

This form of overt warfare extends north of Bangladesh into the Indian state of Assam and beyond. There, the Indian army fought with the Naga tribe for decades following independence from Britain in 1947. Similarly, the Karen peoples and their neighbours, such as the Karenni, are still fighting the Burmese army over sixty years later. Many of the tribes in these parts were championed by the British colonists because they were impressively fearless fighters against the Japanese in World War II. When Japan's defeat was swiftly followed by the demise of the British Empire, it had the opposite effect to ending the subjugation of the tribal peoples. The new masters, independent national governments unwilling to tolerate an independent way of life for the tribals, unleashed decades of armed assaults.

The Asian conflicts of the twentieth century include of course the revolutions in China, which began in 1925 and climaxed in 1949, when the communist party and its 'Red Army' took control. Generations of people saw almost constant conflict as well as extreme and deadly famine; the country shut down to outsiders and information about the many tribes remains scant today. It is clear from the areas which are better known, such as Tibet, that any notion of peoples having a degree of say in their own development was alien to the Chinese elite. 'Minorities' (which can be majorities, as in the case of Tibet) were suppressed by the rifle, prison, and torture chamber. Ideas of distinct 'culture' were tolerated only inasmuch as they were confined to displays of folklore in the way I have described. The many peoples of China were allowed to showcase these, but were also forced to join the mainstream belief in the infallible and unquestioned dominance of their masters in government, even to the point of children denouncing their parents for 'incorrect thought'. Things are a little better today, but not much.

This extreme form of totalitarianism was reproduced in other Southeast Asian countries, as well as in communist Russia. There are more than thirty Russian tribes, comprising about two hundred thousand people in the huge Siberian part of the country, which extends from the Ural Mountains to the Bering Sea. All of them suffered abuse throughout the twentieth century and continue to do so into the twenty-first. From the 1920s, under the all-powerful dictator Stalin, they saw their religious leaders killed and their beliefs outlawed. Their children were forced into distant boarding schools where their languages were forbidden, and their way of life was 'collectivized'. This meant that activities such as reindeer herding, vital to their ability to feed themselves, rapidly disintegrated into hopelessly inefficient, state-controlled versions of the vibrant ways of life they once had been. The result in many areas today is advanced social breakdown; alcohol-induced early death is the usual escape from the extreme poverty that comes from a life sapped of meaning. It is a tragic irony that, as I will describe, indigenous peoples who were subjects of wealthy liberal democracies, such as Canada and Australia, ended up in much the same condition as those who faced Stalin's tyranny. An Armageddon, which the Cold War chess game between the United States and Soviet Union managed to avoid for most of us, was in fact visited on the indigenous peoples of both sides, and its fallout still damages and kills people today.

India

One of the biggest concentrations of tribal peoples in the world is found in India. Until recently, it was thought that the country's prehistory could be summarized as a very early occupation by indigenous tribes which were then largely destroyed or absorbed by waves of peoples coming from what is now Central Asia, starting around six thousand years ago. Those beneath the Hindu caste system, the 'untouchables' – now known more politely as 'Dalits' – as well as the hundreds of tribes, called 'Adivasis', who live in the country today, were thought to be largely descended from the original inhabitants, whereas the upper castes, who tend to be lighter-skinned, were thought to be descendants of the Central Asian immigrants. However, there is little evidence to support this, and some studies have suggested that much of the Indian population was genetically isolated for longer than was previously thought. In short, India is full of tribal peoples but no one knows to what degree they are 'more' indigenous than others. They are however clearly defined as 'tribal', both in my definition and by the government, and are regarded by many Hindus and others as backward and inferior.

Many are agriculturalists. They speak their own languages, retain much of their own distinctive religions and customs, and see themselves as separate peoples, but they otherwise live in a broadly similar way to millions of rural Indians. Some, however, are very different: there are still hunter-gatherer peoples in east and south India, and some are, or until recently were, nomads like the Korwa of Bihar, living in small bands in the forested hills.

Industrialization has had the same detrimental impact on tribal peoples in India as it has elsewhere. The same projects – mainly dam building, mining and deforestation – displace them and take their lands, with the same effects. In eastern India, for example, the Dongria Kondh face having part of their homeland destroyed by a bauxite mine. Of particular concern is that it is supposed to go on the top of their most sacred place, a forested hill called Nyam Dongar, which they see as God. As well as its immense spiritual significance, the area provides the tribe with the deer they hunt and a host of other wild foods, comprising much of their extremely healthy diet. Numbering some eight thousand, the Dongria Kondh are keen to avoid joining the millions of desperately poor rural Indians, and are determined to keep their land. Echoing tactics employed by the Malaysian Penan, but with more visible hostility, they regularly resort to blocking the roads and threaten to 'cut the heads off' the miners, though they have never actually done so. Retaliation is fierce, and bands of thugs roam the area determined to stamp out opposition to the mine, knowing the police will turn a blind eye to their crimes.

The Dongria Kondh can see only too well the real effects of 'modernization', as opposed to the propaganda they are bombarded with by the miners: many of their neighbouring tribe, the Majhi Kondh, were moved to make way for a refinery controlled by the same company, Vedanta Resources. They were put in a guarded compound, built by the firm, where they were afraid to speak out and conditions were intolerable. Harassment by so-called 'security guards' and the local police, directed at anyone who opposes the company's work, remains common in the area.

Philippines

Most black Asian tribes are now found in the Philippines, where it is thought they arrived between thirty-five and fifty thousand years ago. They are, or were until recently, predominantly hunter-gatherers or fisherfolk. Estimates of their total population vary widely, from about fifteen thousand to double that number, speaking nearly thirty different languages.

There are also vastly more individuals – about twelve million – whose forebears resisted colonization by Spain and the United States, and who also now identify themselves as indigenous. They are ethnic Malays, like most people in the Philippines, and predominantly farmers who are thought to have first arrived from the Asian mainland perhaps four or five thousand years ago. Some of the largest groups in this category are the Igorot or Cordillera peoples, comprising several tribes, and numbering more than a million individuals. They have been in the vanguard of indigenous rights since the 1970s, and have repeatedly fought unwanted development projects, successfully opposing some potentially very destructive ones, notably World Bank-funded dams.

Many of the hundreds of farming and herding peoples, from Turkey in the west, to Pakistan in the east, as well as north into Central Asia, also fit my definition of tribal or indigenous well enough. Some are also nomadic herders. However, none have positioned themselves within the indigenous peoples' movement.

There are about one hundred and fifty million clearly indigenous individuals in Asia, of whom perhaps seventy-five percent are also tribal. Most live in India, with large numbers also found in Bangladesh, as well as all countries of the southeastern mainland – China, Burma, Thailand, Vietnam, Laos, Cambodia, and Malaysia. Others live in the thousands of islands of the Philippines, Malaysia and Indonesia.

The line dividing 'Asia' from 'Australasia' and 'the Pacific' is blurred but, even if only to subdivide this vast area somewhat, it makes sense to deal with the Pacific Ocean islands – both the huge and the tiny – as a separate continent.

Australasia & Oceania

Every man among us owns a plot of tribal ground which he calls 'my country'. Mine is an area sixty square miles, south of Roper River. I know a white man who grazes his cattle there and he thinks it's his.

Waipuldunya, Australia

If the tribal overview of Asia is the most complicated, that of Australasia and the Pacific can be sketched fairly simply, though as everywhere there are underlying complexities. Broadly, there are two types of indigenous peoples in this huge, largely watery area. Some of the earliest out-of-Africa colonists, the black Asians, settled New Guinea, Australia and the small islands nearby, probably beginning around fifty thousand years ago. A very long time afterwards, only about three thousand years ago, the settlement of the deeper Pacific Ocean began: seafaring tribes took the next two thousand years to complete the human colonization of the world's largest ocean. Amongst the last major lands to be inhabited, in about the ninth century AD, was the huge archipelago of New Zealand. But before describing what happened there, I look first at the far earlier settlements of the giant islands of New Guinea and Australia.

New Guinea

There are many features making New Guinea unique for indigenous peoples. To begin with, it remains largely inhabited by them, so it goes some way to contradict my definition: in much of New Guinea, tribal peoples comprise the mainstream – though not the governing – society. The island is home to about a thousand languages, about fifteen percent of the world's total, spoken by six million people, only 0.1 percent of the world's population. It is also home to some tribes, or parts of tribes, who remain largely isolated and uncontacted by outsiders, though this is now difficult to state with certainty as the Indonesian government makes travel to half the island extremely difficult.

Although parts of New Guinea were colonized by different European powers in the nineteenth century, the dense forest and high mountains kept most whites close to their coastal towns. Those who did venture inland made surprising discoveries of peoples, animals and plants unknown to the outside world. As recently as 1938, the huge Baliem Valley was first seen from the air. It was, and remains, home to more than a hundred thousand tribespeople, mainly Dani and Lani. Today, these peoples are still often described by the stereotype, 'Stone Age', which is another 'Amish error', and one with distinctly racist overtones. There is, in fact, evidence that the Dani developed agriculture at least nine thousand years ago, probably far in advance of the British.

As well as growing sweet potatoes and other fruits and vegetables, gathering wild foods and keeping pigs, the Dani also hunt in the forests for birds and animals such as tree kangaroos. Their agricultural refinements are another example of how peoples readily take ownership of things which come from outside. For example, sweet potato, which has been a principal staple throughout New Guinea for generations, is not indigenous at all: it was imported centuries ago from the Americas. It is widely favoured over the nearest local equivalent, taro, because it is easier and quicker to grow.

Pigs are the most valued Dani possessions of all. They are slaughtered and eaten, but they also form the core of ceremonial exchanges. Their fat is used for hair styling as well as a body rub, and other parts of the animal are used in decoration and for magic. Their owners can form such a close attachment that women may suckle piglets if the sow cannot cope. As with hunting dogs, the death of a treasured animal can plunge its owners into long mourning.

Another distinctive feature of many New Guinea tribes is that men wear the most elaborate clothing and body decoration imaginable, particularly for special occasions. Thick and bright face paint, complex and large feather headdresses, sticks, bones and leafy branches, embellished nowadays with all manner of coloured artefacts from the outside, are used to enhance men's beauty, leaving the women relatively unadorned.

Men hiding or enhancing their genitals – often both at the same time – is quite common in many societies, including in the West, of course. This is carried to an extreme with some New Guinea tribes. The men insert their penis and one testicle into the end of a hollow gourd, which can be so long, half a metre or so, that it can only be worn if supported by a tie around the body. The size and shape of his gourd can be enough to identify a man's tribe but, perhaps contrary to appearances, has nothing to do with assertions of virility.

New Guinea today is split between independent Papua

New Guinea in the eastern half, and Indonesian-occupied West Papua in the west. The colonization of West Papua is one of the greatest violations of tribal peoples, and ongoing human rights abuses, in recent times. It started in 1963, when the United Nations handed the country from Dutch colonial rule to the Indonesian occupying force. In the words of a White House adviser, this simply 'traded white colonialism for brown', but it went ahead anyway, largely due to the urging of a United States fearful of communist escalation in Asia. Six years later, the invading Indonesians arranged a 'vote' to determine whether the country should become independent. Their army rounded up hundreds of tribal leaders, threatening to kill any who did not declare in support of Indonesia. Officially called the 'Act of Free Choice', little more than a thousand individuals out of a total population of about a million were allowed their say. West Papuans call this colonialist charade the 'act free of choice', and began an active resistance to the occupation which continues to this day.

Indonesia used several tactics to quash this, with a constant theme of force and terror; tribal villages which were thought to harbour so-called 'separatists' used to be bombed, and are now occupied by soldiers who kill and rape routinely. Captured leaders were once pushed out of airborne helicopters, and even small symbolic acts, such as raising the 'Free Papua' flag, are still met with fierce reprisals. The army is estimated to have killed a hundred thousand Papuans, but as most atrocities take place in remote areas, the number is only a guess. Another colonial device deployed was the so-called 'transmigration' programme, in which the poor from the country's overcrowded islands – mainly Java and Sulawesi – were shipped to West Papua and given rudimentary housing and small plots of land. This was the largest organized voluntary population transfer the world has ever seen. It peaked in the 1980s, when it was funded by European, American, and some Asian taxpayers through the World Bank and Asian Development Bank. Many hundreds of thousands of people, all about as different to the Papuans as Europeans are to Africans, and most with similar views about their own superiority, were taken to the island under the guise of 'development' to try to swamp the local tribal population.

As well as violence and the 'transmigration' just described, another plank in Indonesia's attempts to get rid of the Papuan tribes was 'operation *koteka*', named after the gourd penis sheaths. This was a 1970s 'educational' programme, to convince the local people that they were hopelessly backward, and that progress lay in embracing Indonesian culture. The message was not much different to that promulgated by the many Christian missionaries, who had also tried to get rid of the *koteka* penis gourd decades before. Ironically – for Indonesia is a largely Muslim country – West Papua remains replete with missionaries who have had a good deal of success in converting many tribespeople to their own distinctive types of Christianity.

As well as Cold War politics and land grabbing, New Guinea's vast mineral wealth was a key incentive for Indonesian domination. The world's largest copper and gold mine, Grasberg, is in West Papua, on the lands of the Amungme tribe, and remains a simmering cauldron for both tribal resistance and government repression.

Before looking south to Australia, it is worth taking a step east to the independent half of the island, to the country of Papua New Guinea, a name often shortened to 'PNG'. Although the whole island, all of geographic New Guinea, is broadly similar in terms of its tribal peoples, the political situation could not be more different between the two halves.

PNG became independent of Australia in 1975, and is one of the very few places on Earth where tribal peoples not only comprise most of the population, but occupy much of government as well. This has not resulted in a problem-free existence. There are hundreds of different tribes speaking eight hundred languages, and rivalrous conflict is far from unusual.

Shortly after independence, Bougainville, one of the tiny coastal islands, rose in a bid for its own separate statehood. This led to years of violence which only ended in 1997 when it was granted the status of an autonomous province. About twenty thousand people were killed in the struggle, which ignited over a copper mine owned by British company, Rio Tinto: the mine shored up the economy of the entire country but did not return enough to the local people to assuage their sense of being invaded and occupied.

Although beset with problems, PNG remains one of the very few countries where an appreciation of tribal peoples is, at least supposedly, enshrined in the country's constitution: it asserts 'traditional villages and communities' should 'remain as viable units'. Until 2010, PNG recognized concepts of native title and indigenous land rights which many other, apparently 'more advanced', nations vehemently opposed. Unfortunately, the situation was then reversed, when the government suddenly dissolved the constitutional rights of all landowners, including tribal people, in order to open the entire country to resource extraction.

New Guinea is usually classed as the world's second largest island (after Greenland), and lies to the north of the vast island continent of Australia, which is nearly ten times bigger.

Australia

When the British first claimed Australia in 1770, there were probably nearly a million Aboriginals there, speaking around nine hundred different languages (though these are guesses). Perhaps unfortunately for them, none had a fighting tradition to match that of the African Maasai. The British were afraid of Maasai spears, but were unconcerned with Aboriginal resistance to their invasion. Most Aboriginals lived in small bands with no custom of political leaders able to organize serious opposition to the colonists, so the settlers, unopposed, spent the next hundred and fifty years trying to get rid of them. It was not very difficult. The majority were annihilated, largely through disease but also through violence. Whites hunted and killed Aboriginals at least up until the 1920s, and perhaps even later. Such extreme behaviour was relatively rare, but forcing children to attend boarding schools, deliberately located faraway from their parents, continued as government policy into the 1970s. The idea was to ensure the remaining Aboriginals were absorbed and disappeared into the mainstream. The colonists succeeded in many places, especially in the most fertile areas where no Aboriginals survived.

For decades it has been assumed that there were no Aboriginals left who had managed to avoid some contact with the colonists. Then in 1984, to everyone's amazement, nine such individuals were 'discovered' in the Western Desert. They were moved to a fixed Aboriginal community but one of them decided he had had enough, and 'disappeared' back into the bush a couple of years later. They were Pintupi-speakers and many of their language group had been forced off their lands to make way for test launches of Britain's 'Blue Streak' nuclear missiles from the secret Cold War base at Woomera (named after the Aboriginals' spear-thrower device). Blue Streak turned out to be a futile waste of money: it was proposed in 1955 and only a handful were ever built and tested before the project was cancelled. Though never launched against the Soviets, it nevertheless played a role in destroying the lives of many Aboriginals.

Aboriginals who still see themselves specifically as 'tribal' are now a minority of the half million or so Australian Aboriginals living today. They have their own settlements, and largely speak their own languages, of which between fifty and a hundred are still in use. Most hold on to a sense of ownership, at least over some aspects of their way of life.

One of the most vital of these is knowledge about 'sacred sites' and the role they play in elaborate tales about the origins of the people, animals and landscape which make up their world. Different tribes have their own sites and distinct stories. Commonly known as 'the Dreamtime', both the stories and the places they refer to are 'owned' by special 'caretaker' families charged with maintaining the knowledge for future generations. It is believed that if life is to continue at all, the sites must carry on being used, the stories told, and the rituals performed. The creation of the world is seen as a constant, ongoing process, which requires the repeated re-creation of the ancestral beings through the re-enactment of their stories. Much of this is secret, even including the location of the particular sites, which may be just a few square metres of desert indistinguishable from the surrounding countryside. Although details about each tribe's Dreamtime are only ever divulged in small segments, even to members of the tribe, an awareness that this mythic age of creation has not been forgotten plays a crucial role in Aboriginal self-image today.

It is a general principle – not restricted to Aboriginal Australians of course – that the closer a people feels to its roots, and the more it feels it 'belongs', the higher the self-esteem of individuals and the better their physical and mental health. This appears to be the case even when most people do not themselves witness the traditions being played out: simply knowing they are there in the background can bolster people's wellbeing and sense of their place in the world.

These tribal Aboriginals whose Dreamtime is more or less alive and functioning, have fewer problems than others, but only relatively so. Even they are dependent on welfare money which has done nothing to relieve generations of poverty, and which some now see as a problem in itself, perpetuating a cycle of dependence. Tribal Aboriginals may still hunt for the large goanna lizard, emu or kangaroo, or fish the rivers and coasts for food, but daily life is usually passed in special settlements where government employees – many, nowadays, with laudable motives – still attempt to instil an alien way of thinking and living which has failed to convince the vast majority of Aboriginals. The biggest problems are alcoholism, other substance abuse, and the domestic violence, imprisonment and suicide which result. Added to this, are the same diseases of poverty which increasingly afflict poor (and not just indigenous) areas of the richer countries, and which are largely caused by a diet heavy in junk food and fat, but light on nutrients, combined with an inactive lifestyle and a resultant loss of self-worth. This fatal spiral drags people down into obesity, as well as catalyzing high levels of diabetes, kidney disease and other illnesses.

The same pattern is echoed in other countries, principally in North America, where the mainstream population is relatively well off, but where the indigenous peoples live only on the margins. In many cases, they feel they have been kicked into the gutter and trodden on with such force and frequency that picking themselves up again can seem too much effort for too little return.

The resulting statistics are shocking. In Australia's case: Aboriginal men live on average only fifty-four years, twenty-five less than others; although only two percent of the population, they comprise twenty percent of those in prison; child mortality is six times higher than for others; and they are more than six times as likely to die from self-harm. When I look more at the illnesses which indigenous and tribal peoples face today, I will characterize these diseases as belonging to the third, and last, 'stage' after contact.

There is not much brightness in this miserable history. However, there is also an active Aboriginal movement which has achieved some noteworthy achievements. Beginning in the 1960s, it was galvanized by Aboriginals who had been schooled in towns and cities, but still respected more 'traditional' groups. It garnered support, both from them and some liberal whites, and was partly inspired by the ideology of 'Black Power', then growing in the United States. The Australian movement did not produce orators with such power and appeal as America's famous Martin Luther King, perhaps because of the Aboriginals' cultural background, which actively prevented the emergence of powerful leaders. Even now, Aboriginal decisions emerge from discussion and consensus, and they are fond of neither leaders nor followers. This does, however, put them at a distinct disadvantage when dealing with outsiders.

The Aboriginal movement nevertheless produced notable successes, including a powerful symbol: its own flag. It continues to be used in Aboriginal protests since it was first designed in 1971. Featuring prominently in the so-called Aboriginal tent 'embassy', which began as a Canberra demonstration the following year, it has been carried by Aboriginal athletes during important competitions, including the Olympic games. The Australian government even gave it official status in 1995, and it now flies on some public buildings.

A flag of course is both a symbol and a picture, and it is probably no coincidence that, amongst the few indigenous people with their own widely-recognized flag, Aboriginals are also the only ones to have carved out a serious niche in contemporary high-value fine art. Beginning in the 1930s with watercolours, and in the 1970s with larger works in acrylics, some Aboriginals have embraced a Western artistic tradition and used it to produce their own works, in their own styles and sometimes using their own materials. The finest are paintings, which have met immense critical acclaim and which can be priced at hundreds of thousands of dollars. The subjects depicted are more often than not colourful Dreamtime narratives.

Interestingly, most of the artists who have commanded high prices have not used their new wealth to adopt a Western way of life. On the contrary, they have remained in their communities, living much as they did prior to their fame, and distribute their money in much the same way as meat is shared out: handed to relatives and others with whom the giver has an established, often ceremonial, relationship. Money is rarely saved, or invested in land or property, but it is given away or spent, often on things Westerners think 'wasteful', such as trips to town for gambling, fast food, and alcohol.

Although a significant part of the money generated by Aboriginal artists has been taken in commission by non-Aboriginal gallery-owners and agents, the example stands as a good illustration of two related points: even where a different way of life is available to indigenous people, they do not necessarily choose to adopt it; and ideas about what money is actually for – attitudes which lie at the root of Western industrialization of course – differ widely between different peoples (just as they can differ between the wealthy and poor citizens of rich nations). I will return to this point.

A major feature of the Aboriginal movement is that it has spent decades working through the legal system. This climaxed in a 1992 ruling, which reverberated throughout the world of indigenous rights. Called the 'Mabo case', after one of the Aboriginals in whose name it had been brought ten years before, it rejected for the first time the principle that Australia was legally *terra nullius* (nobody's land) when the British first arrived. It confirmed that the indigenous people's view of their own customs and laws, in which they owned the land, whether or not they had written contracts, was valid in today's law. The decision established the legal concept called 'native title', which is now recognized on some continents (though usually not applied).

It was also in reference to Australia that, in 2002, a major mining company (Rio Tinto) first said that, irrespective of whatever loopholes there were in local law, it would simply not mine Aboriginal land if it did not have the proper agreement of the indigenous owners. This was the culmination of decades of protest organized against the company by indigenous peoples and their supporters, and it was considered revolutionary by the extractive industries – a key step in their beginning to move away from being the all-devouring agents of an invading society. Of course, to be meaningful it must be enacted; usually it is not, and the same company seemed to moderate some of its commitment after only a few years.

Despite such advances, many Aboriginals have been able

to do little to curb the cycle of deprivation to which they are subject; although some have succeeded in wresting back at least some measure of control. A group of Martu people evicted from the Western Desert in the 1950s for the missile tests, returned thirty years later to re-establish a community where they forbid themselves alcohol and have gone a long way towards rebuilding their pride. They are not unique, and form part of what has become known as the 'outstation movement' – another powerful riposte to those who think that everyone wants to live like Westerners.

At the same time, although the racism which views Aboriginals as inherently inferior may be slowly diminishing, it remains a potent force in white Australia today, both in government policies and public attitudes. The prevailing view is not so much that Aboriginals are a dispossessed people, suffering a long legacy of, at worst brutal and at best profoundly ignorant, treatment at the hands of an occupying force, but that many of them are violent drunks, largely incapable of helping themselves. The situation is unlikely to improve in any depth until this attitude changes.

New Zealand

The problems faced by Aboriginals in Australia are replicated in New Zealand, though the situation is perhaps not as bad. For example, there are probably more indigenous individuals there now than there were when the British first turned up. The indigenous peoples, the many Maori tribes, are not black-skinned like the Aboriginals or Papuans, but are amongst those peoples, called Polynesians, who colonized the ocean from the Asian mainland, starting around three thousand years ago.

These tribes were expert seamen – far more accomplished than the Europeans of the time – who organized themselves with cohesion and discipline under accepted leaders. Without this quality, they would have had little chance of navigating their huge hundred-crew canoes across the world's largest ocean. They numbered perhaps a hundred thousand in New Zealand when the British arrived, and they put up stiff resistance to the occupation, using the firearms they acquired from the newcomers to fight both the invaders as well as each other. After many hostilities, the British drafted the famous Treaty of Waitangi, named after where it was first signed in 1840, and then spent years getting hundreds of chiefs to agree to it. Although the document stands as a milestone in indigenous rights, the Maori translation is significantly different from the English version. This is not surprising: it was hastily translated overnight by a missionary working to secure New Zealand for the British Empire. The Maori copy, in which the tribes agree to give up 'governance' but nevertheless retain possession of their lands, and just about everything else, is at odds with the English translation, which gave 'sovereignty' to Britain. The treaty ushered in years of serious conflict that lasted until the end of the nineteenth century and has far from disappeared today. Disagreements are no longer settled by firepower but, even in recent decades, over a thousand treaty violations have been investigated, and the Treaty of Waitangi remains a serious issue and the source of much confrontation.

The half million or so Maori in today's New Zealand are largely relegated to the most impoverished sector of the population, where they suffer similar problems to Australia's 'urban' Aboriginals: high rates of alcoholism; imprisonment; suicide and so forth. New Zealand has nevertheless gone significantly further than its larger neighbour towards recognizing them as the country's living and legitimate indigenous people – the Maori language is now routinely taught in schools and broadcast on the radio, and Maori occupy a number of parliamentary seats. However, hostility towards them has far from disappeared: in 2006, for example, racist slogans were sprayed on some of the country's most ancient rock paintings.

Continuing our journey east takes us next to the Americas, where indigenous peoples have probably become more famous than anywhere else on Earth.

North America

They made us many promises but they only kept but one: they promised to take our land, and they took it.

Red Cloud, Oglala Lakota, USA

Human movements can be dated by the established method of looking for the scant remains of people and their artefacts, but also nowadays by examining linguistic and genetic divergence from common roots, though these sciences are in their infancy and subject to much conjecture. Whatever method is used, and as I have pointed out, no one knows even approximately how many thousands of years have passed since tribes first walked from Asia to Alaska. What is certain is that the Americas were the last continents, excluding the Pacific Islands, to be colonized. In that sense, they really are a 'New World' to humankind.

Inuit

As many tribes headed from Alaska south to warmer climes, others – specialists in northern hunting – stayed in the High Arctic islands, tundra, and at the forest edges. All were eventually to be displaced or absorbed by more recent migrants following similar routes, armed with their dog teams and skin boats, and bringing a unique hunting technology: toggling harpoons (which remain embedded in the prey); bows and arrows; and the famous 'igloo'. Their descendants still live in Alaska, Canada and Greenland and are collectively known as 'Inuit' (though some are not strictly-speaking Inuit, but rather Aleut, Yupik, or Inupik). Like the Indians, Bushmen, Pygmies, Aboriginals, Maori and so forth, the Inuit are not one tribe, but a term for many different peoples who share both a geographic area and genetic heritage.

The Inuit were mainly hunters and fisherfolk, living largely off their catch and eating relatively few vegetables, in many cases just berries and seaweed. Contrary to the edicts of Western nutritionists, some thrived for centuries in one of the world's coldest environments without bothering too much about cooking. Even today, the Inuit of Baffin Island can put whale blubber in their electric freezers, not for storage but in order to eat it well frozen!

Some Inuit still hunt seals, waiting at the creatures' icebound breathing holes; some still stalk whales from kayaks; sled-dogs are still used in some areas; and the snow-house or 'igloo' (which means 'interior space') is still built here and there to provide shelter at hunting camps. But all these things have been disappearing for decades. The outside world has come in the form of settlements of wood and concrete, television and electronics, firearms and powered harpoons for hunting, shops with imported food and goods, transport by snowmobile, and salaried employment, especially in the oil and gas industries.

There are about one hundred and fifty thousand Inuit in all. Many live in the north of Canada, where their autonomous region called 'Nunavut' was created in 1999. The fifty thousand Greenland Inuit also live autonomously: they are technically within Denmark, but their country is self-governing and moving increasingly towards more independence. As with Papua New Guinea, this means that many Inuit are in the unusual situation for indigenous peoples of being both the majority where they live, and having political control over much of their affairs. In these ways, they could be said to fall outside our definition of indigenous peoples, but what autonomy they now have is recent, and followed generations of domination by others. Unfortunately, it has not provided much escape from the same problems that plague indigenous peoples everywhere. The Inuit still have similar health problems, for example, as those faced by North American Indians and Aboriginals in Australia. They too are physically and psychologically built for frequent vigorous activity, but nowadays sedentary boredom brings obesity and, all too often, alcoholism, and economic and social breakdown.

In the nineteenth and twentieth centuries, many Inuit, like their Siberian relatives in Russia, became embedded into the world economy by hunting and trapping for the fur trade. This market collapsed in the 1980s, as Europe's vigorous anti-fur campaign succeeded in putting off buyers. Inuit communities, formerly reliant on fur for an income, became destitute almost overnight. Fathers who had been breadwinners found themselves with nothing to do, and no way to support their families other than through government handouts. More drink and domestic breakdown were inevitable. Attempts to convince anti-fur campaigners in Europe to make an exception for indigenous-trapped fur fell on deaf ears. The Inuit smarted under what they saw as a crippling injustice and hypocrisy: they had once been pressed into hunting for fur instead of food, only to be now told it was worthless. The feeling of victimization was not helped when they discovered that there was especially fierce opposition to the fur industry from the Netherlands, a country where hundreds of thousands of muskrats are killed every year to prevent damage to the dykes. The Dutch could kill furry mammals to protect their livelihood; the Inuit could not.

In many ways, the outside world has made life harder for the Inuit than it once was, though it remains the case that most other people continue to find their climate unbearable, and this gives them a degree of protection from some of the invasions which ravage other indigenous peoples. Paradoxically for those who live in the coldest places, it now seems that global climate change is affecting the Inuit more than others. The biggest problem seems to be the increasing unpredictability of the seasonal cycle: people are nervous of venturing on long trips as they no longer know what weather to plan for.

American Indians

South of the Inuit live probably the most famous indigenous peoples in the world. As their ancestors moved down from Alaska, taking several thousand years to reach South America's southern tip, they first encountered all the richness and variety of North America and they adapted accordingly. The northern subarctic pine forests, the Northwest Coast, the eastern woodlands, the Great Plains, the deserts of the southwest. All gave rise to thousands of tribes who lived by varying degrees of fishing, hunting, gathering, and cultivating crops. Many dwelt in sizeable towns, others preferred a more mobile 'camping' way of life. Some formed large alliances with complex forms of government, others preferred small bands, free from the constraints of leaders. Some fought each other, sometimes over land and territory, sometimes more ritually, others steered clear of conflict as much as they could. Then the Europeans arrived to change everything.

There had been Viking camps in Labrador centuries before Columbus, and by the time of his famous voyage in 1492, Basque fishing expeditions were probably already exploiting the plentiful cod around Newfoundland and Labrador. After Columbus, Spanish colonies were soon established in the southwest United States, but the first settlement which turned into the irreversible and total colonization of North America began in Virginia, where an English colony called 'Jamestown' was founded in 1607. The English proved hopelessly ill-equipped to deal with their new environment. As the Bantu in southern Africa turned for help to the Bushmen, the English would not have survived without the assistance and highly-attuned knowledge of the local Indians.

The colony was established to seek wealth to enable England to compete with Spain's successful sacking of South American gold. Thirteen years later, the famous Mayflower landed with the 'Pilgrim Fathers' who went on to establish a society based on their view that they were God's elect, and that they had the duty to direct everyone according to His will, which was also theirs. If the Indians did not convert, and quickly, the settlers believed the tribespeople faced eternity in hell, which justified, in their view, any degree of coercion they chose to exert. The 'heathen' natives might serve and help the colonists, but the land and its resources naturally belonged to the invaders, as it was only they who were favoured by God. They thought they had a divine right both to be there, as well as to take anything they wanted. Fighting quickly erupted as the colonists, escaping religious persecution in Europe, foisted their own religious persecution on the natives. With the exceptions of Australia and the Bushmen of southern Africa, nowhere else on Earth was the colonization so brutally total as it was in North America.

Fighting was not restricted to whites against Indians. Many European countries vied for North America's riches, and different Indian peoples formed alliances with some and fought with others. The struggles between the Spanish and English in the south, the French and English in the north, and between the American colonies and the British over the future of the United States itself, all saw Indians fighting for both sides. Their expert tracking and hunting skills, and of course their ability to live off the land, often gave them a crucial edge, and they made many friends as well as enemies.

The 'Far West' of the United States was not fully taken over until the mid-nineteenth century. The names of the famous Indian individuals in this long struggle, heavily anglicized, but referring to identifiable historical figures still resonate throughout the English-speaking world today: Hiawatha, Pocahontas, Geronimo, Sitting Bull, Crazy Horse – all were real people with fascinating, usually tragic, lives.

As the European wagons rolled west, the Indians moved away, or stood their ground and fought when there was nowhere else to go. Indians were resisting the armed invasion of their lands throughout the nineteenth century: their final military subjugation is usually dated to the 1890 massacre at Wounded Knee creek, when the United States Seventh Cavalry attacked a camp of Sioux Indians, killing at least 153 and perhaps twice that number. The importance of this 'battle' is recognized in different ways by each side: despite being a massacre committed by professional cavalrymen against lightly-armed families, who were actually camping there in order to give themselves up, the American army awarded its soldiers more Medals of Honor (its highest award for gallantry) than it has for any other engagement in its history.

Force of arms was far from being the only tactic deployed to dispossess the Indians: in an attempt to make the land grabbing appear 'lawful', the colonists signed hundreds of treaties with many tribes (a nicety dispensed with entirely in Australia, incidentally). Many stipulated that particular areas were 'reserved' for Indian use, with the indigenous people 'accepting' the loss of sovereignty and territorial reduction. Many of the Indians who apparently agreed to these conditions did so with little understanding of what they meant or even said; others had no mandate to represent their people. None of that mattered much anyway, as most of the obligations undertaken by the invaders were broken almost immediately: an increasing number of colonists demanded more and more land, and valuable minerals began to be discovered on Indian territories.

The treaties may have been a way to cheat the Indians out of their land and resources, but they have come back to bite, throwing up a legal quagmire which has ensnared Canada and the USA – and the Indians, of course – in lengthy and costly law suits right up to the present. In Canada, and initially in the United States, King George III's Royal Proclamation of 1763 declared that Indian land belonged to the Crown, but confirmed that the indigenous peoples had certain rights to it. It still forms the basis for many legal claims two hundred and fifty years later. Many Indians, often through their own native lawyers, have used the treaties to wrest back some self-respect, and even land. It is also true that several indigenous land claims have proved strongest where there were no signed treaties at all – such as in the Canadian north. The Nisga'a Indians of the Pacific coastal forests negotiated their first treaty only in 1999; it gave them control over most of their land, as well as their own schools, health clinics, and even police force.

Perhaps the strangest manifestation of how the treaties are applied today is a result of United States Indians realizing that they were not liable to pay gaming tax inside reserves. Some then built casinos and found they immediately had an important economic advantage over ordinary gaming establishments outside Indian land where profits were taxed. Descendants of the Mashantucket Pequot people in New England took this gambit to an extreme. A few hundred individuals, each needing to show only one-sixteenth Pequot descent – a single Pequot great-great grandparent is enough to do the trick – now take an annual income counted in millions of dollars from one of the world's biggest casinos on their reserve.

The wealthy Pequot are an exception. Most North American Indians, including other Pequot, live in crippling poverty. They have succumbed to alcohol and cheap drugs, including sniffing gasoline. They suffer high infant mortality, low life expectancy, low literacy, high suicide rates, a high proportion of imprisonment, much obesity, and the resulting diabetes leading to amputations and other complications – in short, all the diseases and problems arising nowadays from extreme poverty and alienation in a wealthy country. They no longer starve to death, as they did during the 1830s 'trail of tears', when tens of thousands of Indians were forcibly moved off their lands, but they still die early nonetheless.

Resistance

In the 1960s, some college-educated Indians, who had tasted life in the cities as well as the reservations, began a movement partly inspired by the 'Black Power' ideology which, at that time, was proving so beneficial to blacks (now also called 'African Americans'). They named it the 'American Indian Movement', AIM, and it quickly drew support, particularly from more energetic young Indians. As AIM grew, it also attracted the worried attention of the government.

The United States authorities were frightened that a rise in Indian power might prove a destabilizing force in an America already shaken by numerous threats: losses in Vietnam, as well as the exposure of terrible atrocities committed by both sides there; the election of a socialist government in Chile; the rise of guerrilla movements closer to home in Central America; as well as the increasing stoking of Black Power at home by charismatic African American leaders. Anxieties escalated as some other Indian organizations actually began to receive funding from the Cold War enemy, Soviet Russia. Fear finally tipped into an armed confrontation on the South Dakota Indian reservation, Pine Ridge. The location was a powerful, and deliberately chosen, symbol for Indians as it lay near the site of the famous massacre, which had become much better known because of the popular book, 'Bury my Heart at Wounded Knee'. The young Indians of AIM felt the time had come for change.

The 1973 armed standoff between the FBI and AIM at Wounded Knee lasted over two months, with the FBI eventually calling up tanks to try and flush the Indians out. In the end, two Indians and two FBI agents lay dead.

Leonard Peltier, the Indian convicted of one agent's killing – albeit on highly questionable 'evidence' – remains in prison at the time of writing, nearly forty years later. He has himself become another symbol of the unfairness with which Indians are still treated in the United States.

Although they are citizens of the world's richest nation, the twenty-six thousand Indians from Pine Ridge today have a life expectancy lower than any world average bar some African countries and Afghanistan. A Pine Ridge Lakota baby boy can expect to live to only forty-seven, sixteen fewer years than one in impoverished Bangladesh.

AIM was far from being the first national Indian movement. For generations, many Indians had seen themselves as both members of their own tribes and a united people living under the invader's shadow. At the height of the nineteenth-century Indian wars, American soldiers were astonished to realize that many Indians believed bullets could not harm them: they had joined a new religion, the 'Ghost Dance', which they thought made them invulnerable. The sect was founded by a Paiute shaman in 1890 and quickly spread to other tribes.

Another important movement was the 'Native American Church'. Its popularity was partly catalyzed by the healing of a famous Comanche leader, Quanah Parker, through using the hallucinogenic peyote cactus after a bull gored him in the 1880s. Peyote had been used by Mexican and southern United States tribes for thousands of years, but the movement now spread through the country where it still remains a powerful force. It takes elements from many tribal beliefs and blends them with aspects of Christianity: responsibility to family and work, a shunning of drugs and alcohol, helping others, as well as the adoption of Christ as a key cultural icon, are all key elements, with many local variations.

Quanah Parker, who was half European, had a very interesting history. His mother, of Scottish-Irish descent, was captured by the Indians aged nine, adopted into the tribe, and then kidnapped back by white colonists twenty-five years later. She was desperate to stay with the Indians, and eventually starved herself to death in protest at not being allowed to. Amongst other lessons, this is a brilliant illustration of the limitations of descent in defining indigenous and tribal peoples: forebears of the most famous nineteenth-century Comanche shaman were probably in Ireland before the Romans conquered Britain.

Two devices used to complete the colonization of the United States subsequent to armed invasion are worth noting. One is the 1887 Dawes Act, a law designed to break Indian reserves into small parcels, each one held by individual Indians. This legislation, which was not repealed until 1934, made it easy for outsiders to buy or steal small plots of land, eventually eroding the whole territory, which was of course its purpose. One result is that much reservation land today is not actually in Indian ownership. Other countries have enacted almost identical legislation to try to fragment and destroy tribal peoples. Chile did so in 1979, whilst a prominent economist in Peru recommended the same in 2010, falsely claiming it would help the Indians.

The other device was the government's establishment of 'tribal councils' whose leaders were paid, and sometimes even selected, by the federal authorities. Many were, and are, loyal to their tribe, but the imposition of leaders favourable to the dominant society is a usual tactic of colonialism, commonly practised in the building of empires, from the Roman to the British.

The predicament facing Indians in Canada is not dissimilar to that in the United States. For example, one community of Innu Indians in Labrador (despite the similarity in names, they are not Inuit) was reckoned to have the highest suicide rate in the world in recent years. Many teenagers there sniffed gasoline to escape the misery of their lives. When that eventually failed to bring solace, some just shot themselves.

At the same time, it is true that Canada did not see the same brutality and widespread killings of the United States Indian 'wars', and that more has been achieved there for indigenous peoples' rights. In several Innu communities, for example, the worst excesses of recent years now seem to be gradually improving.

The 'Curtis device'

An enduring image of North American Indians is of a noble 'brave', bedecked in magnificent feather headdress, sitting astride his 'war' pony. It is a symbol which curiously echoes that of medieval Arthurian knights – which may be an element in its enduring popularity. It derives partly from a wonderful collection of photos, made from 1895 to 1907, by Wisconsin-born Edward Curtis. He took tens of thousands of iconic pictures of Indians, leaving what is often the only image of them at the time. They are largely accurate and undoubtedly beautiful, but Curtis was also a subject to a compulsion which remains prevalent today: he portrayed the Indians as they would have been years before. He often removed manufactured items from his images, sometimes in the darkroom after the photo was taken, and used captions such as 'war party' decades after the wars and inter-tribal disputes had finished. The same practice – editing out 'modern' items from images of tribal people – remains very common, and is so determining of the way tribal peoples are portrayed in the West that we might give it a shorthand name. I have already coined the phrase, 'Amish error', meaning the mistaken assumption that, for example, using horses instead of cars makes a society 'backward'. I will now call the deliberate exclusion of manufactured goods from images of tribal peoples, the 'Curtis device'.

Perhaps the most famous Hollywood portrayal of Indians, the bison-hunting peoples of the Great Plains, who figure in so many 'westerns', illustrates an interesting inversion of this Curtis device. There is something which appears in thousands of Curtis photos and Hollywood films, and which is embedded in our view of how these Indians lived, but which is as alien to 'traditional' Indian life as the manufactured goods Curtis excluded: it is the horse or pony. By the nineteenth century, the Plains Indians were indeed as expert with and dependent on their ponies, as Hollywood depicts. They rode to hunt the bison which provided their food, clothing, and building materials; they rode to defend themselves against the invaders; they rode to skirmish and war, most famously to annihilate General Custer's Seventh Cavalry at the Battle of Little Bighorn in 1876.

By that time, the Indians themselves had probably forgotten that, only a few generations previously, their forebears had barely seen a horse, except for a tiny prehistoric variety which had long disappeared (possibly hunted to extinction by their ancestors). The European horse was a sixteenth-century Spanish import.

Incidentally, most of the Plains Indians had been farmers only a generation before their discovery of the creature transformed their lives. In a reversal of the chronology normally taught in human 'development', farmers adopted a new technology – the horse – to become hunters.

In historical terms, the initial contact with many Indian tribes was extremely recent, and so was their destruction. Many people assume that Amazon Indians have been contacted more recently than those in the United States, but this is not always the case. For example, the earliest Spanish missions in Amazonia date to around three hundred and fifty years ago, well before the subjugation of many North American tribes. However, the Indian peoples near those same Amazon missions today, which are now within Ecuador, are far more intact than others who have survived near San Francisco or Vancouver.

The European invasion of North America was extremely bloody. A current guess is that about seventy-five million Indians and Inuit lived there before the Spanish, British, French, and Dutch arrived, and that about ninety percent succumbed to the brutality of the invasion and the previously unknown diseases the Europeans carried to the New World. It was genocide on a par with any in history. Today, there are some six hundred Indian tribes, or 'nations', in Canada and the United States, comprising almost three million individuals.

Before moving on, it is worth noting an interesting anomaly: whereas the descendants of colonists in most of the Americas strenuously deny any indigenous ancestry they might have (as I will describe shortly), the reverse is the case in some liberal areas of North America. In fact, a surprising number of Americans claim Indian descent, often from a famous forebear or supposed 'princess', rather than a more anonymous Indian. Many celebrities say they are descended from a single 'tribe', the Cherokee. These include Kim

Basinger, Cher, Kevin Costner, Johnny Depp, Cameron Diaz, Demi Moore, Elvis Presley, Jimi Hendrix, Michael Jackson, Eartha Kitt, Burt Reynolds, and Tina Turner. Conversely, the most influential nineteenth-century Cherokee chief was largely of Scottish ancestry. Some of these celebrity claims may well be real; on the other hand, asserting such indigenous heritage could come as much from a desire to belong, and to lessen any guilt about the Indians' treatment, as it does from genes.

Continuing in our world tour, the human geography south of the Rio Grande, in Mexico and Central America, is in marked contrast to that in the north; it is as different for indigenous peoples as for everyone else.

Central America

She just looked at me and did not speak because they had cut off her lips. This poor woman had been raped. She had no skirt, so I put a skirt on her and offered her water. She was like a child.

Maya Achí woman, Guatemala, testifying anonymously about army atrocities

Central America - for these purposes Mexico to Panama - might be the smallest area described here but it is of enormous importance for indigenous peoples, not least because it witnessed the most significant historical event to affect them – the 'discovery' of the Americas. It is even arguable that if the Americas had been totally uninhabited when Europeans first arrived, our definition of indigenous peoples might now be different to what it is.

Columbus

In 1492, a Genoese navigator and his crew landed on an island in the Bahamas, so changing the world. He was of course Christopher Columbus, the first non-American who both visited the New World and reported his findings. In spite of what generations of schoolchildren used to be taught, and as I have already pointed out, he was certainly not the first European to reach the continent, which is a good illustration of how events can force a rethinking of history.

Throughout this book I describe what is believed to have happened many thousands of years ago; but Western thinking was proved quite wrong about the relatively recent 'discovery' of the Americas.

There is, however, no dispute that Columbus is where the European colonization of the Americas begins, and it is fascinating to read how he describes the Indians he came across. Given how European views were to shift in the following years, morphing into the racist images which still echo today, Columbus's account is surprising. He found the Indians, *'An affectionate people... without covetousness... There is no better people or land in the world. They love their neighbours as themselves... (they) are always smiling... They are so... free with all they have, that no one would believe it who has not seen it... Of anything they possess, if it be asked of them, they never say no; on the contrary, they invite you to share it and show as much love as if their hearts went with it... There is not in the world a better nation. They love their neighbours as themselves, and their discourse is ever sweet and gentle.'*

Although such lyricism might nowadays be derided as overly romantic, there is no compelling reason to suppose it was not heartfelt. The Spanish crown however was not interested in friendly encounters with different peoples, or even in the pursuit of knowledge: it was simply after money. That meant the promise of gold, as well as spices, some of which were more valuable, weight for weight, than the precious metal. The Europeans expected the Indians both to convert to sixteenth-century Catholicism, as well as to work as servants or slaves. Largely the Indians did neither; attempts to enslave them failed, the Indians simply refused and were killed, or died in chains. This set the seal on the brutality which streamed down the generations. As elsewhere, new diseases claimed a high proportion of Indian lives. These were especially smallpox and typhus and, possibly, syphilis (though some think that scourge was not imported into the New World, but originated there).

There was one vital difference between the colonization of Central and South America, as compared with North America, and virtually everywhere else. In Latin America, the Spanish and Portuguese soon mixed with the Indians to such an extent that today most people have some Indian ancestry. This applies to much of the Mexican population, for example, including those who have never spoken an Indian language or lived in an Indian community, and who would vigorously deny any Indian heritage. As I have already suggested, many Mexican city-dwellers find it insulting to be thought Indian.

The most famous of the pre-Columbian ('before Columbus') Indian peoples are the so-called Aztec and Maya. This is because Europeans saw them as being a rung higher on civilization's supposed ladder than other tribes: they had large stone buildings and empires forged by conquest, and so echoed European ideas.

Europeans thought 'civilization', whether in Egypt, Athens or Rome, as well as in Mexico, Guatemala and Peru, meant having stone buildings and empires. The parallel can be taken further. The biggest buildings in Central America replicated the model found in ancient Europe: they were not dwellings or palaces, but symbols representing beliefs and religion. Just as in Europe, their construction needed intensive labour, usually provided by slaves. They could not have been built without the empires, and the class divisions these invoked. Even some academics, who should know better, still parrot that Mayans and Aztecs were more 'advanced' than their rural neighbours.

Anyway, as European colonization took hold it crushed both Aztec masters and their slaves. New slaves then appeared from over the seas. The European conquest brought the largest enforced population movement the world has ever seen – the shipping of millions of West African slaves to the New World. On the Caribbean islands, they virtually replaced the Indian population, which disappeared from disease, killing or absorption. On the mainland, the Africans stayed largely near the Atlantic coast, where they also mixed with the Indians to such an extent that some peoples, who today identify as Indians, are descended at least as much from Africans. In other places, often in dense tropical forests which were difficult to search, escaped slaves established their own societies and began to live a tribal life much like the Indians, sometimes mixing with them. Some of these still exist, particularly around the northern coasts of South America. They are known by a variety of names such as Maroon, Black Carib, Garifuna, and Quilombola. They are largely tribal peoples, though are obviously not indigenous.

Those known as Miskitu, in the east of Nicaragua, however, are a good example of a people descended partly from Indians, partly from Africans, who have identified themselves as indigenous. They played an important role in twentieth-century history. To see how this came about, in fact to understand the region at all, it is important to have a grasp of the regional geopolitics of the last half-century. The dominant feature is the fear which pervaded the United States about communism following World War II. The American authorities often saw this in religious terms: communism was a threat to them and their way of life, founded on a Christianity which was enmeshed with free-market capitalism. Capitalism was seen as God's way, whereas communism was simply the work of the devil. This was not thought to be in any way metaphorical, it was believed to be literally true (and still is by many).

'Yanquis out!'

Communism was seen as the biggest threat to the United States, not only through its adoption by Russia and China, but also from much closer to home. When they looked almost everywhere south of the Rio Grande marking the Mexican border, the American authorities saw a potential breeding ground for a monstrous communist anti-Christ. That river, of course, divides the continent roughly into the English-speaking north and Spanish-speaking south, a divide as sharp economically as it is linguistically: people in the north are often rich, some are very rich of course; people in the south are mostly poor, many are very poor indeed. At the simplest level communism was perceived, by both sides, as the poor threatening the rich.

Those south of the divide were polarized. The political and business elites – the Central American rich – were pro-American; the great mass of the poor were anti-American, often violently so. They saw the *gringo* as the root of most, if not all, problems, and felt that that their labour and resources were endlessly and cruelly exploited to feed the all-devouring *Yanquis* in the North. It is a simple view, but it remains persuasive throughout the region.

The results of this left-right divide were revolutions, wars and widespread appalling atrocities. Cuba, where the Indian population had been long eradicated, famously fell to Marxist rule in 1959, so did Chile to socialism in 1970, and then Nicaragua nine years later. The United States failed to stop the left in Cuba, but they succeeded in Chile by engineering a brutal coup in 1973 and the murder of thousands of government supporters. When Nicaragua turned to socialism some years later, the United States was determined to stop it.

The American government had already poured huge resources into halting a leftist rebellion in neighbouring Guatemala – this resulted in a vicious thirty-year civil war which raged until 1996. The conflict followed a clear 'ethnic' divide. The Indian peasants were prominent in the struggle to overthrow the corrupt pro-American regime, and so they suffered the brunt of retaliation. Hundreds of thousands of men, women and children were killed, often savagely and in circumstances similar to the nineteenth-century Indian wars in the United States. Thousands of innocents died or fled abroad. Ironically, many went north, to Mexico and then to America.

The war threw up an unusual winner of the 1992 Nobel Peace Prize, the Guatemalan activist and K'iche-Maya Indian, Rigoberta Menchú. Her 1983 book, 'I, Rigoberta Menchú', outlined the atrocities committed by Guatemalan soldiers (many of whom were Indian themselves) against the indigenous peoples. It captured imaginations at a time when the war was at its fiercest, and so perhaps played a role in helping to end it. Although it did not always distinguish between events actually lived by the author and others she had simply been told about, its descriptions were accurate enough to provoke widespread dismay and anger at America's backing for a particularly dirty war.

America and 'the right' succeeded in Guatemala, but it failed in Nicaragua: the 1979 'Sandinista' revolution, named after one of its heroes, was swift and decisive. Hailed as an enormous victory by the left all over the world, it ushered in events which disappointed many indigenous rights supporters. It tore up former alliances, and left a legacy of mistrust of indigenous peoples, the reverberations of which can still resonate today.

The first step was taken, shortly after their revolution,

by the new Sandinista cadres. These were composed of young, idealistic men and women for whom any pretence at diplomacy was drowned out in their ecstasy at having defeated 'Uncle Sam' and evicted the American-backed regime. They strode into the land of the Miskitu peoples, who had been largely ignored by the old dictatorship, and explained to the Indians that they were now 'liberated' and must work hard to produce for the nation. Not surprisingly, misunderstanding and disagreements escalated. The Indians who objected were physically attacked, sometimes with great brutality. The CIA spotted an opportunity and secretly began to train and arm the Miskitu to fight against the government. A minor war waged for some years, failing everyone in the end. The Sandinista government, later to fall prey to corruption itself, did not persuade the Indians onto its side. The Miskitu won a few concessions, but most had never particularly wanted to topple the government, so the United States also failed in its aims.

The reason why this sorry episode brought such mistrust was that the pursuit of indigenous rights, particularly in the face of the rapaciousness of extractive industries, had previously been a rallying cry of the Latin American left. The belief that the United States lay at the root of both imposed poverty and human rights' violations had been a leftist axiom for decades. The fact that indigenous rights were trampled in Sandinista Nicaragua in the early 1980s by a popular leftwing government which enjoyed considerable international support, shook former alliances amongst indigenous rights' defenders. To a certain extent, all players in this drama were naïve: after all, neither communist Russia nor Red China had ever displayed any more respect for indigenous peoples than had capitalist America. Why should the Nicaraguan left be expected to do so?

The same political fissure rifts the continent right up to the present. Since 1994, it has crystallized in Mexico in a leftist movement known as 'Zapatista', which emerged largely from Indian peoples in the state of Chiapas – though its famous secret leader, so-called 'Subcomandante Marcos', is not from an indigenous background himself. The Zapatistas think Mexican poverty originates in the United States. They also lay the blame for the routine brutality dealt out by the state, through its police, army and legal systems, at the same door.

About a third of Mexico's population is predominantly Indian, though only about one third of those live in indigenous communities: the rest are in towns and cities and could not properly be described as tribal people. Almost all are poor or very poor, and the same goes for Indians throughout Central America.

In the forests of Panama, the Emberá live much like tropical forest Indians in South America, through hunting and growing crops. Otherwise, most Central American Indians live largely from their agriculture and are somewhat self-sufficient, though all are also connected to wider markets.

In total, there are about seventeen million Indians in continental Central America, two-thirds of them in Mexico. Most speak Spanish; and a few still have their own languages as well. Almost all now see themselves as Christian, largely Roman Catholic, though just as their genetic heritage remains Indian, so do many of their beliefs and rituals, including those expressed through the church. When I look at missionaries later, I will describe the most famous early priest, Bartolomé de las Casas, who instigated a movement in support of Indians that still echoes today.

Five centuries of invasion have reduced the Indian population of the Caribbean islands to virtually nil, though about three thousand descendents of the Caribs are still found in Dominica.

Broadly, the position of indigenous peoples in Central America is similar to those in the Andes to the south. These peoples constitute a rural underclass, which might be called an 'indigenous peasantry', with a long history of interaction with outsiders. Their main problems stem from impoverishment, though as everywhere land struggles are also common.

Before continuing our journey east, to Europe this time, we must first turn to South America, the continent which remains a key for tribal peoples' issues.

South America

We have a place in Brazilian society, we do exist. I want to say to the world that we are alive, we are here and alive, and we want to be respected as a nation.

Marta Silva Guarani, Brazil

The highly politicized indigenous movement of the late 1960s and 70s emerged mainly in North America and Australia, but it was the treatment of Indians in South America that drew most international attention. A colonial frontier was confronting tribal peoples in Amazonia, killing them with disease and violence, and taking their land for road building, ranching, logging, and mining. This invasion replicated what had taken place in North America a century before. It was dramatic and brutal; it still is. South America remains central to international concern for tribal peoples' rights and is the principal crucible where these issues are thrashed out.

Although a huge landmass, South America is one of the easier continents to describe from an indigenous viewpoint. Amazonia covers much of its heart, blanketing a good deal of nine countries under the planet's largest tropical rainforest. The Amazon used to be occupied almost everywhere by tribes which lived to varying degrees from hunting, fishing, gathering, and growing some staples, particularly the root vegetable manioc or cassava. Some were extremely mobile, never building houses, but camping in bands of a few dozen,

138

moving every few days. Others built permanent houses, sometimes huge ones, home to many hundreds. The first European explorers described large towns on the banks of rivers, and although such accounts were dismissed in later years, there is no real reason to think they were not pretty accurate. Many of these tribes have disappeared, particularly from the bigger rivers. Roughly four hundred Amazon tribes remain today, comprising about one million individuals, with the largest Indian populations found in Amazonian Peru and Brazil.

The other principal zone is the massive Andean mountain chain, running almost the length of the continent. Here, the famous Inca Empire was forged in the centuries before the Spanish invasion. It was a kingship that, like the Maya and Aztec in Central America, conquered neighbouring tribes through force. Bizarrely, it initially fell victim to only a few dozen horse-borne Spanish *conquistadores*, perhaps partly because the Indians thought it had been prophesied and so was inevitable, though later rebellions against colonial domination did boil up for centuries, and were often fairly successful. The descendants of these tribes now constitute the majority of the Andean population: they are the Aymara-speaking peoples of Bolivia and Peru, and the Quechua-speakers, from Chile in the south, through Peru and Ecuador, to Colombia in the north. Andean Indians today number some twenty million. They farm, particularly their potato staple, keep herds of sheep and goats, and use guinea pigs as a back-up food. They also employ the American variants of small humpless 'camels' – llamas, alpacas, vicuñas, and guanaco – for transport, wool, and meat. Incidentally, it is thought that the llama could have been one of the earliest farm animals ever domesticated.

With their numerous votes, Andean Indians play an important role in national politics, and sometimes lend their backing to leftwing revolutionaries and armies. They are indigenous of course, and many communities, living largely off their own resources, easily fall within my definition of tribal. In general, however, they are closer to what I have called an indigenous peasantry, as in Central America, and they have not participated much in the indigenous peoples' movement. The exception is in Colombia where they have been in its vanguard, and I will describe this shortly.

The Amazon and Andes Indians constitute the large majority of indigenous and tribal peoples in South America, but there are others too, including several tribes in the tropical forests on the north and northwestern coasts. Although not part of the Amazon basin, these peoples live in a way almost indistinguishable from Amazon Indians.

Orinoco and the plains

The Orinoco, a large river basin straddling the Colombia-Venezuelan border, produces a different landscape – grass plains crossed with 'corridors' or 'galleries' of tropical forest snaking along the riverbanks. These are only a few dozen metres wide but often dozens of kilometres long.

One tiny Orinoco tribe, usually called 'Cuiva' in Spanish, acquired an unenviable claim to history in 1967. Some were invited to a feast by a Colombian rancher who wanted them off 'his' land because they would occasionally hunt a cow or two. Following the meal, sixteen unarmed Indians – men, women and children – were shot and killed. This was far from unusual, and the locals had even coined a new verb, '*cuiviar*', meaning 'to hunt Indians'. The 1967 massacre was actually rather a small affair: in 1870, two hundred and fifty

Indians had been similarly invited to a meal, and all but seven killed.

The more recent killing turned out to be unusual because some missionaries pressed the police to take action, and the killers eventually found themselves in court. Their astonishing defence made front-page news. As well as admitting to killing more Indians over the years, they pleaded that they did not know it was against the law or even wrong to do so. This was convincing enough to see them acquitted, although the resulting international outcry saw them finally imprisoned.

The 'Wild West' is still played out in the Orinoco, or was until very recently, and it is difficult to think of two societies more different than these nomadic Indians and the surrounding ranchers and cowboys, who rightly see themselves as tough frontiersmen. Many of the latter are heavily armed, drink excessively, and bet on cockfights as a favourite pastime.

The Cuiva lived in bands of a few dozen, mostly in the gallery forest, and split into smaller groups for some of the year. They hunted and gathered, travelled by canoe or on foot, and lived in shelters made of branches and leaves, which they erected in half an hour or less. They were amongst the gentlest people imaginable, unusually making large hammocks for spouses and children to sleep together. A friend of mine spent several months repeatedly timing the lapse between a Cuiva suggesting it was time for the band to move on – which happened every few days – and the whole group pushing their canoes away from the riverbank, loaded with all their possessions: it consistently took less than seven minutes. Dozens of reasons were given for moving: a particular tree might be in fruit, there might be more game elsewhere or, most simply, they just wanted to see another place. Even more surprisingly, they did not have to move at all – all their food needs could have been met by staying put.

When two Cuiva bands came across each other, which was not rare, they would begin a long and ritualized exchange of pretty much everything they had. This comprised hunting dogs, cooking pots, knives, bows and arrows, and not much else. Of course, settler society seeks to accumulate things. This would have been pointless as far as the Cuiva were concerned: possessions made it harder to move, and, in any event, everyone would have to give everything away periodically. There was simply no point in one Cuiva owning more than another.

The observation that colonist society was violent, grabbing, misogynist and unforgiving, whereas the Cuiva were peaceful, non-materialist, socially cohesive, egalitarian and gentle may appear 'romantic' caricature, but it struck those lucky enough to know them with considerable force. Such a clash of opposites pushed the Cuiva way of life into oblivion. It is not clear, for example, what has become of one of the bands I visited in the 1970s: some might have been killed, or perhaps retreated further from contact, seeking increased isolation. Others have joined settled Indian communities as their former way of life became less and less tenable because of the surrounding cattle ranches.

The Orinoco plains lie north of Amazonia, and there are other grasslands to the south – such as the Brazilian Mato Grosso – and, further south still, the dry scrub forests of the Bolivian and Paraguayan 'Gran Chaco', and the 'pampas' of Argentina. The plains eventually give way to the freezing mountain crags of Tierra del Fuego. All were once occupied by Indians and many still are.

The Chaco is now one of only a handful of areas in the world where uncontacted tribal peoples still live with no peaceful contact with outsiders. There is a group of Ayoreo Indians there called the Totobiegosode. Like the Cuiva, they too have an unwanted claim to fame. A North American evangelical organization, the New Tribes Mission, has been trying to find them for decades, and I will look at the disastrous results of this later. These uncontacted Totobiegosode have even fewer possessions than the Cuiva: they have no need for canoes in the dry, thorny environment, and have to carry everything with them. Needless to say, they do not own much.

The Indians of Tierra del Fuego, at the tip of South America, have now gone, wiped out by diseases and violence brought in by colonists. Although relatively little known, these peoples also deserve a mention in history, and not only because Charles Darwin said they were the most interesting thing he had ever seen: they were also the southernmost indigenous peoples in the world. They lived in their harsh subpolar climate, which rarely climbed above freezing, but they often went without clothes, slept out, and happily swam in water cold enough to kill Europeans (the Inuit, at the other end of the Americas, generally do not swim). Their hardiness in cheerfully withstanding the cold made a deep impression on early Europeans. Although these lands at the tip of Patagonia remain remote even today, the Portuguese explorer, Ferdinand Magellan, sailed through them less than thirty years after Columbus's Caribbean adventure, and it was probably seeing the Indian fires on the hillsides which prompted the name 'land of fire'. At the time I am writing, only a single speaker of the Yahgan language of Tierra del Fuego is believed to be alive. The Indians started to fall ill and die shortly after missionaries made them wear clothes. The clothing itself was not directly to blame, but it stands as an accurate metaphor concerning this particular genocide and I will expand on the clothing-missionary-disease relationship later.

The 'elder brothers'

Before turning to perhaps the most famous tribal peoples in the world, the Amazon Indians, it is worth looking to the northernmost part of South America, where there is another unique cluster of peoples, in the hills of the Sierra Nevada de Santa Marta. Despite being close to the Caribbean coast of Colombia, this is a cold climate like Tierra del Fuego, growing colder of course as the uplands climb towards the snow peaks. It is home to the Kogi, Arhuaco, and other Indians with a history very different to the Tierra del Fuegians. Even today, these Sierra Nevada Indians retain a fierce pride, which is founded in their religious conviction. They think that it is the offerings and rituals they make to the Earth which keep our planet in harmony. They go as far as blaming their own failings for natural disasters, such as storms or earthquakes – even those they hear about happening thousands of miles away.

For generations, the Arhuaco were the victims of Roman Catholic boarding schools; the missionaries fiercely opposed the Indians' religious experts, and preached a rigid discipline backed up with harsh physical punishment. The Indians eventually had enough, and threw the priests out in 1982. Today, the Arhuaco remain surrounded by Colombians who look down on them as 'primitive' and 'ignorant'; worse, they live in an area well known for both its drug production and its plethora of armed militias. The two are not unrelated: both the leftwing guerrillas and the paramilitary forces that

Savages. Brazil. The Yanomami were called 'the fierce people' by 1960s anthropologists who claimed warfare there was routine. This is wrong: in fact, they are generally peaceable.

Disease. Brazil. Gold miners brought massacre and disease to the Yanomami in the 1980s. One in every five Indians died before worldwide protest forced the government to evict the miners

Image. USA. 1905. Outstanding photographer Edward Curtis airbrushed 'modern' items out of his pictures, in order to present an image of earlier times. Similar manipulation remains common on TV today.

Uncontacted. Brazil. 2008. Indians shoot at a plane, overflying to try to protect their land. The story was world news until a newspaper called it fake. The paper later conceded that it was genuine.

Killing. Brazil. This 1963 newspaper photo shows the aftermath of a massacre of 'Cinta Larga' Indians. After shooting the head off her baby, the killers cut the mother in half.

Finished. Andamans. Boa, the last surviving Bo. The British killed or captured many other Andamanese tribes. All 150 babies born in the home they were confined to in the 1860s died before their third birthday.

North. Siberia. Reindeer in Europe and Asia have sustained tribal peoples for millennia. Stalin had their shamans killed or imprisoned; the oil industry is now destroying the lichen the reindeer live on.

Land. Canada. The Innu relied on caribou hunting until the 1960s. Since nickel was discovered on their land, the government says it will only negotiate about land rights when they agree to give up their 'native title'.

Law. Botswana. 2006. Bushman leaders and their lawyer go to court. The Gana and Gwi Bushmen, evicted from their land for diamond mining and tourism, fought the longest case in the country's history and won.

Hunters. Borneo. Many Penan were nomadic hunter-gatherers. Men hunt; women collect plants. To sustain themselves, 'modern' city dwellers have to spend more than twice the amount of time working as hunters do.

Nomad. Botswana. Bushmen did not simply roam around the desert, but occupied well defined territories and moved from camp to camp depending on the rain and the game. Some still rely on hunting.

Language. New Guinea. Occupied almost entirely by tribal peoples until recently, New Guinea has over a thousand languages – 17% of the world's total, spoken by just 0.1% of the world's population.

War. DR Congo. The Pygmy tribes are hunter-gatherers. Many are victims of murder, rape, mutilation, forced labour, and even cannibalism, at the hands of the militias hiding in their forests.

Protest. England. 2005. Screen icon Julie Christie demonstrates against the treatment of Bushmen in Botswana, where they are held in contempt by the racist views of the governing elite.

Naked? Ecuador. Waorani women and girls wear only a string around their waist, but would feel naked without it.

Lobbying. 2007. Davi Kopenawa, a Yanomami leader and shaman, visits Downing Street, London, with the chairman of the parliamentary group supporting tribal peoples.

Drugs. Canada. In the 1960s, Innu children were forced into mission schools and punished for speaking their language. Sex abuse and beatings were rife. Many are now drug addicts; others have committed suicide.

Roads. Andamans. The Jarawa may have been there for fifty thousand years. A policy to force them to settle, which would have killed them, was halted in 2001. A road through their land still threatens their survival.

Symbol. Australia. 1994. Defying officials, Olympic sprinter Cathy Freeman parades the Aboriginal flag during her victory laps. Designed in 1971, it became an official Australian flag in 1995.

Support. London. 1995. Expert climber Johnny Dawes led the first 'free climbing' ascent of Nelson's column. Innu children danced at the bottom as the banner unfurled opposite Canada House.

they have fought for decades rely on trafficking money. This results in a fantastic mayhem (reminiscent of the fictional world of Gabriel García Márquez novels) in which Indian leaders are often killed, or 'disappear' never to be seen again. In spite of facing such perpetual hostility, the Sierra Nevada Indians remain some of the proudest tribal peoples in the world. They think of themselves as 'elders' and call everyone else the 'younger brothers'. This extraordinary self-confidence is a major contributor to their having survived centuries of intense contact, and why they continue to do well.

In fact, the contrast between how tribes like them have fared, as compared to, say, the Incas who capitulated quickly to outside rule, is a good illustration of the role psychology plays in the demise of tribal peoples. Tribes who believe those who tell them they are backward seem to fare very much worse than those who know the outsiders are wrong.

Amazonia

As can be seen, South America consists of more than just the Andes and the rainforest, but it is still in the legendary Amazon that the majority of South America's lowland Indians live; it is there where the colonial frontier is still invading indigenous peoples' lands, over five hundred years after Columbus, and it is there where much of the world's attention on tribal peoples rightly remains focussed.

The biggest Amazon people is the Asháninka, largely of Peru, numbering about fifty-five thousand; the smallest tribe consists of a single survivor. In one known case in Brazil, the last of his tribe is an Indian who is so traumatized by the colonist attacks he has witnessed for so many years that he now lives in a pit inside his house, emerging only to hunt, when he is frequently shot at. There are doubtless others in a similar predicament, and not only in South America. Scattered around the world, there are several tribes now numbering fewer than a dozen members each.

One extraordinary story of survival concerns Karapiru, an Awá Indian from Brazil. He lived for years on his own, talking to no one, so that his voice shrank to a permanent whisper. He had fled a massacre in which he saw ranchers shoot his relatives, including his son; he had himself been wounded, but had succeeded in escaping. When he was 'discovered', ten years later, officials spent months trying to work out which language he was using, before asking another Indian to visit him and try the Awá tongue. In a barely imaginable Shakespearean denouement, this turned out to be his son, who had only been wounded in the shooting. Father and son both thought the other had been dead for a decade.

There are at least two or three dozen Amazonian peoples who have no peaceful contact with outsiders. These are the 'uncontacted' tribes who are sometimes now referred to, in Peru anyway, as 'in voluntary isolation'. The existence of several is known only to local people, and then sometimes only hazily. I have personally been in more than one place where local Indians have told me, entirely matter-of-factly, that they often saw signs of uncontacted tribes. In recent years, some peoples have emerged from isolation surprisingly close to quite heavily populated areas. There will certainly be others: it is extremely easy to hide in the dense rainforest, especially when it is home.

'Uncontacted' does not mean the tribe has never encountered anyone else: the history of humankind renders that impossible. Some tribes may have had contact with others, including with colonists, generations or centuries in the past, but subsequently fled into remoter areas to protect themselves against violence or disease. Many uncontacted tribes have also acquired imported goods from inter-tribal trading and raiding. Nevertheless, the concept of 'uncontacted' denoting, 'without peaceful contact with outsiders, except perhaps for some neighbouring tribes,' remains a meaningful description for the world's most vulnerable peoples.

Nowadays, killings and even the occasional massacre still take place, but not on the scale of decades ago. In 1963 for example, the 'Cinta Larga' Indians in Brazil had dynamite dropped from a plane onto their village by rubber-collectors who wanted them out of the way. When brought to trial, twelve years later, one of the killers openly boasted, 'It's good to kill Indians.'

Although a stereotyped image of Amazon Indians is that their societies rapidly fall apart when contacted by outsiders, this is not in fact the case. On the contrary, if their land is left to their control, they are usually resilient peoples, easily able to cope with the new problems that contact with others throws up. All too often, of course, that is not what happens. The land is taken for large-scale ranching, often for bio-fuels or cattle, as well as for mining and timber. The extensive Brazilian road building programme of the 1970s and 80s harmed many indigenous peoples, and destroyed several.

As well as being one of the main focuses of those concerned with indigenous peoples, the Indians of South America are also amongst the principal protagonists of their own rights. The modern indigenous peoples' movement there began in the 1970s, with local, regional, and finally national Indian organizations forming, particularly in Colombia and

Peru. Both countries had helpful historical antecedents. In Peru, there was a 1742 revolt of the Asháninka and other tribes which defeated Spain's soldiers, and closed a large area of Amazonia off to colonists for a century. It was led by a highland Indian, Juan Santos, who called himself 'Atahualpa' after the last Inca king. In Colombia, another highland Indian, Manuel Quintín Lame, led a largely nonviolent opposition to the colonization of his homeland, the Cauca, from the 1920s.

The Cauca is in the lower Andes, not Amazonia, and it was here in 1971, four years after Quintín Lame's death, that the first solid Indian rights' organization – the prosaically named Regional Indian Council of the Cauca (CRIC) – was founded. CRIC developed a technique of passive resistance which proved extremely dangerous, but effective. They took over and ploughed 'white-owned' ranch land, and then accepted arrest and imprisonment, knowing that more Indians would come in to continue the occupation. The local prisons filled to the point where the authorities realized they simply could not arrest any more people. The idea was simple. It largely worked, although dozens of CRIC leaders paid a very high price, and were assassinated over a period of many years. Nevertheless, a good deal of land was eventually legally returned to Indian hands.

The organizational model for Indian resistance has taken off spectacularly in Colombia since CRIC's foundation. Nowadays, literally dozens of indigenous organizations have helped many Indian peoples wrest back land, a good measure of control over their own lives, and a great deal of self-respect.

Indian organizations in Brazil are perhaps not as strong, which is paradoxical because there are more non-Indian support organizations in that country than elsewhere. It may even be that too many support groups can discourage the formation of indigenous-run organizations, or perhaps stifle some that do emerge.

Theft of Indian land continues in South America, but in large areas the situation is now more stable than it has been in the past. Governments recognize indigenous peoples' rights, even when they do not apply them, and the balance has certainly shifted, at least amongst much of the South American intelligentsia, to recognize that the Indians deserve respect as the 'first owners' of the land.

The total indigenous population of South America is some twenty-two million; about six percent of them can be counted also as tribal.

Before leaving this 'world tour' of indigenous peoples and turning to some important, and controversial, aspects of their lives, I will look briefly at the situation in Europe.

Europe

Modernity does offer certain advantages, but each day it nibbles away at our freedom. My children won't be reindeer herders, but I'll do everything I can so that they remain Sami.

Karen, Norway

The several million Romani (or Roma) peoples, or 'Gypsies' as they have been more commonly called, are not indigenous to Europe, nor can they be called 'tribal'; however, their situation is worth mentioning, as they do share certain features with the peoples I am looking at, and they are often invoked in debates about indigenous affairs.

The Romani are, at least in part, descended from people who left India for the Middle East a few centuries before their arrival in Western Europe around the 1400s. It is possible many may have initially been employed in Persia as entertainers and court musicians. Anyway, they spread through the region, and the largest populations are today found in several European countries, though there are also Romani people now in all other continents. A few maintain a mobile way of life, or did so until recently, and largely reject attempts to settle and assimilate them into mainstream national life.

They have faced repeated persecutions more or less everywhere; which has included several attempts to eradicate them completely. The Nazis in the 1930s and 40s considered them 'subhuman', and subjected them to the same horrific treatment they inflicted on Jews, homosexuals, and the mentally ill. That crime was rapidly followed by another in the new communist regimes of postwar Europe, where Roma were denied the ability to move around, and many were forced into a conventional way of life.

Some Romani have nevertheless proved extraordinarily resilient: rejecting house ownership and literacy, refusing to keep their money in banks, and insisting on marrying within their group. Racist feelings towards them are still prevalent, with many non-Roma believing them to be potential thieves or, at best, vagabonds. However, they have traditionally been providers of a variety of services, such as expertise with horses and music, and have also held more commonplace employment, such as blacksmithery and carpet selling. Some Roma claim that their approach to making a living is the more sophisticated, as they enjoy performing the services they provide, rather than taking humdrum work just to earn a living.

In Hungary, where they have long been despised, Roma tend to reciprocate by looking down on other citizens as mere 'peasants'. (When the authorities threw hundreds of them out of France in 2010, it did not go unnoticed that the eviction was ordered by a president, Nicholas Sarkozy, whose father was Hungarian.)

Some people believe them to be unique in their attaching little importance to a geographic place – either of origin or dwelling. In the same vein, they have rapidly adopted all kinds of other, often core, markers of whatever mainstream people they live alongside; for example converting to the local religion. Indeed, this willingness to change many aspects of their beliefs and way of life may be a key factor in their ability both to survive and to retain some other values which they deem the most important of all to their self-identity.

If the Romani are neither indigenous nor tribal, is there anyone in Europe who does fall within the definitions? Some of the Russian tribes already described in the Asia chapter are geographically also inside Europe. It is also true that the Basques, from the western side of the Pyrenees, almost certainly predate the arrival of other Europeans in their area, nevertheless only one European people has joined the global indigenous movement: they are the Sami (also spelt 'Saami') of the far north.

The Sami used to be called 'Lapps', which is now considered derogatory, and it is possible that their ancestors arrived in the area soon after the ice age retreated, about nine thousand years ago. They used to comprise fisherfolk, hunters and trappers, as well as the famous reindeer herders, but nowadays only a minority still lives off their reindeer and sheep. About a hundred thousand Sami survive, half in Norway and most of the rest in Sweden, with smaller numbers in Finland and Russia.

Some governments of these countries recognize the Sami as a distinct people, and use the dozen or so Sami languages as the key identifier. In Norway, those with one Sami-speaking great-grandparent are recognized; Finland requires a grandparent to have spoken Sami as a first language. In Sweden, reindeer herding is used as a defining characteristic, though the state has severely reduced the amount of land available for pasture, so making it increasingly hard to be Sami.

Sami languages, music and costume have all enjoyed revivals in recent decades. Although a Sami Council was formed as early as 1956, it was not until 1979 that a proposal to dam the Alta River in Norway united many of them in opposition. The dam went ahead, flooding much valuable herding land, but led to an important Sami resurgence, which seven years later prompted them to devise their own anthem and flag. In 1989, they formed their own parliament in Norway. They now have a measure of control over their own lands, and have facilitated, often with financial grants, the emergence of indigenous peoples' movements in other continents.

This completes our lightening tour around the world. I will now turn to some more general aspects of how tribal peoples live, building on the most important – how they get food – already described.

Lifestyles – variations on a theme

A more accurate description would have been Mesolithic, middle Stone Age or hunter-gatherer. Why this perfectly acceptable, biological, evolutionary description should cause offence I do not know.

Baroness Tonge, UK, disparaging Bushmen in 2006

In my 'world tour', I have mentioned some of the problems faced by indigenous and tribal peoples in particular countries. I will outline their difficulties in a more general way later, but before doing so, I describe some other aspects of their ways of life and thought, including some very controversial ones which are still widely used to denigrate them.

Some of these have little or no basis in fact; others are more legitimate. But even the latter should be examined in more depth than they usually are. For example, if some tribal peoples are indeed 'barbaric' at times, are they any more so than industrialized people? This chapter, then, is intended both to challenge some common prejudices, as well as to stress that *all* of us share *all* the most important aspects of human life.

A good place to start is with the widespread prejudice that many tribes are 'naked savages'. You might think that whether someone is 'naked' or not is simply an objective observation, but even that is wrong. When looked at from a tribe's own point of view, it is just an opinion based on cultural expectations.

Naked, or not?

People wear clothes, paint, jewellery and other things for various reasons: as protection from the weather, plants and animals; from embarrassment about their nudity; to show what tribe, class or profession they belong to; out of an urge for decoration; or simply to conform. This is as true for tribal peoples as for everyone, and it is surprisingly difficult to place the reasons in an order of importance.

Warmth might appear the obvious priority, and clothes are obviously used to protect from the cold, but there are peoples who live with great cold who do not bother much with them. An extreme example is the Indians of Tierra del Fuego, already mentioned: they happily used to swim and sleep in very low temperatures with very little covering. The temperature of hot deserts often plummets at night, sometimes to below freezing, yet the Kalahari Bushmen and Australian Aboriginals relied more on their own hardiness and on fires than on wrapping up. Some still do. The same is true in the New Guinea highlands, where nights are cold, yet the people remain largely unclothed, relying on fires, hugging themselves closely with crossed arms, and rubbing pork fat into their skin for warmth. Even tropical Amazonia can be very cold in the damp nights, but this does not overly bother the Indians who simply climb out of their hammocks or beds several times a night to build the fire.

If some people do not use clothes to keep warm, even when it is cold outside, a similar paradox can be found with feelings about nudity. Some of the most apparently naked peoples are actually extremely prudish. For example, a number of Amazon tribes go naked apart from a waist string. In some, the men tie their foreskins into this so that the penis is always upright against the belly (which has the – intended – effect of largely concealing erections). An Indian would be as embarrassed to be seen without his or her waist string, as would a sleepwalker, waking up naked in a city street. Even tiny girls, 'dressed' only in their string, are routinely admonished to sit with their legs together to maintain a sense of modesty.

Shame about nudity is embedded into human thinking in a large number of places, though it does not always apply to the same body parts. For example, it is worth remembering that there are branches of Islam which require women's hair to be covered, as did some Christians once (which is why the British Queen wears a hat to church!). Some tribes in Muslim regions have followed suit: women's hair is not openly displayed.

Women's breasts, on the other hand, are freely exposed in many places. For example, Emberá women in Colombia go topless, but must keep the sides of their thighs covered. Even a Western one-piece bathing suit would be thought indecent there.

The mistaken view that tribal nudity fomented licentiousness was common amongst nineteenth century missionaries, and has not disappeared. Conversely, some Western liberals welcome tribes' lack of clothes, thinking it means a freedom from inhibitions. Both are wrong: not only are tribal people not naked in their own eyes, but the rules and conventions about who may have sex with whom, and where and when, are often observed far more strictly than in the West.

Notwithstanding this, one of the core tenets of the missionary endeavour was, and remains, to clothe the naked natives. This simple prejudice became one of the most deadly weapons in colonialism. Clothes were an important agent of the fatal diseases which destroyed more indigenous people than anything else, eventually killing millions all over the world. Several reports say that clothes and blankets carrying deadly germs, especially smallpox, were deliberately given to indigenous people in the Americas. There is one substantiated case of this: in 1763, a British officer had a couple of blankets from smallpox victims passed to the Indians besieging his fort in what is now Pittsburgh. Germ warfare had been practised in Europe and the Middle East since classical times, so there seems every reason to suppose it was deployed in the destruction of American Indians. However, even if clothes did not carry contagion by intent, they were still part of the process of killing.

Rainforest peoples who have recently been exposed to new (for them) viruses, like simple colds and influenza, often sit around apathetically, not knowing how to respond. If a whole community is stricken, people often stop getting food, and so become weaker and weaker. The cycle can quickly descend into deadly pneumonia, made worse if people are in damp and unwashed clothes.

Clothing can of course be a marker of tribal or group identity, rank or profession, and so can hairstyles, body paint, jewellery and scarification. All can also be used for nothing more than simple embellishment. Tribal people often take as much care over their appearance as anyone, particularly if a party is being planned or they are seeking attention (often to do with sex, of course). Maasai men can spend longer over their elaborate coiffure than a Berlin teenager preparing for a night out clubbing.

Much decoration might be without deep significance but, even so, what it expresses seems to stretch back into deepest prehistory. Beads many tens of thousands of years old have been found, and there seems every reason to think that simple embellishment might predate other, more 'practical' reasons for clothing. It seems that those, like me, who fail to grasp the importance of 'accessorizing', are simply wrong!

It is also worth noting that 'hairstyles' includes body hair as well. Some tribes have extremely little, and only the sparsest beards. Both pubic and facial hair might be shaved with sharp wood or stone, or nowadays razors, or simply pulled out. Indeed, what people do with their hair is often as important to them as whether or not they wear clothes. Of course, this applies to many Westerners too, of whatever sex. But there are also many other things, particularly to do with so-called 'work', which are specific to either women or men.

Division of labour

A sexual division of labour is found everywhere. I have described this in connection with getting food: in hunter-gatherer communities, the men hunt large animals, and the women gather 'wild' foodstuffs and trap smaller game. With shifting-cultivators, the men do the heavy work of plot clearance, and the women plant and pick the vegetables. In the case of many pastoralists, it is left to the men and boys to tend the herds. Almost everything to do with childrearing falls, everywhere, to women and girls, and the same is true for a good deal of food preparation and cooking.

That is the simplest overview, but there is also a good deal that both sexes do together, as well as much crossover. For example, a widower might work in the gardens himself, as well as gathering and cooking his own food. In the South American Chaco, men can choose to adopt women's roles, take feminine names, and be largely incorporated into the female side of society. They may also have sexual relations with other men, but not invariably so. As a general principle however, particularly in smaller tribes, there is little which is not gender-specific when it comes to food: all the men do pretty much the same thing as each other, as do all the women.

Lifespan – and barbaric practices

Birth is, of course, the province of women, and everywhere it is subject to rules, mainly about where it happens and who can attend. Although tribal childbirth is also regulated in this way, it is usually regarded as an everyday event, attracting no fanfare, with little special attention given to either baby or mother. In Amazonia, for example, a woman leaves the house and goes into the forest interior to give birth, either alone or accompanied by another woman. When she returns with her baby, often after only an hour or so, life carries on as before. In many places, the placenta may be treated in a special way, for example by burying it in a particular place, which can remain significant for the child throughout her life. When the Bushmen of the Kalahari walked from place to place more often than they do now, birth often happened on the move. The mother would simply carry the baby and catch up with the band.

This matter-of-fact approach is easily explained. Firstly, tribal people tend to have a far greater intimacy with a larger number of individuals than most city dwellers. Those in longhouses live under the same roof as dozens of others. The result is that even young children have seen many more new-borns than have most city folk; childbirth is just part of ordinary life. Additionally, all societies without access to expensive health care – which of course includes many in industrialized societies – know that infant death rates are high. A new-born, particularly in times of scarcity or sickness, is lucky to survive, so society puts less effort into immediately acknowledging him. This is not to say that indigenous people do not love their babies as much as anyone: of course they do, but waiting to see if a child is going to live, before becoming too emotionally attached, is a sensible defence against repeated heartache. As the baby grows and becomes stronger, steps such as naming follow, sometimes with ceremonies and rituals, and the child takes her place as a recognized member of society. The Amungme in West Papua, for example, charmingly wait until his first smile before naming the baby.

The first, and completely dependent, stage of life does not last long: by the age of four or five, children start to join adult activities. Boys hunt or herd, girls look after smaller children, and help at the hearth or in food gathering. This is not viewed as a drudge, for there is no separation between 'work' and daily life. Play continues alongside, and merges into, grown-up activities. No one visiting any relatively intact tribal community can possibly doubt the happiness of their children.

However, one aspect which outsiders can find shocking, is the degree to which even toddlers are allowed to play in a way industrialized societies now find unacceptably dangerous. People who live in houses raised on stilts, even high ones, seem unconcerned about infants playing at the very edge of the floor, or climbing unaided on ladders or trees. Small children ride large horses in Mongolia, and larger camels in Africa. Sharp knives are never out of reach, and playing very close to blazing fires is normal. There must be occasional mishaps as a result, but I have not come across anyone who has seen anything too serious. (In industrialized societies, on the other hand, serious accidents in homes are common: Western-style houses are not the safe havens we often imagine. In the UK alone, one million emergency hospital admissions result annually from household accidents to children.)

Puberty brings a few years of adolescence, which is soon followed by marriage, often in the teens. This might be thought relatively young, but it was similar almost everywhere until recently. In many places, marriage is less likely to be marked by any ceremony than is the step into puberty. This is what social scientists call a 'rite of passage', a ritual marking the move into a new stage of life. It often involves some discomfort, or even pain. In Africa, some of the more common practices include cutting patterns into the chest or face to leave permanent marks – called 'scarification' – as well as male circumcision, which is cutting off a boy's foreskin, subincision, which is a more drastic cutting of the penis, or a form of female genital mutilation, such as cutting off the tip of the clitoris or edges of the vaginal lips. These practices are common in some herding or agricultural communities, as well as amongst many non-indigenous peoples, but very rare in hunting societies, apart from in Australia where circumcision is common. In their milder and more common forms, both boys and girls submit to them because they see them as a badge of adulthood. In the more extreme variations – particularly with female genital mutilation – some degree of coercion may be applied and serious medical complications, even death, occasionally result. In most societies where this is the case there are now movements from inside the groups to stop the practices.

(Although such mutilation is widely practised amongst non-indigenous peoples, and female genital surgery, for purely cosmetic reasons, is now a growing practice in some Western countries, the custom is sometimes used to attack those who support indigenous and tribal peoples' rights. Why should anyone defend such a barbaric practice? In fact, few do, and most of those who stand for tribal rights are also unhesitating in its condemnation. There is no dilemma here: most human rights defenders believe that cultural practices, hurtful ones at least, should not happen through coercion. In other words, if an individual does not want something to be done to them, they should not be forced to submit, even if 'tradition' requires it. Supporting people's rights has never implied standing by everything they do to each other.)

There is another practice which is even worse than severe genital mutilation. It is infanticide, the deliberate killing of children – particularly newborn babies – or just leaving them to die. It arouses extreme emotions, of course, but on deeper investigation it can be seen that it happens everywhere; limited infanticide is the norm, not the exception. For example, in industrialized societies, just as in tribal ones, babies born with deformities which will make it difficult to survive are almost always left to die. Obviously, the degree of disability which leads parents and society to think death is a kindness is different when expensive health care is available. The principle, however, is no different in European cities than it is in the middle of the jungle or desert: in most industrialized countries it is both legal and routine to withhold care, including food and drink, when babies are born so deformed as to prevent a decent life. As with genital mutilation, there are far more cases in industrialized societies than in tribal ones.

Not all disability brings an early death. There are many cases of tribal individuals with, even quite severe, mental or physical problems being cared for just as well – sometimes better – than they would be in the West (where many sufferers of physical and mental illness are relegated to permanent, and often inadequate, institutional care).

Letting babies die is not just a result of birth deformities though, and some of it amounts to murder. This too is sadly found everywhere. It is likely that the greatest proportion of babies being wilfully killed after birth occurs in places of very high population, like China and India; it has nothing to do with tribal peoples.

The figures are sobering: it is reckoned that about two thousand girl foetuses are aborted daily in India. In this vast and democratic country, which claims the world's earliest universities and where primary schooling has been a norm for generations, about fifty million girls are reckoned to have been killed before or shortly after birth. Many parents want sons rather than daughters, and the problem is worse in towns and cities than in the countryside. The huge numbers approach the total killed in the world's deadliest conflict to date, World War II. 'Modernity' has made it much worse: ultrasound examination of pregnant women, which is heavily promoted in India, reveals the babies' genders and makes it easier to 'weed out' unwanted girls. Interestingly, of the babies that survive birth, a higher proportion are girls in tribal communities than in the population at large. Figures also indicate that more babies actually survive birth in these communities than in the wider population. Accurate statistics are not available for China, but are likely to be even worse than for India. European nations have little cause for sanctimony. In the United States, over four percent of all children who die are murdered; in England and Wales a child is killed by a parent about every ten days.

Some Amazon Indians believe that multiple births are not human, but animal-like. This makes them afraid of twins and, mothers might, on some occasions, abandon one or both babies at birth. As many twins result from inherited genes, it follows that multiple births are rarer where none survive to reproductive adulthood. Most Indians say that the killing of twins is a very unusual occurrence and is dying out, but all data must be treated with caution: women are ashamed and saddened by having to abandon their babies and tend not to speak about it, even within the tribe.

In fact, all accounts of infanticide should be carefully scrutinized: many are invented by extremist missionaries to justify their conversion work, colonial administrators to excuse foreign occupation, or just copied from earlier reports. For example, much anthropological literature on Bushmen states that, in extreme circumstances, small children are buried and left to die. An example even appears in Alexander McCall Smith's popular detective stories about Mma Ramotswe, set in Botswana. This is supposedly based on a real case of a girl who saved her brother from being buried many years ago, but it is impossible to corroborate her story.

Several anthropologists refer back to a single forty-year-old study where three percent of child deaths amongst Kung Bushmen were reported as infanticide. This is of course a small, though significant, proportion (incidentally, a smaller figure than in the United States today), but most researchers say they found no first-hand reports at all. One anthropologist, Elizabeth Marshall Thomas, who worked with the Kung fifty years ago – a time when any infanticide would most likely have been more common than now – states that she did not know of a single case. She wrote, 'Every shred of evidence that any fieldworker has learned about (infanticide) shows that it was exceedingly rare.'

However rare it may be, as with genital mutilation, only extremists would attempt to defend infanticide on the grounds that it may have been 'traditional'.

Many tribal peoples practise contraception. Foregoing sex, and either eating or abstaining from certain foods, are all fairly common methods, and it is true that some foods and herbs can affect fertility, or induce early-stage abortion. Babies often continue to suckle at the mother's, or another woman's, breast for much longer than is usual in the West, and this too can inhibit conception, and ensure a wide gap between children. However, childbirth and parenthood usually follow on the heels of a young marriage, which means that grandparenthood often arrives before the mid-forties.

Many societies believe that real knowledge or wisdom takes this long to acquire; the people who are felt to know most about life are the grandparents or 'elders'. This leads to one of the most frequent upsets when tribal peoples come more into contact with outsiders: the balance of knowledge shifts to younger people. This is similar to the way that technology has left many of the old in Western societies feeling less informed than their children. The young know most about the outside world, so the role of the old is devalued, bringing a breakdown of respect, and accelerating further erosion of other social norms. This is true today much more than it was in the past, and it is more harmful.

This fact aside, and apart from the obvious slowing down as youthful energy runs dry, there is little change in the lives of the tribal old as time passes. Hunting and other vigorous activities give way to more sedentary, but nonetheless useful, occupations, such as making and repairing artefacts and tools. Story telling and a full participation in talks and debates often increases; the old both speak and are listened to more. Generally, they tend to be cared for in most indigenous and tribal societies until they die.

With peoples who used to walk everywhere, such as the Bushmen, the really old, who could no longer keep up, might ask to be left in their hut, with as much food and water as could be spared. The group would move on, and leave them to their own devices and eventual death. Those who find this objectionable, might bear in mind that in spite of being illegal in most industrialized countries, euthanasia has been widely – but very quietly – practised by Western doctors and nurses for generations. Doses of pain-killing drugs given to the dying, which also have the effect of suppressing their breathing, are often substantially increased to hasten their end (as I have seen myself).

Incidentally, some tribal people think that the West's tendency to shut the very old into special homes, where the care is often inadequate and given by strangers, is extraordinarily barbaric. In fact, leaving old people without enough food is also common in the West. It is thought that one pensioner dies – malnourished – in a UK hospital about every ten minutes. The problem is not just an institutional one: there are reckoned to be over a million malnourished old people within the community as well.

The existence of the homeless, forced to sleep on city streets, seems equally as inhumane to many tribal people. After an Amazon Indian friend and I observed this in New York City, I showed him an entire supermarket aisle which,

I explained, was dedicated solely to pet food – I simply could not persuade him that I was not joking.

Another 'barbaric' practice worth citing is a custom of American Northwest Coast Indians, which was deemed extremely uncivilized when colonists came across it. A missionary went as far as calling it, 'By far the most formidable of all obstacles in the way of Indians becoming Christians.' It was outlawed, and carried an automatic jail sentence until as recently as 1951. It was called 'potlatch', meaning 'to give away'. The Indians acquired prestige by redistributing their wealth and goods, or by simply destroying them during a ceremonial feast and dance. It is easy to see why a colonist society and government – based on commerce, above all – should find the idea utterly barbaric!

Tribal and indigenous peoples tend to be much more aware of the differences in the stages of life than those in industrialized countries. Knowledge is both acquired and passed on as the years roll by and everyone recognizes that youths have much to learn. At the same time, the young tend to be much better acquainted with birth and death – and indeed with the social responsibilities with which they will be required to comply – than are many in the West today. It is true that several indigenous peoples do indeed have 'barbaric' customs; so do industrialized societies.

To go further into the rules governing how people treat those around them, the best place to look is within family relationships.

Family

Every society has rules about whom individuals cannot marry: brothers, sisters, parents, and grandparents are off-limits everywhere of course; and some other relatives are deemed too close as well. Marrying within that group is incest, the most powerful taboo there is. It still occurs, but those found out usually face extreme forms of punishment. In spite of this, secret brother-sister partnerships – particularly when the two led separate childhoods – do not seem to be quite as rare in the West as many suppose; in closer knit tribal societies, they would be unthinkable.

Who is forbidden as a sexual partner, or which relative might be a preferred one, can be complicated. Quite a lot of tribal societies distinguish between children born to a person's father's brother (or mother's sister – in other words, two siblings of the same sex), and a person's father's sister (or mother's brother – siblings of different sexes). Both are 'first' cousins in Western terms, but the former, called 'parallel' cousins by social scientists, are regarded by many tribes as much closer in kin, often as close as a sibling. In some tribes, a parallel cousin is actually called 'brother' or 'sister', and is strictly taboo as a partner. Conversely, the latter category, the children of a person's father's sister, or mother's brother – a 'cross' cousin – is regarded in many tribes as being an acceptable marriage partner, and even a preferred one if he or she is of appropriate age and sex. Parallel and cross cousins are only the simplest categories in a large web of kin relationships which are often more important, and frequently much better known, in tribal communities than they are in industrialized ones.

Partly because they are apparently comparable, many anthropologists have devoted considerable time to constructing kinship charts, though their biological accuracy can only ever be an approximation for two important reasons. The first is that tribal individuals often use terms which might not mean the same to them as to their questioner. My 'grandmother' might be any woman of appropriate age who had a hand in looking after me as a child. In some societies, she might just be any elderly woman. My brother might be my real brother, a male parallel cousin, more distant relative, or even just a friend. Obviously, good anthropologists are aware of this and will crosscheck carefully, but that does not mean that all their colleagues have always taken so much care, so comparing one tribe's kinship structure with another can be misleading.

There is another reason why kinship can lay a false trail, and be more about perception than reality, and it exists everywhere: not every man who points out his children is correct. He relies on his spouse's truthfulness to confirm he is their father; yet not every mother can be certain who fathered her child. This can of course be important in societies where goods or roles are inherited, but it also impacts on how marriage preference rules are applied. If I ought to marry my mother's brother's daughter, and her father is not really who everyone thinks, then the 'rules' relate more to belief than biological fact. Kinship rules can in fact be rather like the silent Amazonian ritual I describe later, which turned out noisy in real life!

The reason why incest is such a strong taboo is usually explained scientifically in terms of disease. A larger gene pool generally means a healthier society, because a recessive gene, which can bring a weakness or disability, can become more prevalent with 'in-breeding'. However, this is less of a problem where only healthy children survive to reproductive adulthood, and in many numerically small societies there really is a lot of 'in-breeding' anyway. It is also true that most peoples are adept at bringing in partners from outside, but there are cases, such as the Andaman peoples, where it could be that some tribes of only two or three hundred individuals have brought in very few outside marriage partners for a very long time, yet they still remain robustly healthy.

This is probably rare. Of course, there may have been other tribes, with similar histories, who did not survive at all, precisely because of inbreeding. However, considering our species once numbered only a few thousand individuals, and the direct maternal ancestry of all of us originates with one woman, the fact is that we are all pretty much 'in-bred' anyway.

A single mother-father partnership is the norm in most places. In others, a man can have a few wives at the same time, which is called 'polygyny'. In a handful of places, especially in and around Tibet and the Arctic, a woman can have more than one husband at once. This is called 'polyandry', and often the husbands of one woman are two, sometimes even three, brothers. Both variants are termed 'polygamy'.

Probably far more significant than the 'mechanics' of kinship, is the fact that there is any structure at all. Together with language, it is one of the most important factors in moving human life away from a state of apparent confusion, and giving it discernible order. Partners exchange things; they have 'rights' over, and duties toward, each other. This obviously extends beyond the 'nuclear family' (the smallest biological unit of mother-father-children) and out into the wider community. Certain sectors of society must not exchange partners, whilst others can, so they establish more, and wider, ties of rights and duties. Groups have a sense of solidarity and exchange with their 'affines' (the group where individuals seek partners); they are unlikely to be hostile towards them.

Kinship underpins wider notions of what is permitted and what forbidden, and so gives rise to law and order; it also reflects on what is deemed to be fair, in both exchange and gift giving, and so forms the basis of economics. Indeed, in many ways, it is root and branch of society itself. Many indigenous people tend to see relationships as a form of 'wealth' to be amassed, and they use gifts and exchange to increase it. They become, in this sense, 'wealthier' by enlarging the number of individuals they have reciprocal relationships with. It is a wonderfully sensible way for the individual to ensure there is always someone to look after his or her interests, and so might be seen as the primal key to the unlocking of our human potential.

Law and order

There are literally thousands of different 'legal systems' in the world. As with kinship, all peoples have codes about what is acceptable; all have boundaries beyond which behaviour is judged to have gone too far; all have ways of bringing it back into line. As a general rule, the smaller the population, the fewer punishments are needed. Where everyone knows everyone else, no one can get away with much transgression, so very little actually occurs.

As well as using physical punishment on offenders including, in extreme cases, killing or forcing an individual out of the community, a very common deterrent is the use of shame. For example, in some Amazonian tribes, if a young man – for it is usually young men – behaves rudely at a party, he may be encouraged to take rather too much tobacco juice. In tiny quantities, this is a strong stimulant producing a pleasant 'buzzy' high. A little too much and it acts as a powerful relaxant, with a violent effect on the muscles controlling bladder and bowels. The rude youth quickly collapses in his own mess. As the shame would be as bad as it could possibly get, the restraint is never actually needed!

Deterrence is the most powerful policeman. It also applies to other draconian punishments, never or rarely practised. Many tropical forest hunting tribes have little or no notion of private property. In some western Amazon tribes however, a man's hunting weapons are personal and may not be touched by anyone else, including children. Kids are told that flouting this will result in having burning chilli rubbed in their eyes; they do not misbehave.

Of course, numerically larger peoples have more elaborate codes; these may include edicts which are widely accepted, and sometimes written much like Western law. The United States Constitution of 1788 may be based partly on the oral laws, called *Gayanashagowa*, of the Iroquois Indian confederation. These Indians' 'Great Law of Peace' could even predate Britain's Magna Carta of 1215, often regarded as the first step of what became law in the English-speaking world.

On the other side of the globe, the Maori in New Zealand also have complex codes. An important concept governing these is *mana*, meaning prestige, power and influence. This can be inherited, for example from a chief, but also accrues or diminishes throughout life depending on a person's actions. Another important feature is *tapu*, which governs what is considered sacred and desirable, and conversely what is taboo and off-limits. If the norms governing *tapu* are not properly observed – for example, if someone takes shellfish from a part of the sea where a man has died, before *tapu* has been lifted by ritual – then sickness, and even death, can result.

Another important Maori concept is *turangawaewae*, a place of physical belonging, social empowerment, and family connections. A person's turangawaewae represents 'home', and usually confers an authority to speak and act within a particular group of people. I have already described how different Bushman clans do not have the right to hunt others' land. Indeed, all peoples have a sense of where their territory's boundaries lie, just as the Maori *mana* and *tapu* have obvious parallels in industrial societies.

Many believe that one of the unique markers of 'civilization' is a codified body of law, but some tribal peoples had these before many Europeans, and all human societies have concepts which point in the same direction: in brief, everyone lives under a law, though the degree to which it is explicitly defined is very variable.

The 'law' must of course be accepted as largely reasonable and fair if it is going to survive for long (which dictators, on the other hand, never do). What is considered fair exchange forms, of course, the foundation for economics.

Money and exchange

Some indigenous peoples use or used their own form of currency, for example cowries and other shells, often more for ceremonial exchanges and gifts than for making purchases. North American Indians stitched hundreds of shell beads into wide wampum belts, and it is thought these could have been used by Dutch colonists to 'buy' Staten

Island, New York, from the Lenni-Lenape Indians in 1626. The similar and more famous story about the 'purchase' of Manhattan is not really supported by much evidence. Nor is it likely, in either case, that the Indians realized that the colonists thought they were signing away their land.

Although acute poverty is a serious problem widely faced by indigenous peoples, particularly in rich countries like the United States, Canada, Australia and New Zealand, as we have seen not all indigenous people are monetarily poor. For example, I once calculated that some Maasai, in the rather 'traditional' area of the Loita Hills in Kenya, had herds worth more than a central London apartment, yet they still possessed practically no manufactured goods. This was not because they could not afford them; when they drove their cattle to Nairobi markets, some concealed rolls of thousands of dollars in their robes.

Although hard currency, in the form of notes and coins, may seem the most straightforward of tools, indigenous peoples can use it in ways which often surprise and can even dismay Westerners. In societies where goods are not hoarded, money might be treated in the same way and rapidly dispersed or, when it is accumulated, it is not saved for later purchases, or even to use in emergencies: rather, it is given away, or spent on transient things which might appear 'wasteful'. I have given an example concerning payments made to Australian Aboriginal artists, but a similar situation is found in many places. Some southern African Bushmen tend to disburse freely what little money they get, either giving it to friends and relatives, or simply spending it on rather unnecessary food and drink. Parties are traditionally held in New Guinea to give away valuable pigs, and money is nowadays added to the gifts. I have mentioned the potlatch ceremonies of North America, where goods are given away or ritually destroyed.

Exchanging identical things when meeting people is widely practised. Many South American Indian men swap a small handful of coca leaves, or coca powder, with every man they encounter (similarly to the way, until recently, Western smokers used to offer each other cigarettes). These are 'ritual' trades, in which neither party gains anything different to what he had in the first place.

Giving away money and goods, or making identical exchanges, may seem economic nonsense, but that is not the point at all. The prestige acquired, and the relationships fostered, can be worth more than the cash, or anything it might buy. The individual might be economically no better off after the transaction – he might have simply exchanged like for like, or even be 'poorer' through gift giving – but society as a whole becomes richer: everyone involved has enlarged the network of people they can rely on. It may be a cliché that the poor are more generous than the rich, but it is often seen to be true, and it can make very good economic sense. Spending what little I have on 'purchasing goodwill' from others may be a much better bargain than hoarding goods or money. Accruing wealth can have the reverse effect, risking making others jealous and hostile.

Attitudes towards money also differ greatly between sectors of industrialized societies, where the poor use their modest resources for different things to the rich, and where prestige can be acquired in different ways. In some areas of Europe, for example, the daughters of poor families are bought fabulously expensive wedding dresses, even though these are worn only once, and can plunge the bride's parents into great debt. Goodwill can be worth a lot and might cost very little, but another of the most valuable things money can buy is prestige, and it can sometimes prove very expensive.

When things are given away, repayment is usually expected, whether monetary or not. What is fair exchange, as opposed to what is viewed as theft and cheating, requires the consent of all parties. This leads to a consideration of how people arrive at decisions more generally, and what happens when people fail to agree.

Conflict, class, politics

Conflict is rare in small, egalitarian societies. A group of forty or so nomads, for example, includes only a handful of adult men. They avoid fights with other groups, and if there is serious internal disagreement, the band simply splits into two, each going its own way. In larger, more settled societies, attitudes to conflict depend largely on cultural expectations and individual characters. Some avoid it; others embrace it.

Contrary to much popular Western belief, where there are fights, and even war, they are often connected to feelings of insult and lost prestige, rather than about land or resources. The results can be pretty bloody, with entire communities massacred, but they can also be highly ritualized, where conflict continues only up until the moment someone is killed, when hostilities cease. Rituals like this are found in the New Guinea highlands where men used to throw spears at each other from long distances – ensuring far more misses than hits – and then stop when someone died. Another variation is to stop fighting when the same number has been killed on each side. A similar approach is found in some Yanomami groups in Amazonia, where ritualized combat between two men armed with clubs is used to resolve extreme disagreement. The whole community gathers to watch the protagonists strike at each other, each blow received followed by one given, until one falls to the ground, defeated but alive, when the duel ends.

The Shuar in Ecuador and Peru were the famous Amazonian 'head-shrinkers'. They had a different approach to conflict. Some families bore long-term grudges against others which would fester until, usually only after some years, the men would set off to attack the enemy's house. They would cut the heads off their dead victims, and take them away to make into *tsantsas*, or shrunken heads. The skull itself was not reduced in size, but the skin around it was peeled off and boiled until it was about fist-sized. The lips were then sewn closed. That was the important part: it stopped the spirit of the dead enemy emerging through the mouth to seek revenge. Unfortunately, the system did not work well. The spirit's retaliation might be sewn up, but his relatives would certainly claim it, and the mafia-like cycle would continue, often for generations.

This resulted in a society steeped in mistrust. For example, a Shuar visiting another's house for the first time would be invited to sit opposite the house owner, the latter prominently displaying his ancient firearm across his lap. The newcomer would then be aggressively – and somewhat theatrically – questioned to establish who his relatives were. Was there any reason to seek revenge, or was he a potential friend? The latter was the inevitable outcome, as no one who thought he might not be welcome would dare visit a stranger's house anyway. Once friendship was recognized, one of the householder's wives would hand the visitor a bowl of alcoholic manioc juice. As she presented it to him, she would dip her finger in and lick it, to demonstrate that it was not poisoned!

What was behind these cycles of occasional, but brutal, killings? The reason often given was that a woman had been molested or insulted, many years prior to any attack. This was sometimes so long in the past that no one knew when or where it had supposedly taken place. Some young Shuar women had their own way of reacting when they thought they had been slighted: they threatened suicide, and even attempted it by drinking poison. Fortunately, they usually failed.

Conflicts like this have nothing to do with 'class' divisions of course; this is a concept which does not exist at all in smaller societies. In larger ones, on the other hand, role differentiation, often coupled with the idea that some people are superior to others, enters the picture. This can have little or nothing to do either with the skills different 'classes' possess, or the amount of resources they control. I have described how the Maasai look down on their farming neighbours; they also feel superior to the specialist blacksmiths living in their communities, though they are dependent on both. The fact that both farmers and blacksmiths are highly skilled, and that they both control access to a necessary product, does not stop them being thought of as beneath 'proper' cattle-owning Maasai.

The smaller the human group, the less need there is for specialized structures to govern decision-making. Almost every conceivable political model is to be found amongst indigenous peoples. The range extends from the Jumma tribes of Bangladesh, who have a king, to Amazonian hunters, who have no leaders at all and are truly egalitarian. In some cases, different models apply to distinct sectors of a tribe, as with the 'age set' chiefs of the Maasai. They have authority only within their group, and it can be a position which is neither sought nor desired, conferring far more responsibilities than advantages.

As we have seen, many smaller tribes have no concept of leadership at all; they may also have social mechanisms which work to prevent anyone trying to gain power. There is an apt, and rather good, anthropologists' pun reflecting this: 'One word from the chief and everyone does whatever he wants!'

As these smaller tribal societies enter into a closer interaction with mainstream society, their lack of leaders gives rise to problems. Outsiders want to deal with representatives and spokespeople, not with whole communities. Trying to establish a tribe's views on a new proposal can be confusing for everyone: all decisions are subject to long debate which continues until everyone agrees. If no consensus is reached, discussions just continue, or fizzle out with nothing decided one way or another. To make things more problematic for outsiders, tribespeople might consider it perfectly normal to change their minds, more than once, even after arriving at what might look like a firm decision.

The manner in which many tribal people converse and debate can also differ significantly from Western norms. Tribal speakers can talk at length, with others simply acknowledging that they are paying attention with an oft-repeated affirmative word or noise. The normal to-and-fro interruptions of much Western dialogue – replying constantly to what has just been said, and then leading in new directions – is considered bad manners in some tribal societies. So is any disagreement that is openly expressed. It might appear that two protagonists are agreeing with each other, when actually they are not. When tribes which have such characteristics attempt to form their own organizations to represent themselves to the outsider world, enormous confusion can result.

Other factors can further complicate matters. I have touched on the fact that tribal leaders nowadays are often literate, younger people who speak the national language and have some understanding about the changing future, or at least think they do. If the tribe formerly heeded the older and more experienced, this shift in authority can be difficult for everyone. Such characteristics mean that few small-scale tribal peoples have successfully managed to establish enduring organizations to represent them.

Even when they do, the tribe does not necessarily benefit, particularly when money enters the picture. Leaders can become seduced by their role as intermediaries. They might be asked to negotiate between the tribe and industries seeking to exploit timber or minerals, or with aid agencies offering project funding. Tribal spokespeople can use this role to accumulate money and goods to which others have no access. Some of them, newly enriched, can take the money and spend it on themselves and their families, living in nearby towns, and even running houses and cars with servants and drivers. They might try to cling firmly to their role, in a bid to ensure all future transactions pass only through their hands. Class divisions can then begin to emerge where formerly none existed.

An example of this is government-funded Bushman 'leaders' from Botswana. In one case, a man who opposed the eviction of his people to make way for mining appeared to change his mind as he began to receive a government salary and be taken on official foreign trips. Although he might not have recognized it, he was being paid to tell outsiders what the government wanted them to hear – that the Bushmen wanted to move, when they did not.

Such problems may be a relatively recent occurrence in Amazonia and the Kalahari, but they have a longer history elsewhere. I have pointed out how many tribal Indian councils in the United States are financed by the government, but still genuinely speak for the peoples they represent; however, that is not necessarily always the case.

Some tribal leaders might be seduced by displays of wealth and power, but there is another side to this coin. Small and traditionally leaderless tribal people can also be unimpressed and unintimidated by the shows of wealth which are used by governments to impose their authority. It is also the case that, where there are no leaders, there is no one who can be bought off or otherwise corrupted, or even targeted for killing. Such factors can confer enduring strength and independence to tribal organizations. In spite of their difficulty in forming organizations, or paradoxically sometimes actually because of it, many small-scale tribal peoples have proved tenacious in their refusal to disappear into the mainstream.

To summarize, smaller societies usually have no leaders and are egalitarian; larger ones tend to have hierarchies. Lack of leaders makes it harder to cope with outside pressures, but can also bring some strength. Where class divisions emerge in the confrontation with outside society, they always have a weakening effect.

Governance and decisions are of course almost entirely expressed through the medium of language, and this leads to some observations about tribal and indigenous languages.

Language

Some tribes use very few numbers, as I have explained and notions of how to measure time differ widely as well – not surprisingly, the concept of a year means little or nothing in the tropics, where all days are of equal length – but with language more generally the picture could not be more different. There are thousands of indigenous languages and many are far more complex than European tongues. Contrary to the conceits of nineteenth century explorers, no one has ever come across a 'primitive' one. Bushman languages, for example, have vowels and consonants like everyone, but also five distinctive clicks, and several other click-like 'glottal stops'. The Hadzabe hunters of Tanzania also use clicks, and experts increasingly think that such sounds may once have been an integral part of the languages of all our ancestors. Although a human being can physically produce about one hundred and sixty different sounds, the majority of European languages use much less than one third of them. Most tribal tongues, on the other hand, employ many more, with some Bushman languages using as many as one hundred and forty.

A famous example of the sophistication of tribal languages concerns the number of words the Inuit employ for different sorts of snow. As the anthropologist Hugh Brody has pointed out, there is actually no word at all for plain 'snow': it is categorized into dozens of different kinds, such as 'drifted snow, overlaying a harder layer', 'settled snow, now blown by the wind', and so forth. Multiple, very specific, nouns, used where Western societies only employ a single name, are not the only way in which tribal languages are complicated: several Amazonian tongues, for example, have special tenses denoting how a statement is known to be true. The remark, 'My friend is in the hunting camp', can employ different words for 'is' depending on whether: I actually saw him there; I have recent evidence that he is there; others say he is there, so it is likely; and so forth.

Western languages have become simpler as schooling and technology have grown; there may be new things to talk about, but there are fewer words in daily use, as many, formerly common, terms are no longer understood. This has accelerated recently with some tongues: the more a language is used for international trade, the more its grammar and vocabulary lose their complexity. Although English has a constantly growing dictionary of new words, the average Briton is reckoned actually to use fewer than eight thousand words to read his daily paper, whereas Shakespeare used over thirty thousand (inventing many new ones as well). Tribal peoples, like Elizabethan Britons, generally have a more complex grammar and vocabulary – used to communicate precise information about their surroundings, societies and ideas – than industrialized peoples do as they seek to communicate simple ideas to a large number of people from widely different backgrounds. It is difficult to see how this cannot eventually engender a corresponding simplification of the ideas that can be expressed and understood.

We all turn the chaos of life into apparent order through language, and many experts believe that grammar may be 'hard-wired' in the brain. Even so, one tribe's view of what that 'order' consists of may well be very different to another's. Early studies on one of the Andaman languages, for example, indicate that parts of the body, including bodily products, give rise to names for many other things as well. There seems to be a correlation, for example, between the words for 'children' and 'sweat', for both come from the body.

Studying these ideas, and looking at the differences in languages, can tell us much about population movements –

even very ancient ones. It can also reveal important clues about how the human mind works and has developed. Although many animals can communicate with each other, complex language is still a key in defining us as human beings.

Numerous languages are now fast disappearing. A far larger proportion of the world's languages are under threat than are its plant or animal species. Most of those already lost are tribal, and many more are likely to be gone long before any records can be made. More than one-third of the world's remaining languages are now at risk; some experts think the picture is even bleaker, and that nearly ninety percent of them are unlikely to survive another two or three generations. Nearly two hundred known languages now have fewer than ten native speakers each.

Language, however complex, might tell us much about how the mind works, but there is a point beyond which it cannot reach. A good deal of human experience seems to belong in a different realm, one which is not really governed by thinking at all, and which is apparently not susceptible to reason or analysis. This is the domain of spirits, dreams, and beliefs, of religion and the shaman, of communing with something outside ourselves, or thinking we are doing so. Although some Westerners now try to belittle its importance and consign it to the category of 'backward superstition', almost all societies take it extremely seriously.

Drugs and plants

There are many ways people use to get themselves into a state different to the everyday. Amongst the most straightforward is to induce a small change in brain chemistry by reducing the amount of oxygen carried by the blood. This can easily be done by prolonged chanting or dancing, and many peoples, including Westerners of course, practise this.

Many people also use mind-altering plants. Amongst tribal peoples, fruits and vegetables, such as manioc or palm fruits, are fermented to produce alcoholic drink; tobacco is smoked, chewed or inhaled as snuff; other leaves or nuts, such as coca (the basis for cocaine, not to be confused with cocoa!) and betel, are held in the mouth where their effect is quickly absorbed into the bloodstream and brain. They produce effects ranging from mild physical stimulation and loss of appetite, through to extreme 'drunkenness'. Powerful hallucinogens are also fairly common in some places; these may be made from bark, leaves, flowers, creepers, cacti or mushrooms, and the effects can vary from half an hour of colourful, patterned visual hallucinations, to a day, night, or more, spent in a deeply 'mind-altered' state.

Tribespeople generally take all this very seriously: it is far from being mere recreation. Hallucinogens are ingested only by those carefully prepared for the event which enables people to 'experience' other worlds, other levels of reality, directly. With such drugs, anyone can see what the specialist in such matters – the 'shaman' – might well be able to see and understand without the hallucinogen, though not everyone can understand it to the same depth as he can. Such 'psychedelic' drugs are especially prevalent in South and Central America, but they are also found in other continents, though they are not used by all tribal peoples.

Medicinal plants, on the other hand, are found everywhere in tribal societies. One Amazon tribe, the Shuar, uses no less than a hundred different species solely for stomach ailments, and a further hundred and fifty for other diseases. It is estimated that the total number of plants used medicinally worldwide could be an astonishing fifty thousand. Many Western drugs were originally derived from indigenous peoples, or from the tribal ancestors of the Europeans. Aspirin, for example, originally comes from the willow tree, and has been used medicinally for centuries. Many manufactured analgesics and anaesthetics come from substances found in plants used by tribal peoples; the best known is probably opium, made from Asian poppies, and its many, very important, pain-killing derivatives, such as morphine. At least a quarter, perhaps as much as half, of all prescription drugs are based on substances originally found in plants.

Another category of plant products, originally used not as medicines, but as poisons, has also become important in Western healthcare. The most famous are the South American arrow poisons called curare. These gave the world a very important muscle relaxant which made techniques such as open-heart surgery possible. The line between drug, medicine, and poison, can also be as blurred as in the West. For example, some Amazon Indians use the same resin both as a hunting poison and a hallucinogenic drug.

When considering the crossover between tribal and Western medicine, it is important also to mention that some practices, which are animal- rather than plant-related, and which were once used centuries ago in the West, are now returning to 'modern' medicine. Honey, for one, has a strong healing effect on wounds; its antibacterial properties have always been well known to many tribes around the world. Some Western hospitals are now using leeches to reduce swelling and bruising, and fly larvae to clean infection without risking the negative effects of antibiotics – both practices known to tribes from centuries ago. There is even evidence that Orinoco Indians realized the importance of regulating body temperature well before the idea was grasped in Western medicine.

In general, tribal medicines and medical practices work. If they did not, most would stop being used, though of course they are no more infallible than Western medicine is, and the 'placebo effect' – something which works solely because the patient believes it will – can be found everywhere. Obviously, high-quality industrialized medicine – available to only a few, even in rich nations – is better in some situations than any alternative: complex surgery, and machine-based life support for severely damaged people, are obvious examples. But in many other areas, most obviously those to do with mental health, there are a host of maladies where tribal medicine might have an edge over Western practices.

It goes without saying – I hope – that what is old is by no means necessarily good, but what is new is not necessarily better. A good example of the former (though not from tribal peoples) concerns the ancient Chinese and medieval European belief that mercury had excellent medicinal properties: it is in fact extremely poisonous.

Having touched on the role of the 'shaman' in relation to mind-altering plants, it is important to describe this much-misunderstood role a little more, and to delve further into religious beliefs.

Religion

If a Roman Catholic smallholder from Sicily, a US evangelical preacher, and an Englishwoman who uses the Church of England for baptisms, weddings and funerals, each described their religion, few listeners would think they were talking about the same thing. They all call themselves Christian, and all know the Bible stories, but the similarities do not go much further. Some in our trio would not even admit the others were Christian at all. This is true in spite of the fact that Christianity looks to its teachings from a single text, which has been largely unaltered for centuries.

With this in mind, is it possible to say anything meaningful about the beliefs of millions of indigenous and tribal people from all over the globe, who have distinctive ways of life, and different histories of interaction with others? However problematic it may be, it cannot be skipped over. Much of the dispossession visited on these peoples was originally done with the supposed objective of changing their religion. Conversely, much of what their supporters think makes tribal peoples important today derives from a view – not necessarily very accurate – about tribal beliefs, especially concerning their relationship with their environment. Of course, all generalizations about their religions (as well as much else) will inevitably go unrecognized by many.

Most tribal peoples' religion is commonly called 'animism' or 'shamanism'. The latter is an adaption of a term applied to the healers, or shamans, of the Evenk tribe of Siberia. Many Evenk are now Christian, but these people's former beliefs have come to stand for a kind of global tribal religion. This is not without justification, for there are some common factors to be found amongst tribal beliefs. It may even be the case that a form of shamanism was the only religion known to humankind before agricultural settlements began supporting large townships.

There are, in any case, a couple of facts which are irrefutable. Firstly, no people has ever been found which has no religious beliefs. Secondly, it is very rare for tribal life to be compartmentalized, as is industrial society nowadays, into aspects which are religious, distinct from others which are profane: in other words, tribal beliefs are never far away from daily life.

Tribal people largely believe that what we see and experience in our ordinary, wakeful state, is not the only important reality. The same might of course be said of all religions (and sciences too, for that matter). In shamanism, there are thought to be a number of other types of reality, often seen as layers or levels. Some of these might look similar to daily existence, however others are very different, and might be peopled by spirits or animals, though these may think and talk rather like humans. Some of these are friendly, others are hostile, and a few may be murderous. Most can transform themselves, or be transformed by others, into different things: these may be other, living, human beings; mythic creator figures; plants; animals; natural features, such as hills and rivers; the sun, moon and other cosmic bodies. In fact, all manner of things and ideas mutate and are mutable. Some of these levels interrelate closely with each other; what takes place in one directly affects what passes in another.

None of this is really so very different from the way most major world religions conceive of good or bad levels, such as heaven and hell, 'above' or 'below' our own world. The parallel is further enhanced by the shamanic notion that the spirits of dead people exist on another level, where they can influence the living. Again, this is not dissimilar from the

189

idea, for example, that some long-dead holy Christians, called 'saints', or even just recently deceased loved ones, can influence and help the living.

The religious specialist in tribal societies, the shaman, can visit levels other than our own, visible, world. He might do so in a dream, or during a dance or trance, or by ingesting a mind-altering substance.

For simplicity, I refer to 'him', though in many places women can also be shamans, most commonly only after aging beyond childbearing. It is often thought that the required dietary restrictions, and some of the drug-taking, could harm unborn babies, and of course childbirth itself is the ultimate regenerative and balancing force for any tribe, more so even than religious belief. Women physically create new life, and this fact alone can make men anxious about their own prowess. One response to this is a belief that women in their menstrual period are 'unclean' and not allowed to prepare food; a girl's first period may even be marked by several days or weeks exclusion from the house. Elsewhere, on the other hand, a girl's first period is enthusiastically celebrated for the new life potential it does actually bring.

Anyway, whether a man or woman, the shaman travels to other levels of reality to gain knowledge and power, and also to change things in everyday life. He might, for example, visit the level where the 'owners' of the game animals live. The idea here is that each species, wild pig for example, is 'managed' by a creature that looks like the animal, but acts and speaks like a person. The shaman, in trance or dream, might converse with the pig 'owner' and arrange an exchange: the tribe will hunt wild pigs in the next few days in return for a gift to the owner, such as tobacco. Following his trance or dream encounter, the shaman returns to our ordinary, daily level, smokes the tobacco, and the wafting smoke carries the present to the pig owner.

The shaman also visits other levels of reality to find the cause of sickness. This could turn out to be the result of an attack by a harmful spirit; in which case the shaman will find, fight and defeat it, or alternatively negotiate a deal, offering a gift to the spirit to stop it harming the patient in our world.

Visits to other levels are usually both exhausting and dangerous. A shaman might protect himself by enlisting the services of an assistant, the two making their shamanic journey together. In any event, whether accompanied or alone, he will need to be very well trained and prepared for his trip.

These other worlds – or other levels of our world, if you like, which might also be characterized as levels of our minds – are thought to be perfectly real. During a journey, the shaman's body remains visible in our world, perhaps in trance, but his spirit – and he might have more than one – is away. On 'return', he can recount his experiences in graphic detail. His spirit might also be able to move separately from his body on the everyday level, becoming an important animal or bird, gathering information, attacking an enemy, or helping his own people.

In some tribes everyone is deemed to have some shamanic ability. In others, it is a speciality that must be learnt during a period of apprenticeship, sometimes from a parent. It never becomes a full-time 'job', as with priestly hierarchies in Western societies: the shaman never stops being a hunter or herder and doing everything that everyone else does. His research and training, however, may take years and involve many deprivations. Dietary restrictions are common: he must not eat certain meats or, commonly, salt.

Seclusion and sexual abstinence are also widespread. A shaman must know how to recognize different spirits and how to communicate with them, to move them to do what he wants. He must be able to tell a lot of stories in great detail. These are about the origins of the world and of life, of the animals, plants and even of the important hunting or agricultural tools; all are thought to come from a primeval time which preceded our own and which still defines the parameters of our lives today. Through their telling, such stories recharge their own regenerative force, which is often thought vital and necessary if ordered life is to continue.

Anthropologists call these important stories 'myths', and they form one of the markers of any society, as we have seen. Human beings – not only tribal ones – define who they are by knowing and believing in the importance of shared stories. Their content might be much less important than the fact that they are known to all: in a way, they are the ultimate 'marker' defining 'a people'. The myths may be very long, and a single one may take hours to relate. The shaman might know them by heart, or adapt and change them as, with experience, he grasps more and more about how the different levels work. The stories may be constantly re-shaped by the shaman's knowledge and interpretations. A creation story told by one shaman may differ substantially from that told by another from the same tribe, though each would still recognize the other.

A shaman who fails to cure illness quickly loses prestige. This, the long apprenticeship, and the repeated and tiring shamanic journeys to other, often dangerous, levels, means that the training is an arduous and responsible undertaking. Those who are aware of the shaman's world and its levels cannot ignore or escape its rules in the same way that a person ignorant of them can. The teenage son of a powerful Amazonian shaman told me that he simply did not want to know anything about it. If he began to learn, he would then have to take on a responsibility he felt was too onerous and difficult (later, he did).

The shaman is both religious expert and healer. Some may also be proficient at harming a tribe's enemies, but it is more common to discover that this is only what the enemies believe. In other words, many peoples think that their own tribe only has healing shamans: the harmful ones always belong to enemy neighbours, or come from somewhere else.

Contrary to colonial fiction, the shaman or 'witch doctor' (a term considered derogatory) often has no political power and rarely has any interest in resisting the adoption of other forms of healing, such as Western medicine. He is far more likely to want to learn about them, adapt them, and use them himself.

As in the West, many indigenous societies think certain places have spiritual significance. These vary from obvious geographical features, such as hilltops, lakes, and waterfalls, to locations seemingly indistinguishable from the surrounding countryside. Such places may be visited for rituals, or just at special times. The most famous are the sacred sites of Australian Aboriginals, which I have described. The idea that a place has spiritual significance may also be extended to particular objects, and to tribal dwellings. Certain parts of the house, or images carved or painted on it, may represent spirits or other aspects of the world or universe, such as the sky or river. The notion that a dwelling has its own spirit or 'god' is particularly common in much of Asia, where many people keep an effigy or altar on a shelf or in a wall recess.

Religion is about spirits and levels of meaning, about sickness and death. It is also about looking into the future.

There are many ways of doing this, and they do not all require shamanic journeys to the ancestor- or spirit-world. Some Maasai, for example, have religious specialists who use a cow horn filled with special stones. The 'priest', or *laibon*, first asks the horn a question, shakes it, and throws the stones onto a blanket. His interpretation of how they fall gives the answer. Similar ways of looking for meaning in apparently random events are found almost everywhere.

To a certain extent what the shaman – and seer into the future – is really doing is interpreting everything that occurs as if it were suffused with significance. This can be grasped, or simply ignored. A non-shaman hears a bird song and ascribes no meaning to it; a shaman understands that the bird is speaking to him personally, and then has to work out what it is saying. As a way of approaching life, this is at the same time both self-centred and very responsible. Nothing is random: everything means something, and should even be taken personally. Non-shamans may believe things to be meaningful, but the shaman sees and grasps what the significance really is. Things can only be made better – and harmful forces can only be countered – when their real importance and origin is understood. This may not be as different from the West's approach to religion as it might at first appear.

Ritual, song and dance are also extremely important of course. Rituals are shared experiences which follow accepted rules and are thought to have a significance beyond the physical actions required. They might be relatively simple, for example to celebrate a certain fruit becoming ripe, or more complex, such as to perpetuate the conditions needed for life to continue without mishap. Through dancing around a fire at night, the Kalahari Bushmen believe that experienced adults can achieve a state, a trance, in which they can talk with the ancestors, passing on advice from them and healing the sick.

Many indigenous people make and wear masks for dances and rituals. The mask might represent a particular spirit, and the dancer believe that he is not merely re-enacting a mythic story: he may think he actually turns into the spirit or character represented. In that sense, a masked dance renews the myth, bringing the story from the distant past right into the present. The dancers are not merely acting out the story, they are actually recreating it.

Rituals have rules, and these are important. 'We can no longer practise that ceremony because no one now remembers how it should be done,' is a common complaint from people who have suffered dispossession over a sustained period. It is also true, on the other hand, that the rules may be applied somewhat laxly. One Amazon tribe spent weeks preparing for a ritual where they go into the forest at the time of a particular fruit ripening. The anthropologist visiting them was invited, and for days beforehand it was carefully explained to him how crucial it was that all participants keep very quiet. Talk could only be in the lowest whispers. Yet when the appointed day arrived, he was astonished to hear everyone laughing and chattering loudly. 'Aren't we supposed to be quiet?' he asked. The Indians quickly agreed: in their excitement, they had forgotten their own rule!

Ritual often involves music and dance, and so leads to a consideration of these and some other aspects of tribal life, which I will look at before turning to an outline of the problems faced by these peoples.

Art, artefacts, music, sport, games, laughter

All peoples express themselves through what the West calls 'art': music, song and dance; the invention and telling of stories, verbally or enacted; making artefacts which have no practical use; and decorating themselves, their tools, dwellings and surroundings. All have been practised since the distant past and, as with religion, it is likely that, until recently, no society regarded any of them as separate from daily life.

Techniques such as pottery, weaving, basketry, and even metalwork, are all very ancient and have been practised by many peoples. As with the supposed progress from hunting to farming, they are often categorized, with the same flawed reasoning, as being on a scale climbing from 'primitive' to 'civilized'. The potter's wheel and, much later, the mechanical loom were supposedly great leaps forward over earlier methods of making ceramics and cloth, but in fact this is just another 'Amish error'. Such machines certainly speeded up production, and so boosted commerce and profit, but not everyone's objective is to produce the most in the shortest time. Coiled pottery, fashioned without a wheel, is still made in many places (pots from the Amazonian Quichua in Ecuador are amongst the finest); and the simple, but very efficient, backstrap loom remains in use all over the world and, in the right hands, can produce the most exquisite textiles. Peruvian cloth predating the Incas by a thousand years still astounds professional weavers today with its seemingly impossible intricacy.

Artistic expression which is not composed of words can rarely be adequately explained through them: reading or talking about a painting or piece of music is very different from seeing or hearing it. A shaman might give his interpretation of a pattern painted on a mask, and certainly a grasp of the beliefs behind it can lead to a deeper level of understanding, but expert theories and explanations, even by members of the same people, should be treated with some caution. They are only ever interpretations, and often differ widely between individuals. The patterns used for Amazonian face and body painting, the handprints in Bushman rock art, the colours of a North American Indian or Siberian headdress, the multi-coloured bead work of East African pastoralists, the weaving of West African tribes, or the carved 'totem poles' of Canadian Indians, can only be clumsily 'explained', even by those who made them.

That is not to say that the artist does not have specific thoughts in mind. Of course, all art is symbolic to an extent, and what the symbols once meant to an artist now dead are often unknown. This is hardly surprising: once commonly-understood European symbolism from only a few centuries ago is often nowadays only the conjecture of experts.

Much tribal art has influenced the West, perhaps most famously with Picasso's infatuation with the African sculptures he saw in Paris museums. On the other hand, relatively little indigenous art has escaped out of the 'ethnic' (or 'primitive') category. One example which has is Inuit carvings, aimed at a popular market, and made from a variety of materials such as soapstone, bone, and tusk. These attracted international attention from the 1950s, and have grown into an important source of income, partly replacing fur trapping in some areas. Woodcarvings by the Asmat of Papua, and highly-prized Aboriginal paintings, are other examples.

The English language aptly demonstrates the connection between art and religion. Art needs 'inspiration', whereas religion is to do with the 'spirit', and both refer to something entering the body from outside it. Indigenous peoples believe the same thing. When a Siberian shaman drums, a Bushman dances, an Amazon Indian tells of the origin of the river, or an Australian Aboriginal paints a 'modern' canvas, all are inspired by an idea of a reality which is separate from and beyond daily life – and is considered more meaningful as a result. Some form of artistic expression, whether or not it is called that, is common to all peoples and, perhaps as much as complex language and rules about marriage partners, distinguishes us from other animals.

All peoples also sing and play music, particularly drums and wind and string instruments. One of the earliest is the so-called 'Jew's harp' or mouth harp, and the oldest recognizable instrument yet found is a flute from Germany, made from bone and dated to at least thirty-five thousand years ago. The small 'thumb piano', or *mbira*, is found in many places, particularly in Africa and Asia. This is a wooden sounding board with a series of prongs, played by plucking with thumbs and fingers.

Music and songs can be used to convey messages. For generations, several indigenous peoples have used song as a vehicle to protest about their dispossession. One of the best-known indigenous singer-songwriters of recent times was Buffy Saint-Marie, a Cree woman from Canada, who rose to fame in the 1960s with records such as 'Universal Soldier'; this was embraced so enthusiastically by the movement against the Vietnam War that it prompted the United States government to try and suppress her work. It failed, and the song became an international hit. More 'traditionally', the massive hollowed-out trunks kept in northwest Amazon longhouses were used to drum out messages. These are technically known as 'slit gongs' and are found in all shapes and sizes and on all continents. Big ones can easily communicate over several kilometres.

Song and sound convey messages; so can many other things. A favourite feature of the comic strip 'Western' is the 'smoke signal', through which American Indians could transmit meaning over distances though varying the amount, and location, of smoke coming from a bonfire. Several other techniques using smoke or fire can be found all over the world.

Tribal and indigenous peoples have art and music just like everyone else. They also have 'traditional' sports, which include wrestling, running with heavy logs, canoe and horse racing, and a kind of polo. Rubber originates in the Americas, and was used to make balls for football, hockey and lacrosse well before European colonization. Variants of football have been played (including of course by Europeans) for centuries. 'Modern' soccer has also now become common in much of the world, and a set of goal posts can be found in almost every Indian community in the western Amazon. In some tribes, teams happily swap members until each has scored the same number of goals, when the game draws to a close.

In many parts of Africa and Asia, a variety of *mancala* board games can be found, consisting of a wooden or clay tablet, with hollowed-out scoops, and counters made of seeds or other materials. Thousand-year-old sets have been found, but the game is likely to be a great deal older. Hollows in the earth can substitute for the board itself, so very ancient examples are likely to have left no trace at all. No one has any idea how long such games have existed.

Finally, no outline, however brief, of tribal peoples' ways can be complete without mentioning jokes. The evolutionary origin of laughter is being studied, but as far as I know no one has looked much at tribal humour. I know of no figures for the time tribal people spend laughing, though anecdotal experience points to it being considerably more than in industrialized societies; in fact, perhaps this is one of the biggest differences between them. I am not alone in observing that the more isolated the tribe is from outsiders, the more its members seem to laugh, and this is often the feature that most forcefully strikes visitors. Everyone has a hearty sense of humour and a keen sense of the ridiculous; people laughing to the point of tears is not unusual, often triggered by the retelling of inherent absurdities in past situations.

Laughter can be a reaction to embarrassment or surprise, and it is common for people to laugh at their own mistakes and accidents, even when they are in some pain. Slapstick is rife in many tribal societies. If someone slips and falls over, he and any onlookers immediately laugh. Humorous innuendo and gentle criticism is also widespread, mocking the way people talk or walk. It may also be about sex; the size of people's genitalia, whether presumed or real, is often a cause of merriment, as is, perhaps more curiously, the sound of farting. This might appear childish, but more 'sophisticated' forms of humour, such as elaborate and complex word play and riddles, are also widespread amongst indigenous peoples. The way similar words can mean different things in different languages can be the source of jokes, as can the ease with which outsiders can be fooled into believing nonsense. One of the early wordlists compiled from a European Romani language, collected by Jacob Bryant in 1776, recorded the name for female genitals, *mindž* or *ming*, in place of the word for 'father'. Tribes have obviously been playing similar jokes on investigators for centuries, and I have already mentioned how urinating on visitors' feet and squirting them with breast milk are unending sources of mirth for some Andaman tribes.

The use of self-deprecating laughter to diffuse tension, particularly immediately following an exchange that is critical or could lead to argument, is a common technique small-scale societies use to avoid internal discord – which is one of their main concerns. A man criticizing another for being bossy might follow with the (false) assertion that he is being bossy himself, and then immediately laugh to defuse the situation. He has succeeded in making his point without risking conflict.

Laughter brings discernible health benefits, which are now being looked at scientifically. People laugh when they are happy, but the action also *makes* people both happy and physically healthier: it is far from being just a laughing matter!

All the aspects of human life which I have touched on, as well as many others, are found amongst tribal and indigenous peoples just as they are in industrialized societies. The similarities amongst all peoples far outweigh the differences between them. It is also the case that the aspects which are considered the most important are also the same for everyone, everywhere. Personal relationships, friends and enemies, children, health, diseases and death, a sense of belonging, meaning and fulfilment, and – by no means least – the pursuit of excitement and fun, are the things that really engage the human mind and spirit and all the societies it engenders. They are likely to remain dominant, whatever the future might bring.

It is also the case that the most important preoccupations for many indigenous people today are the problems they face from mainstream society. The broad patterns of these are very similar all over the world.

What are their problems?

Several years ago when an Innu man went to social services or hospital and was asked his occupation, he said, 'Hunter'. Now he says, 'Unemployed'.

Jean Pierre Ashini, Innu, Canada

The immediate threat to little-contacted tribes is violent confrontation due to the encroachment of outsiders. This usually comes from ranching, logging, mining, or other industries. Some tribes are still shot at, particularly in remote parts of Brazil and Peru. However, contagious diseases that are usually not deadly to others, such as influenza, kill far more people than bullets. Whatever the direct cause, it is normal for at least half the tribe not to survive this first stage of contact.

The next onslaught, for those in more routine contact, is land dispossession bringing poverty, associated malnutrition, and illnesses such as tuberculosis. In spite of this, population numbers can stabilize after a generation or so, though the tribe itself is usually severely fragmented.

Those who survive then move on to a third stage, where they suffer the same problems as other extremely poor citizens, though often on a far worse scale. This applies particularly to indigenous peoples in richer countries. The number of violent deaths rockets – ironically often now originating within the group, from crimes or accidents resulting from drugs or alcohol. In spite of the suicide, addiction, imprisonment, domestic violence, and shorter lifespan, it is not uncommon for population numbers to grow. A different set of diseases appear, especially those associated with junk food and inactivity, such as obesity and diabetes.

The fundamental problem underpinning all three stages is that others want to control indigenous peoples' land or its resources. Before going into this in more detail, it is important to touch on one 'resource' – labour – where the worst problem has now largely subsided. This was of course slavery, and it has left its long and traumatic shadow behind.

Slavery

Slavery, at least overt slavery, is largely a crime of the past. Indigenous peoples were not only its victims: their larger empires such as the Incas and Aztecs had slaves as I have pointed out, as did some Northwest American Indians and others. In parts of Amazonia until very recently, Indian children, particularly girls, who survived raids by colonists or other Indians, might be 'stolen' and brought up as unpaid servants, though often they were free to leave once grown up. Pygmies in Central Africa are forced to work for the militias that litter the region, often as trackers or porters, and the same happens in Southeast Asia. Bushmen in Africa, Australian Aboriginals and many others routinely work as farm labourers or domestic servants – or did so until very recently – and are paid a pittance; sometimes only in food or alcohol. Central American Indians still provide much of the domestic workforce for the wealthy, both in their own countries and in the United States. So it is still the case that many indigenous people are exploited to the extent that they are paid little – sometimes nothing at all – for menial labour, including prostitution; this is obviously a serious infringement of their rights, but it still falls short of slavery as it once was.

There is, however, a kind of quasi-slavery, called 'debt bondage', which still affects tribal people today. Particularly in Amazonia, Indians are forced to collect forest produce to pay a supposed 'debt' that they owe a non-Indian *patrón*, or 'boss', who provides them with a stream of manufactured goods, so perpetually increasing the amount they 'owe'. The Indians' produce, which a few years ago used to be raw rubber and animal skins, and nowadays is more likely to be gold, timber or cocaine, is undervalued and the price of the goods they receive – clothes, tools, shotguns and so forth – is grossly inflated to ensure the debt is never cleared. The Indians have to work for their 'boss' throughout their lives, and their children then inherit the obligation and must carry on working.

This is defined by the United Nations as a form of slavery, and it is of course deeply unfair and exploitative. Some Indians put up with it partly because it brings certain advantages: primarily, it provides a supply of outside goods coming through a known intermediary. Indians may be cheated, and even know it, but they can stay in their communities and work in their own time. For his part, the 'boss' might have an Indian wife and children living in the Indian settlement (in addition to his non-Indian family elsewhere), and so is easily able to create and foster kin relationships with 'his' people.

Debt bondage is gradually disappearing in some places, and neither it nor any other form of labour exploitation involves the destruction of very large numbers of tribal people. However, it is important to remember that even in recent generations slavery plunged many into immense suffering. Most important of all is that the principal victims of the transatlantic slave trade, which saw perhaps ten million African slaves transported to the Americas, were almost all originally tribal people themselves.

Violence

Violence has always been a more widespread problem than slavery. For most of the colonial era, tribes faced open warfare from those invading their lands. Killing parties were attacking Aboriginals in Australia as recently as the 1920s, Bushmen in southern Africa decades later, and Indians in South America occasionally still today. The Central American wars which killed tens of thousands of Indians only a generation ago are now largely over, but violence persists on a wide-scale there, as well as in places such as Bangladesh, India, Indonesia, and parts of Africa, where tribespeople are all too regularly attacked, raped, and killed by government forces, guerrillas or colonists.

Disease

As already noted however, violence was rarely the cause of most deaths resulting from the invasion of tribal lands; this was illness – particularly measles, smallpox, and common viral respiratory infections such as influenza and colds. No one will ever know how many million American Indians died from disease after the European invasion, but it was probably amongst the largest human wipeouts in history – akin to the numbers who succumbed to the Black Death in Europe, or those killed during both world wars put together. If the figures were smaller in Australia and southern Africa, it was only because there were fewer tribal people there to begin with.

Land theft

Violence, enslavement and disease affect fewer indigenous people now than formerly, but the same is unfortunately not true for land theft, which is on the increase. This is the key avoidable issue tribal peoples now confront, and part of the problem is that it is often characterized as either inevitable or for the common good – or even beneficial for the tribe in question – rather than the serious and deadly crime which it really is.

Until recently, the main cause was colonization. The rich have been establishing their farms and plantations on tribal land for generations; they are still there. In South America, huge soya and sugar cane fields, as well as cattle ranches, feed the wealthy world's appetite for food and fuel which cost the consumer relatively little, but have taken an expensive toll in human suffering long before they reach the dinner table or gas station. The 1970s saw an increase in poorer colonists, particularly in Indonesia and Bangladesh, as well as South America: governments pushed the impoverished away from the urban areas, which were potential hotbeds of threatening dissent, and drew them into more remote zones where tribal peoples also lived.

These poor newcomers were often granted a plot, tools,

and sometimes a cow or small dwelling, and told to make a new life for themselves. Many tried, but gave up after a few years, often leaving much damaged land behind. Hordes flooded into the Amazon from Brazil's poverty-stricken northeast; across the continent, thousands flowed down the Andes into the Amazon region of Ecuador. On the other side of the world, the poor were shipped from Java's slums to West Papua. Dozens of tribal peoples disappeared as a result of all this. Some tribes, now rendered landless, drifted to the towns to try and eke out a living as labourers, prostitutes or beggars. Losing connection with each other, and with no home to return to, they disappeared irretrievably as peoples. Others, such as the Guarani in Brazil, hung on desperately, living on shrinking scraps of land, sometimes just on roadside verges, but nevertheless clinging together and to a sense of their identity, and remembering what they had lost. Many are still there. Guarani children still routinely despair and commit suicide, usually by hanging themselves from trees. The youngest recorded so far was Luciane Ortiz, a little girl of nine.

Resource theft

Over the last generation, resource exploration and extraction has become an even bigger threat than colonization. This usually comprises oil/petroleum, minerals, or timber, as well as damming rivers for hydropower. As the world's population consumes more goods and energy, driven by its growing population and huge corporations promoting an unceasing demand for new things, the price of such commodities has increased severalfold, making it more and more profitable to exploit remoter areas, exactly the places where tribal peoples have survived.

These developments vary from major international programmes to those promoted by local companies and individuals, who are often poor themselves. The most destructive schemes of recent decades, all funded by taxpayers from the industrialized world, include the Narmada dam in India, the Polonoroeste and Carajás projects in Brazil, the Chad-Cameroon oil pipeline, and the Indonesian transmigration programme, which I have described. All destroyed tribal communities; most were environmental disasters. They largely benefitted the companies which built them, and the authorities with their hands in the cash register, siphoning off whatever they could. The total cost of these five megaprojects is unknown, but it certainly amounted to many billions of dollars. The real impacts of such catastrophes, rather than the fantasies disseminated in World Bank and government reports, were predicted years in advance and repeated, largely unsuccessful, efforts were made by human rights and environmental organizations, as well as by indigenous groups themselves, to stop them.

The largest copper and gold mine in the world is in West Papua, destroying a mountain sacred to the Amungme people. Dams in Ethiopia threaten the tribes downstream, such as the Mursi, who rely on seasonal flooding to enrich the riverbanks for crops and pasture. A diamond mine lay behind the eviction of Gana and Gwi Bushmen in Botswana. In Brazil, gold miners brought in an especially dangerous form of malaria which killed twenty percent of Yanomami in just a few years and remains a deadly threat. Gold and copper mining in the Philippines, uranium in Australia, coal and nickel in the United States and Canada, all have been acute problems for decades.

Almost everywhere now the race for underground riches has spread into areas once considered safe. Nowhere is this more destructive than in Amazonian Ecuador and Peru, but as the destruction grips, so does opposition to it. The American oil giant, Chevron, was presented with a claim for billions in damages from Ecuadorean Indians, brought through the New York courts. In an attempt to save their lands, Amazon Indians blocked roads and rivers in Peru for some weeks in 2009. Government forces then attacked them, provoking the killing of several policemen hostages the Indians were holding. Such an uprising had been unprecedented for generations. In Peru's 1742 Indian revolt, the authorities characterized the Indians trying to protect their lands as 'savages'. They said the same in 2009.

Capitalism, communism, globalization

It is sometimes argued that the root cause of all these problems is market-led capitalism, but it is also true that both Soviet Russia and communist China destroyed their indigenous peoples as thoroughly as anyone else. This was primarily achieved through timber and oil extraction and the 'collectivization' of reindeer herds in Siberia, and the hysteria of the 1960s Chinese 'cultural revolution', which imposed Maoism with as much brutality as any medieval crusade. It is also often claimed that recent, so-called 'development' projects constitute a new form of destructive 'globalization', though in fact it has been around for centuries.

A good illustration of this fact is the scramble for rubber at the end of the nineteenth century. This was provoked by Ford's mass production of the motorcar in the United States, combined with Goodyear's discovery of vulcanization in Ireland that rendered rubber hard enough to make car tyres. Some of the valuable gum came from the Congo but the major source was Amazonia. Rubber did not adapt to plantation growth: individual trees had to be found in the wild and tapped where they stood. On the Colombian-Peruvian border, the rubber sap was extracted by Amazon Indian slaves, working under henchmen from Barbados – then a British colony – and organized by a Peruvian company, which was floated on the London stock market. As if this was not global enough, the industry later collapsed when the British adapted seedlings in Kew Gardens, London, and successfully grew them in new Malayan plantations. This combination of inventions and markets thousands of miles distant was responsible for some of the most gratuitous and savage violence seen in Amazonia. It is impossible even to guess how many tens of thousands of Indians were killed or how many tribes disappeared. The Andoke were reduced from an estimated ten thousand to just a few dozen individuals. They are now recovering and, a century after the end of the 'boom', today number a few hundred. They were lucky: many were wiped out.

It was not only rubber, and the development of the motorcar (and the eco-friendly bicycle, of course), which was bought with the lives of tribes. The gold and silver resplendent in Spain's grand cathedrals is in fact war booty from South and Central American Indians. In reality, colonialism and market forces have long been global phenomena and their grasping fingers have reached deep into tribal territory for centuries. The pattern continues today: much of the wood used in Japanese houses, and even chopsticks, is from the Borneo forests which really belong to the Penan.

Conservation, climate and carbon

The assault on tribal land nowadays is not confined to stealing it for colonization, farming or mining: with tragic irony, it is increasingly taken for conservation zones. Since the national park movement began in nineteenth century United States, many of its protagonists have thought parks incompatible with any human presence – apart, that is, from conservationists themselves and their retinues. This desperation for 'wilderness' ignores the fact that most of the areas chosen actually owe their physical appearance to millennia of human habitation anyway; but what is far worse is that it has resulted in the enforced eviction of many tribal peoples all over the world. Indeed, this variant of land theft is rapidly emerging as one of the biggest problems confronting indigenous peoples. This is not new: many famous parks, such as Yosemite in the United States and Tsavo in Kenya, involved the destruction of the resident indigenous peoples, and the problem is now growing more acute as conservationists press harder for governments to set aside 'natural' areas, which in reality have been lived on for generations.

In recent decades, other new forms of 'development' have become a scourge for tribal peoples, particularly in the tropics: these are biofuels, especially oil palm, sugar cane and soya bean. The fact that tropical forest is reckoned to be one of the best ways to 'soak up' greenhouse gas emissions has not stopped it being felled to cultivate these wasteful plants. This is underpinned by a short-term logic which declares that burning biofuels is better for the environment than fossil fuels, but which fails to factor in the loss of forest, the destruction of its inhabitants, or the increased cost of food crops which have been displaced. In most areas, the drive behind biofuels is really to do with fast profit rather than any

211

environmental concern. An estimated sixty million indigenous people, mainly in Southeast Asia, stand to lose out.

A theory linking rainforest destruction and global warming was advanced as long ago as the early 1970s, since when there have been numerous schemes put forward to save the forests. Most involve a flawed logic as well as someone from outside making a lot of money, or trying to. In the 1990s, one idea, called 'rainforest harvest', involved putting forest produce, such as Brazil nuts, in cosmetic and food products, and marketing them under the pretence that buyers were helping save rainforests. It was largely a gimmick of the kind known as 'greenwash'. This 'pro-environment' illusion is spreading into many destructive projects today. Malaysian Borneo's Bakun dam displaced thousands in the 1990s, including some Penan; more dams are planned, but now they are promoted in the name of countering climate change. Kenya's repeated attempts to throw the Ogiek out of their Mau Forest is now supposedly about the same thing. The 'environment' is rapidly replacing 'development' as the lie underpinning much land theft harming tribal peoples (as well as many others who also lack the money or power to stick up for themselves).

'Conservation' schemes that steal from tribal peoples – the best conservationists – might be paradoxical, but efforts to combat climate change which trample over those whose carbon emissions are largely nil is doubly so. Unfortunately, this is exactly what is going on now. An important part of the 'carbon offsetting' agenda is that governments and other authorities agree to 'reduce emissions from deforestation and forest degradation' (or 'REDD'). In the talks around this, the 'bigger' environmental picture is deemed too important to get sidetracked with concerns over 'minority' indigenous rights. The result is that those rights are ignored in a way not dissimilar to how religious evangelization was once, and sometimes still is, thought to be fully justified in overriding any rights the 'primitives' might have.

REDD schemes are designed to make intact forests more valuable than felled ones. This was the same ideology behind the phoney rainforest harvest and it also prevailed during the rubber boom. In reality, increasing the value of standing forest is likely to put *more* pressure on tribal territories, lead to more land theft, and do nothing at all to safeguard the rights of the original inhabitants. Many existing 'carbon offset' schemes, for example in Africa, have harmed the indigenous peoples whose lands were involved.

Another recent 'quick fix' to exploit worldwide concern for forests, asks the public in rich countries to 'buy' a piece of rainforest, in order to save it. These fanciful claims are rarely what they seem and are fraught with problems which were clearly not thought through when they were launched. For example, some contracts try to lock local people into generations of compliance, and will simply prove unworkable. Additionally, several rainforest countries do not take kindly to swathes of land falling under foreign control and are prone periodically to nationalize outsiders' interests: the governments simply take the land back.

In general, tribal peoples are used to changing weather patterns and have survived many. It is in the coldest parts of the world that the effects of climate change are having the most impact, particularly in the Arctic where seasonal weather is no longer as predicable as it once was, so hampering Inuit hunting and fishing. The Sami reindeer are declining, as they find it harder to locate food, and the usual migrations of Siberian herders are disrupted because rivers have failed to freeze solid in recent years. Droughts in

Amazonia and the Kalahari have also proved problematic: in the rainforest, because there has been an increased incidence of forest fires; in the desert, because the Bushmen depend heavily on seasonal rain, which is no longer as predictable as it was.

Whatever the impact any changes to the world's weather might bring, and however beneficial some anti-climate change schemes may eventually be, tribal peoples are probably suffering today as much, if not more, from attempts to combat global warming as they are from climate change itself. This is a particularly tragic paradox, given that these days many would actually like to help both indigenous peoples in particular and the planet more generally; it is an indictment of the way such peoples are still denigrated by those who decide the world's priorities.

There may be a certain inevitability in this: national governments are unlikely to see much value in defending peoples who produce little or no money or votes. This leads to a consideration of some aspects of how governments and related sectors have responded to indigenous and tribal peoples.

The world's response

First they make us destitute by taking away our land, our hunting and our way of life. Then they say we are nothing because we are destitute.

Jumanda Gakelebone, Bushman, Botswana

Many past injustices are now recognized for what they are – crimes which rightfully demand acknowledgment and, where possible, some form of reparation. Nazism, apartheid and slavery are all good examples, which only cranks would now seek to defend. Few people would publically defend European colonialism either, particularly in an African context.

However, this is not the case for the criminal treatment meted out to indigenous peoples. The historical destruction of, for example, North American Indians, African Bushmen, and Australian Aboriginals, is still not faced up to by the vast majority of descendants of those who perpetrated these atrocities. Their enduring misery – the aftermath of the theft and colonization of their lands – continues to inflict an enormous price in human suffering, but is met with little or no sense of urgent atonement. Quite the contrary in fact, most North Americans, southern Africans, and Australians, firmly believe in their inalienable right to 'their' country, a right which has – broadly speaking – long ceased to be challenged by the indigenous peoples they dispossessed.

Governments and their clubs

Governments are the main violators of indigenous peoples' rights. They oppose cohesive minorities living within their frontiers but outside the mainstream, not conforming to desired or imposed norms, not buying anything much, rarely paying taxes, and unable to be counted on to support the ruling elite. Until the 1970s, the most commonly encountered government policy was based on the attempt to 'integrate' indigenous peoples into national society. This was hardly ever questioned and was thought to be beneficial both for the country as a whole and for the indigenous minorities. It was in fact extremely destructive and led to the disappearance of many peoples.

A few governments have specialist departments for such issues. Probably the most famous are the Bureau of Indian Affairs (BIA) in the United States, and the National Indian Foundation (FUNAI) in Brazil. The BIA was created in 1824 and its main job nowadays is to administer the land held 'in trust' by the government for Indians. It became particularly controversial in the 1970s when the radical American Indian Movement (AIM) was taking root. When AIM clashed with the authorities, the latter were usually represented by the BIA's 'native police': Indians employed by government fought fellow Indians who opposed official policies.

The BIA started life as part of the United States Department of War, but Brazil's FUNAI has a more surprising history. Initially called the Indian Protection Service (SPI), it was founded in 1910 by a half-Indian soldier, Cândido Rondon, who was charged with laying telegraph lines into the remote interior of the country. He quickly became a hero in 1909, when one of his expeditions reappeared after being thought lost for good. Rondon died, aged ninety-three, in 1958, and now has a Brazilian state named after him. He was generations ahead of his time, and imposed a famous motto on his organization, 'Die if necessary, kill never!'

When Brazil fell to military dictatorship in 1967, scandals concerning SPI corruption were exposed to the media, and the agency was dissolved, to be re-formed under a new name, FUNAI. Since then, it has oscillated between being a force for good or harm, depending on the policies of its senior staff and their ability to stand up to the political, business and military elites which have always held power in Brazil, and which view Indian areas as a source of personal wealth, primarily through ranching, farming, timber, or gold extraction. Unfortunately, with a few notable exceptions, FUNAI officials genuinely supportive of Indians tend to be removed from office fairly rapidly.

Quite a lot of governments have policies that are much better now than they were a generation ago, even if they are rarely, if ever, properly applied. For example, when Peru was taken over by a left-wing army dictatorship in the late 1960s, the authorities allowed progressive anthropologists to write a new law on Amazon 'native communities', which I look at shortly. A similar leap took place in Colombia in the late 1980s when an anthropologist, Martín Hildebrand, was able to use his position as head of the government's Indian department to push Indian control over their own affairs into the first new Colombian constitution for a century.

At the opposite end of the spectrum, many countries do not acknowledge indigenous peoples' existence at all. Everyone is supposedly an 'equal' citizen, and where indigenous rights are acknowledged, they are supposed to apply to everyone, and so are rendered meaningless. This is the case in Botswana where the government claims that everyone is indigenous, in spite of the fact that the Bushmen have been there for tens of thousands of years, in contrast to the majority Bantu-speaking population who immigrated only about five centuries ago. In 2009, one hapless tourist was arrested for remarking that the president, who was actually half-English, looked like a Bushman! By claiming everyone is indigenous, the government certainly does not mean that everyone is part-Bushman: it is just a way of denying the rights of those who really are.

This points to another, especially perverse, reason put forward nowadays to oppose indigenous rights: that there should be no 'special case' for any particular sector of society – all rights must be the same for everyone. Whilst ostensibly based on principles of equality, in fact this demonstrates a flawed reasoning, in addition to a lack of understanding both of the law and human rights, as well as about how people actually function in real life. It is not difficult to see that particular sectors do have rights and obligations which others do not, and that this is both just and inevitable. At a simple level, citizens of a country have a right to live there which may be denied to others. Children have rights that adults do not (for example, they have the right to have their best interests considered at all times). Those who hold particular religious beliefs are also exempt from obligations which others must fulfil (in the UK, Sikhs are not required to wear motorbike or police helmets because it would interfere with their turbans). There are also special provisions for the disabled and elderly, and different facilities and laws which cannot relate to both men and women, such as those relating to maternity. 'Affirmative action' policies in the United States and elsewhere are specifically designed to give individuals from a disadvantaged sector of the population an edge over others, in order to promote eventual equality. When it comes to indigenous peoples, the only real reason to deny they are a definable sector with their own particular rights is to seek their dissolution.

Another way of looking at why indigenous and tribal peoples must be considered as a category with their own special rights, particularly to land, is that they simply do not survive without their territory: if that is taken from them, *all* their human rights are denied.

If some governments remain unwilling to make room for indigenous minorities in policy or reality, the same is no longer true of several major international associations, including the Organization of American States and the United Nations. More curiously, although the World Bank has funded lots of projects which have harmed many indigenous peoples, it also has guidelines and policy directives which can be quite good, though they are unfortunately rarely, if ever, realized.

The United Nations has a good record of supporting, at least in theory, some indigenous peoples over recent years, though it has very little real muscle. Second only to the UN, the largest 'club' of nations is the Commonwealth, comprising almost a third of the world's population. Although claiming to exist partly to further human rights, its record on indigenous peoples is abysmal: of the fifty-three Commonwealth countries, a mere two, Dominica and Fiji, have even bothered to ratify the International Labour Organization's Convention 169 which defines indigenous and tribal peoples' rights.

Moving on from the responses of governments, how have the broader strands of political thinking reacted to the 'indigenous question'?

Far right and left

As we have seen, indigenous peoples were a political football between right and left throughout the twentieth century. The global Cold War following World War II was distinctly hot in many places; some indigenous people joined as willing combatants, some were press-ganged on to one or other side, many were simply caught in the crossfire. The conflict was particularly acute in Southeast Asia, and not only in Vietnam: it spilled over into the archipelagos of the Philippines and Indonesia, and was the reason why the West turned a blind eye to Indonesia's atrocities in New Guinea.

We have looked at the appalling atrocities this gave rise to in Central America; a similar struggle was also waged in South America, where the United States wrestled to maintain its hegemony against popular uprisings in which indigenous peoples often played a role. In Peru, the notorious 1990s leftist guerrilla force, the 'Shining Path', both recruited Indians into its ranks as well as killing many. In Colombia, anti-government guerrilla armies, some of them more than half a century old, still threaten Indian areas on the edge of the Orinoco and the Amazon, as do the government forces which are fighting them. Following the American-engineered coup in Chile in 1973, the incoming rightwing dictatorship did its best to break up Mapuche Indian communities. Some Indians fled to Europe where they remain as exiles a generation later.

Indigenous rights usually suffer whether left or right is dominant. In the 1920s, for example, some leftist intellectuals in South America argued that chewing the mildly stimulating coca leaf was merely a Western ploy to make the Indians work harder in the Andean silver mines. This was nonsense: coca was and remains central to Andean religion, a food of – and from – 'the gods'.

The theory that tribal peoples are a distraction to the 'real' conflict between right and left has not disappeared today. In one manifestation of this, a small handful of anthropologists argue that any recognition of 'ethnic divisions' plays into the hands of those who support racist ideologies, such as apartheid. Such assertions may sound perverse, and be of interest for academic point-scoring, but they nevertheless distract from the life-threatening problems faced by real people, as well as from their potential solutions. However, the real problem remains the action, and inaction, of governments.

National and international law

Several countries have special laws concerning their indigenous and tribal peoples. One result of the international concern focussing on Amazonia in the 1970s is that the majority of countries there have quite good laws nowadays. An example is the Peruvian legislation of 1974, which saw most Indian settlements' land rights acknowledged. When Indian land was mapped it was usually not enough and left out hunting territories, but it was a lot better than nothing: Indian ownership of territories known as 'native communities' was explicitly recognized. An especially radical provision was that the land was owned in perpetuity: it could not be sold, or even used as security for loans. This neatly solved the problem of Indians being tricked out of their land, or losing it in one-sided commercial deals. It did however give rise to other conundrums: most obviously, why should Indians not be able to sell their land if they all wanted to? However, its main fault was that it was applied only to communities, rather than peoples as a whole, and the land awarded was never sufficient. A riverside village with title to a few kilometres around would be in serious difficulty if, for example, the river changed course (as they frequently do in the rainforest). Nevertheless, it was greatly welcomed by Indians and formal land titling has taken place all over Peru's Amazonia ever since.

That country's recognition of Indian land is not unique: the establishment of 'reserves' legally owned by Indians dates back to 1890 in Colombia. More controversially, Indians in Brazil are treated as 'minors' and cannot own land at all, though this is being challenged. The Brazilian state 'delimits' (on a map) and 'demarcates' (on the ground) Indian 'areas' or 'parks', but ownership is retained by the state. The biggest problem with this is that the government can change its mind and revoke already established Indian zones. Indeed, there is constant pressure on it to do so by local bigwigs with vested interests in profit-making schemes.

I have referred to the fact that the United Nations body handling indigenous peoples' law is the International Labour Organization (ILO). This is primarily charged with employment issues, and is run by governments, employers and trade unions, which probably explains why it shows little interest in indigenous peoples. This curious situation dates from 1957, when the predecessor to Convention 169, numbered 107, was approved. The ILO was looking at that time at the situation of indigenous mineworkers in the Andes, and it simply widened its brief to include all indigenous peoples. However, outside of the Andes and a few other places, labour law is relatively low on the list of problems confronting indigenous peoples, and hardly affects any tribal peoples. Delegating indigenous issues to the ILO has created inherent problems in how these peoples might use the UN system to their advantage; these remain largely unaddressed, and are another legacy of the way the whole question has long been viewed as one of only marginal importance, which has never warranted a more considered approach. Consigning indigenous issues to a pigeonhole intended for work and trade unions happened partly because no one knew where else to put them.

ILO conventions are written and 'adopted' by the ILO itself, and then individual governments can choose whether or not to 'ratify' them. Those that do are supposed to ensure they then become part of the national law. If a significant number of countries do this, those conventions begin to form part of international law. The latter is a loose term covered by several definitions and much debate, but even where a convention has only been ratified by a few nations, it still represents the nearest thing to the minimum required international standard.

The earlier ILO law on indigenous peoples, Convention 107, also affirmed their land rights. This is the most important thing of all and means that the standard in international law has recognized indigenous land ownership since 1957. Twenty-seven countries ratified Convention 107. At the time of writing, twenty-two countries had similarly approved Convention 169, but more are doing so slowly. It is a core principle of the promotion of indigenous rights that as many countries as possible ratify this Convention.

The most important differences between the 1957 and 1989 conventions are that the earlier one makes 'integrating' indigenous peoples a desirable end goal, and refers throughout to indigenous 'populations'. The more recent law abandons the concept of integration, and uses the term 'peoples', rather than 'populations'. This is an important symbolic distinction because the UN's 'Civic and Political

Rights Covenant', which is one of the main cornerstones of all international law, gives 'peoples' the vital right to 'self-determination'. This means that no people should be ruled by another people. The same does not hold true for mere 'populations', which are simply numbers of individuals. Men in Nigeria, for example, constitute a population, but are not a people. Populations can be, and often are, ruled by others. Adults, for instance, rule the underage population everywhere.

One of the most important struggles of indigenous peoples ever since colonization is to be recognized as 'peoples', rather than merely as collections of individuals. This does not however mean that they seek to become sovereign nations, separate from the states they inhabit, and Convention 169 makes it clear that it does not endorse such a step. Those few that do want some such level of autonomy, for example the seven million Karen who have fought the Burmese army since 1949, or the Tibetans seeking independence from China, do not position their struggle within the framework of indigenous rights. There is one major exception to this: most of the original inhabitants of West Papua, all of them tribal, do seek self-rule and an end to Indonesian occupation.

It is true that some indigenous peoples, particularly in North America, have occasionally made a sort of 'unilateral declaration of independence' and pronounced themselves separate from the USA or Canada, but this is mostly for symbolic effect. In 1973, I travelled with a Hopi elder who had his own, homemade and leather-clad, Hopi Nation passport, refusing to use a United States one at all. This prompted some interesting discussions with border guards but, to my delight and surprise, it saw him through. I doubt it would today; the Iroquois lacrosse team was refused entry to the UK when they tried to do the same in 2010.

The ILO conventions are written as laws and use a phraseology which is intended to stand up in a court, though it may not always be especially precise. A different, but also important, document is the 'Declaration on the Rights of Indigenous Peoples'. As a United Nations declaration, this is not written as a law, but is a statement of how countries should behave; the most famous comparison of course is the 'Universal Declaration of Human Rights', adopted in 1948 as a response to the Nazis' attempt to eradicate the Jews, Roma and Travellers, homosexuals, and disabled people. It was written entirely with individuals in mind, rather than peoples, and so reflects an attitude to rights and responsibilities which is not much help to peoples, and is even less so to those who have a very different way of life. Some argue that it is written from a very European perspective and is decidedly 'ethnocentric' (a term which means adopting the narrow viewpoint of one's own ethnic group whilst ignoring, often unwittingly, how things appear from other perspectives).

If the Universal Declaration was ready just three years after the defeat of the Nazis, the one on indigenous peoples' rights was a far more laborious affair. Lobby groups of indigenous representatives, many from the United States, met in Geneva every year for twenty-five years to press for the best possible text. Every year, a phalanx of government representatives lined up to try and weaken it. In the end, after countless machinations and deals, a pretty good paper from the indigenous point of view came for vote to the United Nations General Assembly (which all member states attend) in 2007. There were a few abstentions, but almost all states voted to approve it. Just four opposed: the USA and Canada, Australia and New Zealand. It is not accidental that all share two common features: they were once part of the British empire (today, three are in the Commonwealth and still have the UK sovereign as head of state); and they are the only large regions of the world to have been so swamped by European colonization that the indigenous peoples are reduced to near-powerless minority survivors. A couple of years after the vote, an incoming government made a point of reversing the decision and announcing Australia's support for the declaration. The remaining three opponents followed suit fairly rapidly. No one wanted to be seen as the sole country in the world to oppose the new declaration.

The UN declaration confirms the ILO convention's emphasis on land ownership rights. Its article 26 says: *Indigenous peoples have the right to the lands, territories and resources which they have traditionally owned, occupied or otherwise used or acquired*. But a potential problem is that it avoids any definition about whom it actually applies to. This was deliberate: indigenous leaders at the United Nations felt that no definition at all should be imposed. The declaration simply says, in article 33: *Indigenous peoples have the right to determine their own identity or membership in accordance with their customs and traditions*. In other words, they can simply decide who is and is not indigenous. Perhaps a bigger problem, at least in some parts of the world, is that it does not mention the term 'tribal' at all. This may be because the articulate and internationally savvy indigenous individuals, who attended the United Nations to argue for the declaration, rarely originated from the more 'tribal' end of the spectrum of peoples covered. As I have explained, the ILO convention, in contrast, confronts this problem fairly well.

However, by far the biggest problem with the declaration is that plenty of governments voted for it without the slightest intention of actually applying it. Botswana is just one example: it supported the declaration but pretends, as already noted, that all its citizens are indigenous, and it routinely violates Bushman rights.

Another law often quoted to support indigenous peoples is the United Nations 1948 Genocide Convention, also written in direct response to Nazi atrocities. It is worth citing its definition of genocide: *Any of the following acts committed with intent to destroy, in whole or in part, a national, ethnical (sic), racial or religious group, as such: a) killing members of the group; b) causing serious bodily or mental harm to members of the group; c) deliberately inflicting on the group conditions of life calculated to bring about its physical destruction in whole or in part; d) imposing measures intended to prevent births within the group; e) forcibly transferring children of the group to another group.*

Although the genocide convention is one of the cornerstones of human rights, about fifty countries, including nearly half of all African states, have not even bothered to ratify it. Many places with indigenous peoples, including Botswana, Guyana, Indonesia, Kenya, and Thailand, have not done so.

It is arguable that, especially given the countless historical precedents, removing a tribal people from its land does inflict 'conditions... calculated to bring about its physical destruction in whole or in part,' and so might be described as genocide. The law also requires the 'intent to destroy', but arguments on this point can be complex. If a government does not want a tribal people to carry on living as it has, and if history shows that taking its land will destroy it, then is the government guilty of genocide if it evicts the people from its lands? The destruction of the group is, after all, the inevitable consequence of the government action. However, many lawyers would argue that this does not amount to genocide unless the destruction was actively sought.

Perhaps a clearer argument concerns the enforced separation of families through compulsory boarding education. In Australia, this was consciously intended to 'integrate' the Aboriginals into white society and so to ensure that they ceased to exist as separate peoples. This seems to fit into the law's definition pretty well, although the government did not murder anyone. Deciding what does and does not amount to genocide is far from straightforward, and can lead into many blind alleys. For example, some might say that the root objective of the Nazis was to ensure the 'purity of the master race': even killing the Jews was a means to this, rather than an end in itself. Indeed, there are people who may argue that seeking the 'purity of the master race' is not that different an idea from trying to integrate a minority people into a dominant society. Both lead to the disappearance of the minority, so could both be justifiably called genocide? Of course there remains an enormous gulf between killing people and trying to incorporate them into the mainstream, even against their wishes. All forms of genocide are horrific; some are still worse than others.

The vast majority of peoples who have ever been destroyed by the actions of other peoples are indigenous, whether through disease, force of arms, or the deliberate break up of their societies. In that sense, they have suffered far more genocide than any other sector of the world's population. In spite of this, and in spite of the fact that the states which have signed the genocide convention have a duty to root it out and prosecute, the accusation has hardly ever been levelled in real court cases. Only in Brazil in recent years have charges of genocide against killers of Indians been upheld, and then only against relatively 'small fry'. Five gold miners were convicted of it following their 1993 massacre of sixteen Yanomami Indians, mainly children and the elderly, in the community of Haximú, and an old rubber tapper who killed eight Oro Uim Indians in 1963 was also convicted of genocide, some thirty years after the event.

Before moving on, it is worth correcting a common mistake. Some people think that genocide inevitably involves large numbers of people being killed, as in the European death camps. The word itself was invented in 1944 in response to the Nazis, but there is no minimum number required in law and, more importantly, if there were, it would be extremely problematic. It would mean that entire tribes, which might number less than a couple of hundred individuals, could be wiped out without it being classed as genocide. That would clearly be contrary to justice and any sensible definition of the word.

A frequently-used term is 'cultural genocide', but this does not appear in any official declarations or laws. Indeed, those who concur with my definition of 'culture' will, I hope, agree that it is impossible to kill one, or preserve another (in the same way that it is impossible to stop or preserve the weather). In my view, the phrase is not helpful.

Genocide cases have been almost non-existent in court, but there are several legal actions concerning land rights which have been real milestones in the struggle for indigenous rights. Three are especially worth noting. The first was the 1992 Mabo decision in Australia, which I have outlined in the section on that country. The second was the Delgamuukw case in Canada, five years later, which confirmed the concept of 'aboriginal title' in British Columbia. The third was the 2006 court decision in Botswana, which held that Bushmen did have the right to return to and live on their ancestral land in the Central

Kalahari Game Reserve, although they had no formal title and the government had evicted them. This was the first recognition of the legal doctrine of 'native title' by an African court and was won after the longest and most expensive case in Botswana's history. The government fought hard to defend its crimes, and to make the case as drawn out and costly for the Bushmen as it could, but justice finally prevailed.

The legal principle – that indigenous peoples have rights to their land because they were living on it a long time before anyone else arrived – might seem just plain common sense, but it has taken generations for it to gain widespread acceptance in law. This is happening more and more nowadays, though there is still a very long way to go before it is properly upheld.

Governments are very reluctant to apply these laws and principles essentially because commercial interests want to take tribal land, usually justified by the false assertion that everyone will benefit if they do so. This lies at the core of the 'development' argument.

Development

Development, where it means helping the poor out of poverty, is vitally important and has brought crucial improvements to many parts of the world. The main problem with 'development' more generally is that it can attempt to replicate Western ways of life in areas, and with peoples, which cannot sustain them, do not want them, or both. When it comes to 'developing' indigenous peoples it can do immense damage and has been directly responsible for much suffering and death.

I have touched on this when describing the prejudice which asserts that tribal people are stupid: they must surely be fools not to want to live like Westerners. When people think this – and many do – they usually mean 'to live like affluent Westerners', with good education, health care, nutrition and housing. In reality, there are many people including in the richest countries who live in poverty and have access to none of these. For example, about one in every five American children is considered extremely poor, and more than half of United States citizens will sink below the poverty threshold at some stage in their lives.

There is little doubt that if offered the choice to have all the benefits enjoyed by the well-off in the West, particularly if it included continuing to live on their own land in their own communities, many indigenous people might well opt in. The problem is, that is not what is on offer. There is an enormous trade-off for practically everything that passes for 'development', and it can leave people in a worse state than before, frequently much worse.

An extreme, but common, example is the enforced boarding schooling already described. Even programmes where the benefits should be obvious, such as health care, can bring more harm than good when they are carried out by badly-trained professionals, who have a superior and aggressive attitude to those they are caring for. Unfortunately, this is the case more often than not.

The biggest key to why such projects fail is that the intended beneficiaries have no sense of ownership over them. They are not asked if they want them. Or, if they are, it is frequently in hasty meetings, conducted in an alien environment, with people they have never met before. Indigenous representatives may casually agree to ill-conceived and little-understood proposals on the basis that they have nothing to lose, just hoping that there might be some benefit, somewhere along the line.

The solution to all this is not difficult, but it needs more time and common sense in planning, as well as usually far less money. These factors sit uneasily in the agendas of many development agencies, which are simply not flexible enough and too pressured. Good projects may be cheaper than bad ones, but the job of agency staff is generally to spend money, not save it. Funds remaining unused may result in smaller budget allocations in future years, and no one wants to be responsible for that. The vetting of projects involves time and work, and it is far easier and quicker to approve a few big ones, costing tens of millions, than lots of small ones, costing a thousand each, even though the latter might be preferable and bring much more benefit to those on the receiving end.

For example, in the usual developmental model, and in the minds of many Westerners, 'education' implies buildings, books, children on chairs in rows, teachers from outside the community, and a curriculum dictated by city officials, often bearing little relevance to rural life. The result for indigenous people is that their children learn little which helps them, in an alien environment, and from unsympathetic tutors. Children sitting under a tree, or on the floor, listening to a teacher from their own community telling them things, in their own language, which are going to equip them for their changing lives, are rare exceptions. The same goes for health projects.

Peel away the rhetoric from many development agendas and they begin to look all too closely like the old colonial enterprise: everyone must learn to live like Westerners, like it or not. Dig deeper, and the connection with business and profit is inescapable. Everyone must not only learn to live like Westerners, they must either supply raw materials to

Western markets, or buy their finished products, and preferably both.

Trillions of dollars have been spent on 'development aid' in the last couple of generations and this has undoubtedly both helped many poor people and impoverished others (largely by taking their land for 'development'). The single biggest factor, by far, in enabling people to live healthier and longer is not financial assistance however, but knowledge of simple hygiene – the understanding that human faeces transmit fatal disease through microbes too small to be seen. If people defecate near water supplies, or fail to wash their hands afterwards, or if insects carry the germs into the water, then serious illnesses result.

Western science discovered this link in the mid-1800s, though ideas about hygiene are certainly not a monopoly of the West. It took a century, even in the richest countries, before the infrastructure needed to keep people safe in cities was in place and houses were connected to both piped water and sewerage. (As late as the 1970s, a friend's Paris apartment had its WC sited in the middle of the kitchen, with privacy provided merely by a makeshift screen!) In spite of all that is spent on 'development', most people in the world still live without piped water or sewerage. This is obviously much less a problem in rural areas with low population densities than it is in urban conglomerations where many people are taking water from the same source, and where much more contaminating material is produced. A few people falling ill in cities can rapidly turn into fatal epidemics.

Child mortality rates are not a bad way of judging whether development 'works'. In most countries, they are lower than they were twenty or so years ago, but this is not so everywhere. Kenya for example is one of the biggest recipients of aid, but mortality rates there have actually risen. The large proportion of the Kenyan population which is rated as 'undernourished' – nearly one in three citizens – has only been marginally reduced.

Real facts about whether more people overall are better or worse off as a result of 'development' are difficult to pin down. For a start, a lot of the data gathering is relatively recent, the definitions used can differ over time and from study to study, and they are open to government manipulation. What counts as 'poverty' in one place is different to another. Another problem is that much of the information is, of necessity, presented as averages, and these can hide as much as they reveal. For example, the gross domestic product (GDP) of a country is the apparent monetary value of everything produced there. But if a tiny number of people produce most of the 'value' and most of the rest produce nothing at all, then the average GDP figure per head of population gives only a distorted picture.

Davi Kopenawa, the famous Yanomami Indian, was once in a meeting with the UK government's development agency, trying to explain the needs of his community. After an hour listening to the thinking behind the programmes being offered, he felt it necessary to point out to the perplexed official that the Yanomami were not 'poor': the help they needed was to counter the catastrophic effects outsiders had brought, principally from previously unknown diseases carried in by illegal miners.

Some companies accept that their activities *do* harm some people through making profits for others, so they sponsor beneficial 'development' projects in the hope of mitigating this. The claim is that the locals end up better off overall. In India for example, the Majhi Kondh saw the schools, which were there anyway, acquiring new signs announcing they were funded by the mining firm which had taken their land. Even where a company funds worthwhile projects, there is an intrinsic problem here: if an enterprise is violating the rights of a people, can it 'offset' this by doing good elsewhere? Such a concept would not be accepted for other crimes: someone who had saved the lives of many men could never claim it excused his murder of a few! If funding benevolent projects is seen to legitimize harmful 'development', then the fundamental principles of inalienable human rights and justice quickly crumble.

Nevertheless, such a notion is gaining strength as resource extraction continues to make a few businessmen and politicians rich, and as corporations and governments increasingly fund supposedly independent non-governmental organizations (NGOs). For example, one of the largest American not-for-profits, Conservation International, is controlled by a board which includes the president of the world's largest public company, JPMorgan Chase, as well as the president of Botswana. Both the investment house and the Botswana government have conducted unlawful activities, with Botswana held responsible for the recent inhuman and degrading treatment of Bushmen. What relevance has such behaviour to the not-for-profit sector?

In reality, NGOs now encompass some huge corporations with budgets running into hundreds of millions of dollars. Some argue that this is a sign of their maturity and professionalism, that they are now working for change 'from the inside' and that the earlier not-for-profit model was inefficient and amateurish; others just see an infiltration and takeover of the sector by business and the state. Some of these organizations are certainly a world away from the original NGO stereotype, once dominated by altruism and notions of service that have largely fallen from fashion. The real problem may be the silence of some not-for-profits when faced with atrocities in areas where they work, or their tacit provision of ethical and environmental 'credentials' to those who do not deserve them.

The bigger question, however, remains whether or not the gap between the wealthiest and poorest has narrowed. Has the proportion of extremely poor shrunk as the world's population has grown? The answer seems to be: probably not. There have of course been winners and losers but, by conservative estimates, one in every six people in the world now goes hungry. That amounts to one billion people – more than ever before. About half of all child deaths are specifically related to malnutrition, with a child dying as a result every few seconds.

Governments, their laws, and industry, have taken the principal roles in how the world has treated tribal peoples, but there is another component of nation states which has also played an extremely important supporting role – its churches and missionaries.

Missionaries

Many tribal people's understanding of spirituality and religion is different from Western norms in an important way: for example, after recounting their creation myth some shamans ask, 'That's our story, what's yours?' They know that different peoples have different visions, whereas Western religions tend to think only one account can be correct. Some framework of beliefs is one of the primary ways that human beings define themselves, so it is not surprising that the attempt to eradicate indigenous religions has been one of the most potent weapons used against tribal peoples. Christian missionaries have taken the lead in this destructive role in much of the world, with Muslims also contributing in Africa and Asia. Both these Middle Eastern religions share three important ideas: that they are the only 'right' beliefs; that anyone can convert to them; and, most importantly, that everyone should. Some Hindus also attempt similar conversions in India, and there are fringe Jewish sects at work in South America and elsewhere.

After their arrival in an intact and healthy society, missionaries often begin encouraging people to settle in larger and more permanent communities. This change of habits and, inevitably, diet often makes them ill. The missionaries then ensure the people become dependent on them for medical help. This is a very good strategy for missionary expansion: it ensures the missions are needed and seen to be helping people and saving lives. However cynical such an interpretation might seem, there are many cases where both missionaries and their indigenous 'victims' were clearly aware of these steps and their consequences.

In extreme examples, missionaries have set out to force the first contact with tribes before going on to create this dependence. Instances of this can be found in Paraguay and Bolivia where an American fundamentalist organization, the New Tribes Mission (NTM), used missionized Ayoreo Indians to bring their still uncontacted relatives to their mission bases as recently as the 1980s. Some Indians were killed during these attempts, and when the newly contacted families were taken to live at the mission they often succumbed to disease and more died. Their independent way of life was destroyed; they found little or no hunting in their new surroundings so they had to earn money and food through menial chores. They also had to attend religious indoctrination; unbelievers soon realized that survival meant conversion, or at least a serious pretence towards it.

The NTM is amongst the world's most extreme evangelical groups; its goal is to reach all tribes who have not yet entered into peaceful contact with outsiders. Unfortunately, these are also the planet's most vulnerable peoples. NTM justifies its work through its belief that everyone is condemned to eternal hell unless he or she is 'reborn in Christ'. Whether or not tribal individuals die in the process is relatively unimportant when compared to securing the heavenly eternity which their beliefs confer. As well as 'accepting Jesus as a personal saviour', the evangelicals adhere to a code which includes, for example, not drinking alcohol or smoking. Indeed, it is a safe bet in parts of South America that non-smoking Indians are evangelical, whereas smokers are Roman Catholic!

There are many other American-based evangelical groups working with tribal peoples. Their missionaries tend to hold rigid and rather parochial views; they believe they come from God's country, the United States, which is under attack from Satan's forces. The latter are largely thought to be 'communists', though they include some other Christians, such as Roman Catholics, and nowadays some Muslims. Outside their own circles, their ideas would be viewed as extremist, even medieval, which is of course ironic as they themselves think they bring modernity to 'backward' tribes.

Evangelicals tend to focus on saving individual 'souls', whereas Roman Catholics see their work more in terms of a collective 'flock'. There is no doubt that the impact of evangelical missionaries is generally catastrophic for less contacted peoples. A more widespread missionary practice, which is no better, is the establishment of the boarding schools I have described, where tribal children are separated from their parents and even siblings, physically punished for speaking their language, and taught that their own way of life is backward, and even 'sinful'. These are often Roman Catholic in much of the Americas (but were largely state run in, for example, Australia and Russia).

Such schools were common in much of the world until a generation ago, particularly in places taken over by European colonists. The results were extraordinarily damaging: indigenous children were alienated from their backgrounds, which was the intention, but they had little or no opportunity of integrating into the dominant colonial – and racist – society either, even if they had wanted to. The children's despair and anger led many to drugs and violence which dragged them down into domestic abuse, crime, prison, and suicide. This established a vicious cycle which still cascades down the generations. In Canada and elsewhere some of the priests running the schools routinely sexually abused their charges. When these children became parents they were more likely to mistreat their own children in turn.

Such enforced separation of children from their parents and background was government policy in Australia and Canada until recent decades. Aboriginal children subjected to it are called the 'stolen generations', and the Australian government made a formal apology to them in 2008. Many were of 'mixed-race', and the idea was to remove them from their Aboriginal background, so that their 'aboriginal-ness' would wither as the children progressed from boarding school to become servants or labourers for white Australians. The same ideas underpin government policy towards

Botswana Bushmen, as well as with Siberian tribes, today.

Not all missionaries have a harmful impact – far from it. Several very good indigenous organizations were started or at least assisted by them, and some individual missionaries have stood in the vanguard of working for indigenous rights and are enormously appreciated, indeed loved, by the peoples they serve.

Of all the people who spend time with tribal people, missionaries spend the most. Until relatively recently, some young Catholic priests and nuns were even told at the start of their mission work that they would never be allowed home again: it was seen as work for life. Some (and not only Catholics) live with tribes for decades, learn their language, and even occasionally 'go native' to the extent of wearing tribal clothing, and joining in tribal ceremonies, even including religious ones. A few go as far as partaking in ritual drug taking.

These missionaries do not think they are there to convert heathens, but see their work as helping those in need. This slant on the missionary endeavour was given an enormous boost by the Second Vatican Council which sought to modernize the Roman Catholic Church in the early 1960s; it certainly had a liberating effect on those amongst the missionary clergy who were already predisposed towards notions of 'service' over and above 'conversion'. Many were themselves from a minority background, such as French Canadians or Basques, and they fostered a concept called 'liberation theology', particularly in Latin America: they saw their Christianity as standing with the downtrodden against the violent exploitation of the elite. They were also often the first to report armed attacks against tribespeople. State thugs murdered hundreds of them as a result, including the

Colombian, Álvaro Ulcué, in 1984, who was both an Andean Indian and a Catholic priest. He was one of many missionaries who stood shoulder to shoulder with tribal peoples, and paid the highest price.

In other parts of the world, Christianity has also supported tribal minorities. In India, for example, conversion to that religion can be a way in which Dalits ('untouchables') and Adivasis (tribals) can escape from their position below the lowest rung of the Hindu caste system. In Indonesian-occupied West Papua, where colonial society is Muslim, Christian missions often act as a bulwark against the oppression and killing which government soldiers still routinely mete out to the tribal people.

Individuals convert to Christianity for many reasons: to protect themselves from sectors of the dominant population; to have access to medicines and money; to acquire power; to stop mainstream society seeing them as different; and of course because they have undergone genuine religious conversion. The latter is rarely straightforward however: as I have pointed out, people adopt things from other societies all the time. Swapping a tribal religion for Christianity is rarely like turning one tap off and a different one on: it is more like adjusting a mixer where both streams merge, but one is more dominant. Social scientists call such religious mixing 'syncretism'. In a sense all religions, including the largest, are or once were syncretic, taking some elements of what went before and adding to them. Nowhere is this clearer than in the Catholicism practised by indigenous peoples in much of Latin America, or in the Protestantism of Oceania, where a good deal of the pre-colonial religions have survived in today's Christianity. These are often called 'indigenous churches' and thrive particularly where the incoming belief shares common traits with the old, such as a priestly hierarchy. In both Central America and the Andes there are many other examples of this.

Central America, incidentally, lays claim to one of the first prominent defenders of indigenous peoples: the sixteenth century Spanish bishop, Bartolomé de las Casas, who worked as a missionary there. Surprisingly for his time, he believed that God had charged him with restoring the lands and liberty of the Indians. He is one of the most important founders of both indigenous rights as well as human rights more generally and deserves to be better known. Unlike Father Ulcué in the bloody Colombia of the 1980s, the bishop expired peacefully in 1566, an old man asleep in his Madrid convent.

Missionaries are not of course the only people from industrialized society seeking to defend indigenous rights.

Non-governmental organizations

Apart from indigenous peoples' own organizations, some government and inter-government bodies, and some missionaries, the principal forces to support indigenous rights are non-governmental organizations, NGOs. The oldest is the Aborigines Protection Society, originally established in London as part of the anti-slavery movement in 1837, and still part of the organization Anti-Slavery International.

At the end of the 1960s, an anthropologist, Helge Kleivan, and colleagues from the University of Copenhagen formed the International Work Group for Indigenous Affairs (IWGIA) in that city; and in London, Robin Hanbury-Tenison with a handful of individuals with no particular academic affiliation, founded what became Survival International. The latter was catalysed by a newspaper article about Brazilian genocide by the renowned writer, Norman Lewis. In the years following, other NGOs with similar objectives were formed in several countries, including the United States, where Cultural Survival was started by an anthropologist at Harvard University. Most have since disappeared.

These and other NGOs, as well as less structured groups of individuals, began with broadly similar, if rather vague, objectives – and little clear idea how they might be realized – but they differentiated increasingly with time and changes in personnel. Some, such as IWGIA and Cultural Survival, turned mainly into brokers for government aid to indigenous peoples, and publishers of anthropologists' papers. The largest, Survival International (with which I work), has offices in several countries, and became the exponent of a popular movement designed to help tribal peoples, both through pursuing specific cases, and by changing public attitudes permanently in their favour. It was, and remains, funded by its individual supporters, rather than government or business.

There are a few other NGOs, funded through different sources, with a track record of including international indigenous issues in part of their work. These include Amazon Watch, Forest Peoples' Programme, Gesellschaft für bedrohte Völker, International Rivers, Mines and Communities, and Rights and Resources.

Public attitudes towards tribal and indigenous peoples are often disparaging or paternalistic: many still view them as backward or primitive. But there are other ways of looking at them too, including seeing them as paragons of particular virtues. There are even extremist NGOs which believe that tribes are 'corrupted' from their 'pristine' condition by any and all contact with outsiders, and that total isolation is the only desirable state. I will go on to outline these opposite approaches – if that *is* what they really are – and something of what lies in between them.

Through a looking glass

All the years of calling the Indian a 'savage' has never made him one.

Luther Standing Bear, Oglala Lakota, USA

Attempts to exonerate the illegal occupation of tribal lands are similar to how slavery was justified in the early nineteenth century, or how apartheid was defended a generation ago. People can get away with this largely because tribal voices speaking in their own defence carry relatively little force: tribal peoples are both numerically small and politically weak. But public reactions play a vital role as well. If the treatment of indigenous peoples is going to be acknowledged as a crime rather than an historical inevitability, it is important to understand how these attitudes arise.

Cannibal? Noble savage?

With the exceptions of the devastation wreaked by disease, and difficulties emerging from an unpredictable climate, all other problems faced by indigenous peoples are underpinned by racist prejudice. This dangerous cocktail of beliefs has three main ingredients: indigenous people are supposed to be savage, even subhuman, as well as unintelligent and childlike. Racists believe more or less the same about all who are different. These presumed qualities make tribal peoples inferior to others, which is thought to legitimize the violation of their rights, particularly if it is for the benefit of supposedly more civilized, intelligent and grown-up beings. The latter may take indigenous lands because tribes are thought not to have the capacity to use it properly; they do not exploit it in the way that intelligent adults would.

The first view – that they are savages – encompasses their supposedly being violent, unpredictable, and uncontrollable, as well as dirty and lazy. One of the most extreme accusations of violence can be seen in the charge of cannibalism.

Cartoon cannibalism shows 'primitives' around a pot, boiling up a hapless captive prior to eating him. The image largely originates with a sixteenth century German, Hans Staden, who said he had been captured by Tupinambá Indians in Brazil and claimed he saw them cooking and eating their Indian enemies. It is impossible to tell to what degree his account is true. Many inventive stories emerged from the same era, men with faces in their chests, a single eye in their forehead, and so on. Indeed, a similar, if not as extreme, trait is not confined to past history: modern accounts of travel in 'distant' lands frequently use dramatic embellishment, often largely invented to enhance prestige, book sales and television viewing figures. Staden also had an interest in ensuring his tale would sell. Not surprisingly, it did. His dramatic title ladled it on thick: he called it, *The True History… of Grim, Wild, Naked Man-eating People*. Staden's pictures of huge pots and outdoor barbeques look unconvincing to many, and it would be astonishing if he did not at least over-embellish what he actually saw, but there is no way of being certain. Nor do we know what the

Tupinambá thought of the Europeans, though other South American Indians certainly thought it was the invaders who were the cannibals.

Cannibalism has been reported from elsewhere as well, particularly from the Pacific. Some Papuans claim to eat their enemies, or to have done so in the past, though some think this is largely boasting! In fact, on close examination, there is not one verifiable account from anywhere; in other words, no one who seems credible, without an axe to grind, book to sell, or mission to fund, has ever seen a tribal person kill and eat someone out of custom. Some social scientists think that all accounts are a myth; others believe denying cannibalism is mere wishful thinking, an attempt to turn a blind eye to an uncomfortable reality.

What is certainly true is that some tribal peoples do have a custom of ingesting portions of the ashes, or flesh, of the already dead. These are usually their kin, but some also do this with their enemies. Some Brazilian tribes, for example, say they sometimes used to eat their liver. It is also true that many – non-tribal – people resort to consuming human flesh in times of extreme hunger. There are dozens of eyewitness accounts of this, from times of war, shipwreck, and so forth. The much more extreme step, in similar extraordinary predicaments, of first killing in order to eat is also well known. In addition, there are many verifiable accounts of cannibalism resulting from extreme deviancy. This has happened in industrialized countries recently, and there is little reason to think that similar odd behaviour does not crop up amongst indigenous peoples as well.

Paradoxically, as well as tragically, some tribal peoples who may be the victims, rather than perpetrators, of cannibalism are Pygmies in the Democratic Republic of Congo: as I mentioned before, some have reportedly been killed in order to be eaten in special war rituals by the violence-crazed militias which have fought over the region for decades.

As well as cannibalism, indigenous peoples were also routinely accused of practising human sacrifice. This was used as an important justification for Europeans to invade and conquer them, and was given wide publicity in the colonial era: it was commonly reported from British India, for example, where it did seem to have taken place, though very rarely. There is no doubt, however, that it was formerly practised by some peoples in a ritual context. This is widely known, and perhaps the most famous example concerns the Aztecs. (Those familiar with the Bible will also know that Abraham, ancestor of Moses, Jesus and Muhammad, was going to sacrifice his own son ritually.) The other really savage accusation levelled at some tribal peoples is that of child- or baby-killing, called infanticide, which I have already touched on.

It is – rightly – difficult to look at cruel behaviour with any degree of objectivity. However, even a cursory study will show that tribal peoples have no savage practices which cannot also be found amongst the so-called 'civilized', as I have shown when describing both infanticide and genital mutilation. Indigenous peoples *can* sometimes behave like savages, just like everyone else.

The second plank in the racist view about tribal peoples is that they lack intelligence. This notion can be reinforced because quite a lot of indigenous communities are now home to the decaying remains of aid projects which have fallen apart as soon as the Western agency which instigated them left. New-style housing, water pipes, latrines, and agricultural projects have all been apparently welcomed by communities curious to see what was in it for them only to be subsequently discarded at the earliest opportunity. Although such a scenario is not confined to indigenous peoples, it gives ammunition to the belief that they lack the ability to see the advantages such schemes confer. The reality is that this has nothing to do with any inability to grasp new benefits: usually, the abandoned projects were simply felt to be disadvantageous in the long run, though the reasons are often social rather than economic, and may remain obscure to outsiders.

A very good example concerns Western-style concrete or plank houses which have been built all over the world to 'modernize' tribespeople's 'primitive' dwellings, and which usually stand empty. They are simply not as practical as the houses they are supposed to replace. In Papua, they are often kept for pigs, whilst the people carry on in their former dwellings. Other than in the minds of some development agencies and governments, these houses are not always better than what was there already. For example, an earth floor is easier to keep clean than one made of concrete, dirt is quickly absorbed, or can easily be swept out or dug up, and it never needs washing. Many Amazon Indians are meticulous about cleanliness and the floors of their communal houses are swept several times daily. Similarly, a new tin roof can be much less comfortable than one made of thatch. In the tropics, metal roofs are hotter in the sun, noisier in the rain, decay quicker, and are harder to repair.

Cheapness, the ready availability of local materials, and ease of repair, are only some of the reasons why long-established house design can be difficult to improve on. For example, Maasai houses made of branches, mud and dried animal dung, are very dark inside. This can seem inconvenient to visitors (especially when many Maasai do not bother with electric flashlights), but it keeps away the plagues of flies which swarm perpetually around the nearby cow and goat herds, and which invade any well-lit, 'modern' houses in the vicinity.

In 2011, the Rwandan government tried to destroy all 'primitive' thatched roofs in the country, forcing people to buy metal sheeting. Hundreds of Batwa 'Pygmy' people were made homeless, as the free roofing the 'most destitute' were supposed to be given rarely materialized. It is difficult to escape the conclusion that this and similar 'development' schemes are more about securing profits for manufacturers than merely misguided attempts to 'modernize'. Where indigenous people abandon recently-adopted Western ways, there is usually a perfectly intelligent reason – they are not being stupid (though of course no one would claim that tribal societies are freer of foolishness than others).

The third main accusation – that indigenous peoples are childlike – derives partly from the noticeable spontaneity of hunting societies, where people seem to plan little for the future. They eat when food is available, often gorging, and then go without for days. Of course, a 'civilized' way of life requires more forethought. A hunter-gathering society has, on its doorstep, the equivalent of its supermarket, hospital, place of worship, and entertainment centre, and none are shut at weekends. There are no admission fees, no bills, no tax, no mortgage, and no pensions. A house and food cost nothing, so there is little need to plan far in advance. These are also, of course, the keys to why their land is so much more important for tribal peoples than it is for almost anyone else. It means literally everything to them, including life itself.

It is arguable that such spontaneity, their 'living in the moment', is a key factor behind what might be described as the 'goal' of many tribal societies (if any society can be described as having goals). In their case, it is to maintain a healthy life – in a physical and spiritual sense – rather than share the ambition of the industrialized nations to seek perpetual 'progress' or 'growth', revolving around wealth. Although the benefits of such growth go largely unquestioned by many Westerners, particularly those in positions of power, it is worth remembering that these ideas really only took off when industrialization began seeing individuals primarily as workers, people who earned money in order to buy things produced by other workers. However widely accepted the notion has become – that buying and selling are the keys to a good life – it has far from convinced everyone: there are plenty of people, including many in the industrialized world, who 'opt out', and choose to live rather separately, in communes, religious groups, as Travellers, or just in small rural communities. Unlike tribes, they are not generally held to be less intelligent or childlike as a result.

It is also worth recalling that *most* of the world's societies, as opposed to individuals, do not promote the same obsession with the pursuit of wealth and power as does the industrialized West, and others who now want to copy the model.

Perhaps curiously, those (like me) who assert the realities about tribal ways of life, and refute the racist view that they are savage, stupid and childish, are often accused of romantically portraying the 'noble savage'. This is an old concept that is worth exploring. Although ancient European and Arabic philosophers expressed a similar idea, it first took serious root with the glowing accounts written by the early explorers about Central American Indians and Pacific Islanders. The Swiss philosopher, Jean-Jacques Rousseau, touched on the idea in several works, especially in his famous 1762 book, *The Social Contract*. It is Rousseau who is usually, though inaccurately, credited with inventing the concept of the 'noble savage', and so the view is often named 'Rousseauesque'.

Proponents of the 'noble savage' assert that peoples are corrupted by 'civilization', and live better without it. Some social scientists have gone out of their way to demonstrate that this is wrong, claiming the idea is itself patronizing and even racist. One way of doing this has been to document the incidence of conflict in certain tribal societies, to emphasize their violent, as opposed to any 'noble', side. The best-known example is Napoleon Chagnon's description of Yanomami Indians in Venezuela in the 1960s. This American anthropologist called the Indians, and titled his best-selling book, *The Fierce People*, and produced data and films showing them exercising brutal levels of violence against each other with little apparent provocation. Sir Edmund Leach, the doyen of British anthropology in the 1970s, went further when he wrote that if Yanomami 'traditional culture' was 'protected', the Indians 'would then exterminate one another'! However, researchers working subsequently with the same people found the Yanomami generally peaceable, and certainly not the violence-obsessed creatures they had read about as undergraduates. Some feel this raises serious ethical, as well as scientific, questions over the degree to which anthropological data can be selected, perhaps even unconsciously, to fit a preconceived thesis.

It may not be particularly surprising that tribal peoples are viewed disparagingly. Perhaps most societies, including tribal ones, think those who live differently are somehow inferior to them, that their own homeland is the best of all possible places, and that their way of life is better than others. Indeed, there is nothing intrinsically wrong with this; it is just part of the glue binding a people together. The real problem with racism is that it goes further and leads to – and is used to justify – hurting people. Where societies are portrayed as violent, it breeds violence against them. This can create the sort of situation I have described, where South American ranchers did not realize there was anything wrong in killing Indians because they were 'like animals' – a statement undoubtedly made in all honesty. The same view was frequently echoed in many places until recently, and still is in some, such as in West Papua. The anthropologist's image of the Indians' ferocity was even cited as a reason why Yanomami-run projects should not receive British government funding in the 1990s.

Those who reject the ideas of savagery, stupidity or childishness, can still adhere to less obvious forms of racism, which may be even more insidious, because they can appear much fairer. It is frequently argued, particularly by those who stand to make money out of mines or dams, that a tribe should not be allowed to prevent resources being extracted which could benefit the wider majority, or that they should not be entitled to more land than other poor people. But neither of these assertions is fundamentally any different to the arguments used to justify nineteenth century colonialism: why should Africans not give up their resources when more advanced Europeans could make better use of them? Why should a few thousand Aboriginals occupy Australia, when England and Ireland needed room for their own, 'more advanced', folk?

The answer was, of course, because Europeans thought they were superior to others; it was a conviction substantiated with the soundest science, or so they firmly believed. Darwin's theory of evolution lay behind much of this. Whilst it undoubtedly accounts for some differences, it is often used to make false hypotheses. It is important to explain this in more detail.

Darwinian selection has played an important role in the physical appearance of 'races'. For example, exposing the skin to sunlight stimulates it to produce the principal source of vitamin D that is vital for health. A pale skin works better than a dark one in less sunny climates because it creates more of the vitamin. In fact, dark-skinned people who now live in the north of North America, for example, are particularly susceptible to vitamin D deficiency, and this can lead to heart disease and other problems. As prehistoric humans moved into northern Europe and Asia, natural selection favored those with paler and paler skins, because they were producing healthy levels of the vitamin.

Whether one person is darker than another, or has healthy levels of vitamin D, are statements of simple fact. But to argue that one 'race' is more or less 'intelligent', 'civilized' or 'barbaric' – as Darwin himself did – is nothing more than personal opinion and prejudice: people neither agree on what these terms mean nor how to measure them. Darwin was right about the effects of natural selection on the body, but entirely wrong about thinking it led to his own race's superiority over others. That 'superiority' came not from scientific evolution, but from force of arms and the willingness to use them.

Certain 'races' do tend to do better than others in, for example, IQ tests, but this is only because the papers measure something one particular group of people does well. All this is obvious, but is still used to bolster archaic and racist views. Amazon nomads who do not count higher than three are unlikely to excel in high school mathematics! Were tests contrived by the nomads to establish who can provide their society with the most food, then Ivy League or Oxbridge professors are equally unlikely to impress.

Anthropologists and museums

Like all social sciences, anthropology is little more than a century old. For most of its life it has concentrated on those different from Westerners, and most of its subjects have, until recently, been indigenous peoples.

One branch of the science, physical anthropology, set out to compare indigenous people with Westerners, measuring their bodies, particularly skulls, and comparing their size, colour, type of hair, eye shape and so on. This was supposed to demonstrate the scientific basis behind racist ideas which were already firmly established before the Nazis expanded them in the 1930s to decide who belonged to their 'master race' and who did not. Their scientists advised the Brazilian government to get on with the job of eradicating the Indians. Nowadays of course all this is discredited by all but racist extremists. However, the idea that indigenous peoples are 'backward' ultimately derives from the same roots and is still widely held, as we have seen.

Of course, there *are* obvious physical differences between peoples. They arise from adaptations to local environments, varied notions of beauty, and different ancestry. Sub-Saharan Africans have black skins, except for the Bushmen, who are copper-coloured. The Andaman Islanders and a handful of other tribes in Asia are also black, as are the peoples of New Guinea and Australia. This is likely to be because they are more directly descended from the first migrants out of Africa, as I have said; they have mixed less. Apart from Europeans and many Chinese and Japanese, pretty much everyone else is more or less brown-skinned. The Bushmen have almond-shaped eyes, different from other Africans and Europeans, but similar to many Asians and all American Indians and Inuit. All such traits are inherited of course, and can now be more acceptably looked at with genetic research, rather than a tape measure and calipers.

The other principal branch of the discipline is social or cultural anthropology. This examines what people do and say, rather than what they look like. As with many sciences, only a tiny handful of anthropologists have ever gained popular recognition. Probably the best known was the American, Margaret Mead, who studied the South Pacific islanders and was then enthusiastically adopted by 1960s feminists in the United States. In France, Claude Lévi-Strauss, created a famous movement, 'structuralism', which emerged from his fieldwork with Brazilian Indians. He held that mythology and ritual, and indeed everything else, could be viewed as forming part of an overarching pattern or structure.

Anthropology has never been far from controversy; Nazi theory is only the most obvious example. In the 1960s and 70s, a British-American anthropologist, Colin Turnbull, wrote two popular books. The first, *The Forest People*, told of the BaMbuti Pygmies in the Democratic Republic of Congo. They appeared to live idyllically, and conformed closely to what the hippy movement was searching for at that time: a freedom from restraint, peace, tolerance, and an easy life. Turnbull rather upset things with his next work, *The Mountain People*, which described the Ik in Uganda. According to him, they behaved in a monstrous and inhuman fashion. Many are now sceptical about the accuracy of these accounts, which seemed to court sensationalism, and nowadays they are widely discredited. At the time of publication, however, criticism was muted, and did not stop the works achieving a popularity which even led to one being adapted for theatrical performance.

It is probably unsurprising that some anthropologists, at least those with a fascinating story to tell, have found what they set out to look for, and it is equally unsurprising that many tribal peoples who can now read their books and speak for themselves, have objected to their findings. Radical American Indians in particular can be scathing of anthropologists, and some now refuse to talk to them at all.

Like any profession, anthropology encompasses all shades of responsibility, and lack of it. In the 1970s, a German anthropologist, Mark Münzel, denounced the appalling treatment of a Paraguayan tribe, the Aché. He called it genocide and published evidence to support his conclusion, which was endorsed by a legal expert. Two anthropologists, hired by the United States government, then opposed his account: according to them there was no genocide at all. Why should the accusation warrant the attention of the American government? Because Paraguay's rightwing dictatorship depended on the United States and acted as a bulwark against communism in the region. America had passed a law to stop it supporting regimes guilty of gross human rights violations, so if American aid (which was primarily military) was to continue flowing, it was important for Paraguay to be judged innocent of genocide.

Many believe that the anthropologist's job is to observe, record, and interpret, but never to 'take sides' for or against their 'subjects'. Indeed, some field-working anthropologists assert that they can neither intervene in, nor even report, human rights abuses suffered by those they study, because the government will withdraw their research permits. Others, like Münzel, have stood in the forefront of the movement to assist them. Some academics have always defended tribal peoples, either behind the scenes or more openly. One of the most famous early proponents of this was German-born Franz Boas, who fiercely opposed racist ideas about indigenous peoples for the first four decades of the twentieth century. Others, particularly in Latin America, have also supported the peoples they studied. In 1971, a group of anthropologists signed the 'Declaration of Barbados', which laid a foundation for much of the indigenous peoples' support movement which followed. They put the blame for the destruction of American Indians at the feet of governments and religious missions; and also attacked those social scientists who pretended to be detached from their subjects' welfare. Since that time, many anthropologists have helped tribal peoples' land claims, and assisted them to establish their own organizations.

As well as conducting studies resulting in books and papers, and to a lesser extent film, anthropology also inherited the role created by early travellers – collecting 'exotic' things for display in museums. This facet of the discipline has also become controversial, as now the descendants of the peoples represented often want the objects returned, particularly those with a spiritual significance. Many Western museums have gone along with this and handed items back. In 1998, for example, Glasgow's famous Kelvingrove Museum returned a Lakota Sioux 'ghost dance' shirt, which may have been stripped from a body after the Wounded Knee massacre.

Museums have been criticized for mounting displays about indigenous peoples without explaining their current predicament. This became the focus of an important battle between the British Museum and supporters of Amazon Indians in 1985. Although the museum steadfastly refused to amend its presentation, which completely ignored the Indians' plight, the controversy succeeded in changing the way many exhibitions are displayed: few major museums nowadays omit referring to the descendants of the peoples represented, and several, including the British Museum, have begun to work closely with those peoples when arranging exhibitions about them. It would be difficult or impossible now for any museum in North America to mount a major display of Native American artefacts without first conferring with the descendants of those who originally made them. Apart from ethical considerations, they fear 'repatriation' claims whereby the descendants ask for 'their' items to be returned.

The most controversial topic of all for museums is the display of human bodies, or bits of them. Indigenous peoples in New Zealand have long mounted a vigorous, and largely successful, campaign to insist on the return of Maori body parts. Heads, and even whole bodies, are held in many collections because they bear elaborate and much-prized tattoos. So much so that, in the conflicts with the British, Maori captives were sometimes tattooed before being killed and their bodies sold.

A key case took place in 1988, when an old Maori head was due to be auctioned in London. Indigenous supporters organized a successful legal challenge that eventually saw the relic returned to New Zealand. Australian Aboriginals and African Bushmen have also been subjected to having their dead ancestors displayed in museums, and have often been successful in claiming them back. In the last couple of decades, most of the world's major museums have worked at becoming closer to, and more understanding of, the descendants of those whose body parts they hold. In one surprising outcome, some Torres Strait Islanders, from near Australia, now consider a museum in Cambridge, England, to be an acceptable resting place for some of their ancestral spirits.

Scientists have also found themselves enmeshed in similar controversies. For example, geneticists took blood samples from Yanomami Indians to the United States in 1967, without the Indians being aware that they would be kept for medical research. When a Yanomami dies, his body is cremated and none of his remains or possessions are kept, so the Indians found the idea of storing blood from a dead person barbaric. Years later, when they learned that the blood was still there, they petitioned to have it returned so they could dispose of it respectfully.

Of course, it is not only professionals, such as missionaries or social scientists, who spend time with tribal peoples these days. Tourist visits have become common, often without leading to any appreciation of, or sympathy towards, the tribes concerned.

Tourism

Tour companies in southern Africa often pay Bushmen to demonstrate their 'tracking skills' to tourists and backpackers. One such company, Wilderness Safaris, offered its guests 'an interpretive 'Bushman Walk' with a couple of [Bushman] staff members [to] gain life-changing insights into the unique culture of this fascinating people.' The irony is that the 'ecotourist' lodge was built in 2008 on the traditional territory of a Bushman tribe that had been evicted six years before. Visitors were in fact watching Bushmen demonstrate with pretend bows and arrows on land in which they were neither allowed to hunt, nor even to access their own water borehole. The tourists, on the other hand, were free to quench their thirst in the bar as well as swim in the hotel pool.

Commercial tourism to tribes encompasses trips to a wide variety of peoples. Many are to 'fake' tribals; folk paid to dress exotically and pretend to be something they are not. Some are to genuinely remote peoples who suffer visits because they are made, or paid, to entertain the tourists. Almost always only the tiniest proportion, if any, of the resultant profits goes to recompensing the tribe. At the opposite end of the spectrum, there are a very few enterprises which genuinely bring benefits. These are often run by tribal people themselves and involve small, well-managed and low-impact tours. Of course, many pretend to be in the latter category when they are not.

One of the most famous areas for tribal tourism is the hills of Thailand, where the influx of backpackers on the coast created a ready market for people looking for more than the drugs, sex and beach-oriented holidays available there. A good deal of this is relatively harmless, though the tribes concerned may be exploited by being paid very little. Tribal people turn up in 'traditional' dress, often to villages created or adapted for the purpose (for example, by hiding away all electrical equipment), enact a bit of tribal life, and then go home with their pay. The biggest, closely-related, problem in Thailand is probably that many of the, often very young, sex workers on the coast are tribal children from the hills.

The Kayan in Thailand and Burma have long been famous because their women appear to have elongated necks. Known as 'giraffe women', the effect is the result of wearing necklaces of heavy metal coils for many years that press down their collarbones. Necks appear stretched by a dozen centimetres or more, providing an exotic photograph for which tourists are willing to pay. Some Kayan have become dependent on the income provided, which can encourage girls to have the neck coils when they may well not otherwise have done so. In this and similar ways, tourism can artificially encourage cultural features which many would rather change.

Like everyone, different tribal people react differently to being photographed or filmed. Many are uncomfortable and do not like it, and sometimes this can go further. Australian Aboriginals, for example, often object to the display of photographs of people who have since died. However, the widely held notion that tribespeople believe photographs 'steal their soul' seems to be largely the invention of Victorian travel writers. Some Maasai routinely demand money for photographs but, once paid, are happy to strike a pose. Many tribal people have no objection to being photographed at all; some rather like it, putting on their finery and pressing to get in the frame, especially if they think they will receive a copy. Unfortunately, large numbers of tourists descending on small communities and generally behaving aggressively is the more common experience.

'Cultural shows' in which people enact a variation of supposedly traditional songs and dances are widespread. Many of these are harmless, somewhat akin to English 'morris' dancing. The performers may or may not have any relationship with the traditions they are presenting, some may be enacting something their parents or grandparents did, often adapted for a Western audience, others are simply performers. In parts of Amazonia, for example, tourists are taken to 'Indian villages' and shown hunting, dancing and dress which are created by local folk who are simply play-acting, and who acknowledge no Indian ancestry once the tourist boats have left. This has been going on for generations.

I have mentioned the more sinister way many governments, such as Botswana and China, build 'folklore' into state policies, supposedly to preserve 'traditional culture'. This is about promoting tourism through lip service to a diversity that the authorities tolerate only if they can control it. These governments do not want minorities around who are genuinely different, but they are happy to profit from their dances and costumes.

Tourism to sites, as well as to people, can also be controversial. A well-known example is the impressive rock formation in the centre of Australia, which Aboriginals regard as sacred. Naming it 'Ayer's Rock' in 1873, numerous Australians have visited and climbed over it since the 1940s. Aboriginal ownership was officially recognized in 1985 when the name reverted to the original 'Uluru'. The Aboriginals however were still forced to allow climbing on the rock, and this has become a source of dispute. The Aboriginal owners have also tried, sometimes successfully, to prohibit the photographing of particularly sacred parts of the crag.

Amongst the most impressive rock paintings in the world are those in the Tsodilo Hills in Botswana. The origins of some are at least twenty thousand years old and were painted by the ancestors of Bushmen; others are from recent centuries, and a Bushman community still lives nearby. In 1994, however, their settlement was forcibly moved further away; the authorities objected to Bushmen 'begging' from tourists, and non-Bushman 'guides' wanted a monopoly of showing people around. The tourists came to admire Bushman rock paintings, but the authorities did not want them seeing any Bushmen, unless it was to pre-arranged 'cultural' shows.

Heavy-handed state intervention, exploitative entrepreneurs, and tourist arrogance aside, tourists visiting tribal areas who behave with common sense politeness, sensitivity and courtesy are generally well received. Where they are unaware of local etiquette, they would be well advised to exercise great caution about both gender and age differences, for men and women often occupy different parts of a dwelling and behave differently. Visitors should not make any assumptions about what they might think is just a polite greeting, but which could be interpreted as more intrusive. Amazonian Waorani who visit houses other than their own, for example, announce their arrival with a shout, and then wait outside until invited in; the wait can be long!

Tribal people who have been in routine and close contact with the outside world for decades are unlikely to be more susceptible to most disease than anyone else, though an exception is with new strains of influenza, and care should always be taken about contagion. For example, swine flu seems to affect indigenous people more than others, even in places such as North America and Australia where they have been in intensive contact for generations.

Such advice does not apply to little-contacted peoples. It is extremely dangerous for tourists to be anywhere near them, for both parties. Such peoples are likely to react with lethal hostility towards outsiders, who may well bring in infectious diseases which can reap deadly havoc long after the visitors have left. Tourists are more likely to carry such contagion than local people for two reasons. One is that they come from all over the world, and so carry alien microbes to which local people have established no immunity. The other is that a very high proportion of air passengers develop a cold, or worse, within a week of flying. These people may not realize they are ill, as carriers might show no symptoms for several days (or even at all) but they are still contagious.

This is particularly dangerous in places like the Andaman Islands where most visitors fly in and stay only a week or so – the most contagious period of all. The recently-contacted Jarawa on one island are treated as if they were animals in a game park, with visitors vying to catch photos of them; in fact, some tours are marketed specifically for that purpose. Tourist lodges close to the Jarawa reserve are a dangerous recent development and tourists with a conscience should stay well away from such places. If one day the Jarawa do succumb to a deadly infection, as so many tribal peoples have in the past, the carrier might well have long returned home and never have an inkling of the catastrophe he left behind.

Popular ideas about tribal peoples are formed by tourism, as well as by anthropology, and prejudice. Overwhelmingly however, the public's ideas about such peoples are nowadays shaped by television and film. They are not always helpful.

Films and television

I have already mentioned how many American showbiz celebrities such as Johnny Depp and Cameron Diaz claim descent from an Indian tribe. Hollywood also has an ambiguous relationship with the past. This is not surprising: the film industry moved there less than thirty years after the 1890 Wounded Knee massacre. The Indian wars were almost contemporary with early cinema, and figured prominently in its portrayals. It is Hollywood of course, which projected the 'Red' Indians (a term they largely object to) to worldwide fame. However, depictions of Indians in mainstream art and thinking were already well established. James Fenimore Cooper, for example, published his famous book, *The Last of the Mohicans*, over sixty years before Wounded Knee.

That book is a novel and Hollywood is fantasy, but much of what is presented as fact should be treated with similar caution. I have shown how Edward Curtis deliberately removed anything from his photos of American Indians which he thought too 'modern'. Captions as well as the images themselves, whether still or moving, remain very important in shaping views about tribal peoples. Both are subject to manipulation. It is rare, for instance, to see a photo of young Maasai men today without them being called 'warriors', yet the tribe has fought no one for a very long time. Some of the most powerful modern images of Botswana Bushmen have been taken at camps where Bushmen re-enact their past for the benefit of photographers and tourists, and many television companies do not want the tribal people they are filming to wear watches on screen, or be seen listening to the radio. The desire to make tribal peoples look more 'exotic' than they really are has far from disappeared.

Nanook of the North is probably the earliest documentary portraying a tribal people. Filmed in 1920 without sound, it portrays a staged story of a Canadian Inuit hunter. 'Nanook', which was not his real name, is shown hunting with spear, not the rifle he would actually have used, but the story is nevertheless reasonably true to life and not unsympathetic. Other films have gone much further with their staging. The Belgian, Armand Denis, made many television films about African wildlife in the 1950s. 'Wildlife' included the Pygmies of the Belgian Congo, and in one spectacular episode he showed them building a 'traditional' rope suspension bridge over a river. It was entirely artificial: the people would never have built such a structure if the filmmakers had not told them to.

To a certain degree of course, every documentary is 'staged'. Early, massive equipment required lengthy setting up, and film was heavy and expensive. Every shot had to count; not be left to chance. Nowadays, all this is easier, but the director, camera operator, and editor still select what is filmed and eventually shown.

Starting in the 1970s, the British company, Granada, made a series of television films called *Disappearing World*. Under the leadership of director Brian Moser, it broke new ground. Moser insisted on only filming tribes where there was a resident anthropologist who spoke the language and who would work with the film crew, ensuring the people were treated appropriately, securing their agreement, and explaining what was happening. Moser also wanted the smallest possible crew to remain on site for extended periods of many weeks. The first *Disappearing World* series included the excellent, *The Last of the Cuiva* (1971), shot in Colombia. An anthropologist appeared in the film, explaining what was happening, but what the Cuiva said was subtitled. For the first time on mainstream television, tribal people were talking for themselves. In *Eskimos of Pond Inlet* (1976) the idea was taken much further: there was neither visible anthropologist nor any voiceover, just the subtitled Inuit voices.

Disappearing World covered the threats the people faced, as much as their way of life. *Mehinacu* and *Onka's Big Moka* are two further top-quality examples, filmed respectively in Brazil and Papua New Guinea, which showed how tribes can be sensitively presented as both extremely interesting – even exotic – as well as much like everyone else, at one and the same time.

These films were shown on primetime television and formed part of what some see as a golden age, defining a new, respectful way of portraying tribal peoples. Recent television tends to be much shallower, with more focus on the television presenter or a visitor than on the tribe. The best-known is the BBC's *Tribe* series (2005-2007), presented by ex-marine Bruce Parry, who threw himself into exotic scenarios with infectious gusto. Unfortunately, some imitators have produced material of truly abysmal quality and dismal prejudice, which serves largely to reinforce bigotry against tribal peoples.

More serious films, looking at aspects beyond tribal exoticism or how they cope with television crews, continue to be made outside mainstream broadcast. An excellent example is Hugh Brody's *The Meaning of Life* (2009), showing how a prison in Canada interacts with a nearby Indian community, and the way the Indians can bring a sense of belonging and balance into prisoners' lives.

Even the briefest outline of film cannot ignore the Western. All English-speaking children in the 1950s knew television's, *Lone Ranger*, and the hero's loyal Indian sidekick, Tonto (which is the Spanish word for 'stupid'). Most Indians in Westerns were not like Tonto, but were savage and hostile. This began to change in 1970 with films including *Soldier Blue* which portrayed in graphic gore the real-life 1864 Sand Creek massacre where hundreds of Cheyenne and Arapaho were butchered by the US cavalry. Probably the most famous feature film sympathetic to Indians is *Dances with Wolves* from 1990.

Before looking at other parts of the world, it is worth mentioning the Canadian 'Indian', 'Grey Owl', who said he was half Apache and who made films which garnered an enormous following, so much so that, by the time of his death in 1938, he had become one of the most influential conservationists in the West. His life story was no less extraordinary when it was discovered that he had no indigenous ancestry whatsoever, and that he was not even from Canada: he had been born in Hastings, England.

If thousands of feature films have portrayed North American Indians, hundreds have shown other tribal peoples, mostly depicting them as savages. However, at the positive end of the spectrum is the magnificent 1986 film, *The Mission*, a fictionalized tale of Jesuits and Indians in eighteenth century Paraguay. Another excellent film is *Rabbit-proof Fence* (2002), a profoundly moving testimony about the forcible separation of Australian Aboriginal children from their families, based on the autobiography by Aboriginal woman, Doris Pilkington Garimara.

Several films have been made by indigenous filmmakers in South America, especially by Brazilian Indians engaged in programmes with the 'Video in the Villages' organization, founded by Vincent Carelli, as well as in projects catalyzed by the anthropologist Terence Turner. In North America, an extraordinary feature film, *Atanarjuat – The Fast Runner* (2000) was made and acted by Inuit and recounts an Arctic myth. In Australia, *Samson and Delilah* (2009) is a beautiful love story, which harrowingly captures the reality of Aboriginal life today. It was made by Aboriginal director Warwick Thornton, to much critical acclaim.

Over recent years, the use of short, subtitled, films made on ultra-lightweight equipment and shown on the web, rather than broadcast, has become an important component in the pursuit of tribal peoples' rights. For example, Survival International's award-winning *Mine* (2009), about the Dongria Kondh's fight against a bauxite mine in India, secured many more viewings on the web than it would have on broadcast television.

Books and plays

Tribal peoples' issues are little represented in mainstream theatre. Much – probably too much – has been made of the possible links between Shakespeare's Caliban, from *The Tempest*, and the Carib Indians whose name was adopted for the Caribbean Sea. More recently, the famous playwright Christopher Hampton wrote *Savages* in 1973, based on a massacre of Brazilian Indians. Fringe theatre has dealt with the subject rather more. For example, the South African play *Survival in the Wilderness* by Elijah Molahlehi recounted the story of the 2002 Bushman evictions in Botswana to much local acclaim.

Books about tribal peoples range from anthropological texts, often unintelligible to non-specialists, to a handful of works of enduring popularity. As with film, the degree of veracity presented in books, including academic treatises, is variable.

Works which are controversial with anthropologists, but remain enormously popular, are Laurens van der Post's accounts of the southern African Bushmen first published in the 1950s. The author, who described himself as a storyteller, might have been inventive in some areas, extrapolated from others' accounts, and got some details wrong, but however legitimate such criticisms may be, exactly the same ones can also be laid at the door of many social scientists. His depiction did have the unique virtue of being the first popular account of the Bushmen that was also sympathetic to their plight, and it forced their little-told story into the limelight.

Bury my Heart at Wounded Knee (1970) is an enormously influential and powerful history of North American Indians, which few can read without being profoundly moved. Another good and authoritative outline of the subject is James Wilson's, *The Earth Shall Weep* (2000). Many North American Indians themselves have a tradition of oratory that has spawned some magnificent literature. *Black Elk Speaks* (1932) is amongst the best. Australian Aboriginals have also produced their own writing, and I have already mentioned Doris Pilkington Garimara's moving book. Germaine Greer's extended essay, *Whitefella Jump Up* (2003), is perhaps the most eloquent testimonial to their predicament as a whole, whilst Hugh Brody's *The Other Side of Eden* (2001) is the best introduction to hunter-gatherers.

Victims of Progress by John H. Bodley, originally written in the 1970s, is a good overview of the political issues facing indigenous peoples. It is written for the specialist, as is the material regularly published by Cultural Survival in the United States, and the International Work Group for Indigenous Affairs in Denmark.

As with film, indigenous writers are increasingly writing their own books about their own people. As well as the better-known examples in places like North America and Australia, this development is also leaping forward in more remote regions. The Tucanoan Indian peoples in Colombia, for example, have produced nearly two dozen books about themselves over recent years.

Several publications from Survival International, aimed at the non-specialist, provide introductions to different aspects. They include, *Guardians of the Sacred Land* (on religion and ecology), *Disinherited* (on Brazil), *Canada's Tibet* (on the Innu in Canada), *Indians* (on North and South America), *From Siberia to Sarawak* (on Asia), *Progress can Kill* (on harmful development), and the cartoon parody, *There you go!*, on what much development is really all about.

Survival's large-format collection of high-quality photos and essays, *We are One*, edited by Joanna Eede in 2009, is also aimed at a popular readership and goes much further than other, similar, books at presenting the point of view of indigenous people themselves. (This spawned a powerful theatrical event, created and directed by Mark Rylance, consisting of celebrity and other actors reciting testimony from both tribal peoples and their detractors.)

Of course, today there are hundreds, perhaps thousands, of websites dealing with indigenous and tribal issues, created both by indigenous peoples themselves, their supporters, and even their enemies! The biggest is that of Survival International which reaches millions of people in several languages and also incorporates many books and films.

I cite these not in an attempt to give 'further reading', but rather to point to some of the material that has shaped the public's perception of the peoples and the issues they face. Some texts crop up again and again in this context. One of the most famous of all is an 1854 address by a Duwamish Indian leader, commonly called Chief Seattle, who came from what is now Washington State. The speech was originally given in his own language and after some years, and much translation, printed in English. No one knows how faithful this is to what was originally said. It has been amended and added to over the years, including being entirely rewritten for use in a film in the 1970s. Unhelpfully, it is usually the last version which is quoted in most books and articles. Interestingly, it makes substantially different points from the original.

For example, the earliest version 'sanctifies' the natural world only in the context of human interaction: verdant valleys are hallowed by the Indian feet that walk there; murmuring rivers by the bodies that swim in them. They are not, in themselves, 'sacred' without this human presence. There is also little sense of man's 'brotherhood' with nature, as is suggested in the later, film script, version. The original is better left unadulterated and includes some beautiful and surprising imagery. An extract seems a good way to conclude this chapter.

Our dead never forget this beautiful world that gave them being. They still love its verdant valleys, its murmuring rivers, its magnificent mountains, sequestered vales and verdant lined lakes and bays, and ever yearn in tender fond affection over the lonely hearted living, and often return from the happy hunting ground to visit, guide, console, and comfort them... Every part of this soil is sacred... Every hillside, every valley, every plain and grove, has been hallowed by some sad or happy event in days long vanished. Even the rocks, which seem to be dumb and dead as they swelter in the sun along the silent shore, thrill with memories of stirring events connected with the lives of my people, and the very dust upon which you now stand responds more lovingly to their footsteps than yours, because it is rich with the blood of our ancestors, and our bare feet are conscious of the sympathetic touch. Our departed braves, fond mothers, glad, happy hearted maidens, and even the little children who lived here and rejoiced here for a brief season, will love these sombre solitudes and at eventide they greet shadowy returning spirits.

Chief Seattle

Seattle's lyricism seems to foresee the end of his people. He was largely right of course: most Duwamish were destroyed as settlers took over their land, including where the city bearing his name now stands. Not all disappeared however, and some Duwamish recently opened a new cultural centre, housed in the first longhouse they have built for generations.

The Indian wars of the nineteenth century United States are long since ended, but many indigenous and tribal peoples today are fighting back in different ways. They are articulating their own demands, which are relatively straightforward and very similar all over the world.

What on earth do they want?

If we lose all the things the forest gives us, we will die.

Penan, Malaysia

Land

The small sector of tribal peoples who have little or no contact with outsiders have their own idea about what is correct behaviour, but are unlikely to have any concept of what we call human rights. Obviously, they do not understand notions of exchanging things for money or being paid for work or resources either. These are all things other societies invented to cope with large numbers of people, and they remain alien to those who have escaped their domination.

If no one can talk to them, how can anyone know what they actually want? No one can of course, but it is a fair bet that they want to survive, and to do that requires one thing above all – their land. There is unanimous agreement that this is the most important thing that all tribal and indigenous peoples want and need, whatever their degree of contact with outsiders.

I have already touched on the two other things that push even land theft into the shade: slavery and lethal physical violence. However, most peoples nowadays do not face such extreme threats and so always put land first. As we have seen, the fact that both international law and the United Nations recognize indigenous land ownership rights does not prevent governments and companies, and others too, trying to invade and take their territory all over the world.

Before looking at other needs, it is necessary to deal with a couple of important points. No sensible indigenous person has ever claimed, apart from jokingly, that their rights should extend to the removal of European descendants from the Americas, Australia and similarly colonized places: that would be nonsensical. They ask for those parts of their territories which provide their livelihoods and, particularly in Australia, for their sacred sites as well. In some places, they also seek some form of compensation for land which was taken by force.

Measured against population density their lands might appear relatively large, at least for self-sufficient tribes. Indeed, a common refrain from the opponents of indigenous peoples is, 'Why do they need so much land for so few people?' The answer is not only that a sustainable hunting or herding way of life needs a larger area than is practicable for short-term farming, but also that too small areas of some ecosystems, such as rainforests, cannot survive at all on their own: rainforests create their own microclimates and regenerate from their own rotting vegetation, and so need to cover a significant area. A small patch left standing like an island in a sea of pastureland will dry out and die. It is also the case that game animals need quite a large area to get their own food, so species density is low in such places (meaning that there are only a few wild pigs or monkeys in any block of forest).

Contrary to appearances, most of the world's largest rainforest, Amazonia, grows largely on poor soil. Once felled, the land produces for only a few years before turning into low-quality grassland. In brief, indigenous peoples need a largish area of their land because without it they cannot survive.

Resources

Some care must be taken over the definition of 'land'. Some indigenous people prefer using 'territory', believing that it has a wider meaning, and includes rivers, lakes, seashores and offshore fishing rights, as well as iced areas in the north. Whether one speaks of land or territory however, there is a general consensus that this also includes rights to surface resources, including forests, pastures and, of course, game and fish.

Digging under the ground presents a trickier problem. No countries automatically grant subsoil rights to landowners, whether indigenous or not. Some do recognize that if an indigenous people has long used such resources, they have the right to continue doing so, but it remains true that no one – indigenous or not – has an unqualified right to mine or dig up anything which lies underground, even on their own land.

In practice, indigenous peoples' priority is usually not to exploit such resources themselves, but to protect their land from damaging mining from outside. Often this means trying to prevent it altogether (and then confronting the ire of companies who may stop at little to get their way), though some peoples are willing to negotiate with the company or authority concerned. Those that do tend to look for certain safeguards: limits on the damage; rehabilitation plans for when the mines are exhausted; a sensible recompense, usually royalties; and assurances of paid jobs. Unfortunately, even when such agreements are secured, the indigenous people often ends up with little but the promises and a handful of fairly useless community projects: these are cheap for the company but can make convincing propaganda for shareholders and the press.

Financial compensation sometimes causes divisions between those indigenous individuals who seek money and jobs, and those who do not want the interference from outside. All too often, short-term gains can tempt people away from considering their own long-term survival, and tribal people are not immune to this. This is a real problem, which is becoming more acute as resource extraction reaches into remoter territories where the affected peoples have little experience on which to base far-reaching decisions.

The same applies to some surface wealth, usually timber or other forest or vegetable products (materials which are normally mined, including diamonds and gold, can also be found on the surface in some places). In rare cases, these may be sold off by indigenous leaders, who are not all averse to trading the future of their people for a fast buck. It is not only Westerners who are good at justifying their greed.

As well as resources beneath the surface, an additional problem in a few places is who has rights to the space above indigenous lands. Nation states claim all airspace as theirs, but, for example, low-level warplane manoeuvres are severely disrupting the Innu Indians of Canada. Their problem is far worse than that facing residents near a busy commercial airport: jet fighters scream overhead only a few dozen metres above ground, seriously traumatizing people as well as the game which the Innu still try to hunt.

'Intellectual property'

In recent years, pharmaceutical companies have begun to market a component of a southern African cactus-like plant called 'hoodia'. Certain Bushmen use this as an appetite suppressant and mild stimulant, and this has prompted some Westerners to think it could be a useful ingredient in slimming products. Companies have paid royalties to some African organizations for the fact that the Bushmen originally discovered and used the plant, but so far it is not clear whom this has helped.

This leads to a complex issue about the extent to which peoples own their discoveries and should benefit from them: this is called 'intellectual property rights'. Although it has a long pedigree, much of it is a relatively new concept in Western law; it has taxed the finest legal brains and is likely to continue doing so. The fact that the remaining Bushmen should derive some benefit from the West's use of hoodia seems straightforward: the plant is marketed on a small scale, and there are relatively few people alive with a preponderant Bushman ancestry (though, in one way, everyone has a little!).

However, if living Bushmen eventually benefit from the world's use of hoodia, why should Andean Indians not do so from the world market in potatoes, and traditional poppy growers not gain from the legitimate sale of opium derivatives, such as morphine? Why should Central

American Indians not get a cut from the world market in maize, chocolate and tomatoes? No one has claimed they should, but such questions highlight problems in defining intellectual property and what rights should devolve from it. If anything, Andean Indians have a greater claim to a share of potato profits (a trade worth six billion dollars a year) than Bushmen do for hoodia: after all, the Indians actually created edible potatoes by selective cross breeding, whereas Bushmen are thought to have simply found hoodia growing wild.

Self-determination and respect

As well as their land, and a reasonable say in what happens on, below, and above it, what else are indigenous peoples asking for? The answer can largely be summed up as 'self-determination' – the right to decide about one's own future. This can perhaps best be epitomized in a single word: 'respect'. They want to be treated with decency, to be no longer despised as worthless and primitive. Indeed, in a way this could be said to be the only thing they really want, for their right to live on land occupied for thousands of years, in a way they choose themselves, is surely no more than simply a basic tenet of respect and natural justice.

Those in more intense contact with mainstream society want to be recognized for what they really are, the original inhabitants. They want their story to be taught as part of their country's history, and for it no longer to be censored out and ignored. They ask for an end to the denial of their existence and their significance. Australia did not start with Cook, nor the Americas with Columbus. Although everyone now knows this, the role of indigenous peoples remains peripheral in schools' curriculums, probably nowhere more so than in southern Africa, where the genocide of the Bushmen is barely acknowledged.

The same concept extends to how indigenous peoples are governed. They usually want to deal with crimes that occur within their societies in their own way and through their own law. This can be problematic, but is not as radical as it may sound, indeed their right to do so is recognized in the ILO Convention. It states: *To the extent compatible with the national legal system and internationally recognized human rights, the methods customarily practised by the peoples concerned for dealing with offences committed by their members shall be respected.* In other words, indigenous peoples do have the right to deal with criminals internally, so long as this does not contradict national law or human rights.

The ILO Convention also includes a formula for situations where an indigenous person finds herself before an ordinary ('non-indigenous') court. It states: *The customs of these peoples in regard to penal matters shall be taken into consideration.* It is easy to understand how complicated it can be to apply this in real life. For example, a common problem in some areas concerns marriageable age. Western laws and public opinion about the minimum age permitted for consensual sexual relations have changed a lot over the last hundred years. It used to be around puberty. Shakespeare's fictional Juliet was just thirteen years old when she married Romeo, as was the real mother of England's Henry VII when the future king was born. Sexual relations at that age are still legally allowed in Spain and some other countries today (the age of consent is even lower in Vatican City, where it remains at twelve, though no children actually reside there). In Australia, an Aboriginal girl might be expected to marry at around fourteen or fifteen, but the minimum legal age in some states is now sixteen.

Should an Aboriginal man who marries a fifteen-year-old girl, with her full consent, fairly obtained, be charged with rape even though the couple are complying with normal Aboriginal practice? There are no simple answers, and governments are understandably reluctant to accept a separate legal system within their country. Nevertheless, in both Australia and New Zealand some aspects of indigenous law have gained some formal recognition by mainstream courts.

The idea of respect also applies to the two big shibboleths of development – education and health. I have already explained that indigenous peoples want schooling – which should include lessons for adults in some places – that is appropriate to their needs, rather than dictated by outside teachers imposing an alien and pointless curriculum. Interestingly, and completely contrary to some liberal Western sentiment, tribal peoples do not always want their children taught about their own background in school. Some tribal parents think they can do that better themselves: they want their children primarily to go to school to learn the new knowledge and skills needed to interact with national society. They want their schools staffed with their own teachers, not because they seek an apartheid-style separation from others, but because they know just how much damage outsiders can do. Similarly with health care, they want their own health workers and nurses for the same reason. They look for basic medicine and hygiene to be taught by their own people because others usually treat them badly.

Not surprisingly, indigenous and tribal people who have commercial dealings with the outside world want a fair price for their goods and labour, even if they, themselves, are not strong at keeping records and doing figures.

Most of these issues are best managed by their own indigenous organizations. These have been formed in all continents over the last few decades as I have described in the chapters on specific continents. There are literally thousands of organizations in the United States, as there are in Canada – from the countrywide Assembly of First Nations, down to small local groups. South American indigenous organizations are also strong, especially in Colombia, Ecuador and Peru. Outside the Americas, indigenous peoples have perhaps not embraced the organizational model quite as enthusiastically, though in Bangladesh and the Philippines they are fairly strong. Where organizations are genuinely run by the people themselves – and it is worth remembering that many are not, including some which claim to be – indigenous peoples want them to be recognized and supported.

In spite of the many difficulties they face, there is no doubt that indigenous peoples' own organizations have greatly improved the situation for their peoples over the last generation and have directly led to many people successfully reclaiming an enormous amount of pride and control over their own lives.

Indigenous peoples want to be recognized for who and what they really are. Their self-image is as important to them as it is to everyone: they identify primarily as Innu, not just as Canadians, as Yanomami, not just as Brazilians. If this were not the case, they would probably have long ceased to exist as definable peoples.

Although I have tried to avoid the term 'culture', for reasons already explained, it is important to cite it here as one of the aspects indigenous peoples want respected. Broadly, what they mean by this is that they want to decide themselves what their values are and how best to try and realize them from birth to death. That is what culture really means: it is the way people understand and try to control their lives, including their environments and histories. It is the way they give sense and reality to what they think is important, to their relations with one another. In brief, it is who they think they really are.

When indigenous people seek 'cultural autonomy', or to 'keep their culture', it does not mean they want to preserve an unchanged past. This idea is eloquently expressed by a Manitoba leader from Canada.

Our struggle will be over when we have, in our own way, found our place among the many peoples of the earth. And when that time comes, we will still be a people identifiable and independent and proud... Your culture is not the culture of your ancestors of one or five hundred years ago. Nor is ours. Our culture is creative. We are developing a twenty-first century culture. And it is and will be an Indian culture.

David Courchene

Some thinkers propose that the best future for humankind would be to have common goals, which include a unity and cohesiveness leading not only to equality, but also to an eradication of the differences between peoples. This can look like a reasonable, even laudable, proposition, but there are many problems with it: the most important being that it is always the minority which is required to fit in with the majority. This is of course a step which all too easily leads towards fascism.

Governments can use the concept of 'equality' as a deception, in an attempt better to control or exploit people by trying to convince them to identify with the state, rather with their own specific people. This can turn the notion of 'equality' on its head, and produce injustices just like South African apartheid or Nazi-style ghettoes. In practice, both the enforced separation of minorities from the mainstream as well as an obligatory identification with the majority, are two sides of the same coin: they are political tools to create subjugation, but neither can endure for long if ordinary citizens insist on treating minorities with the same respect they expect for themselves.

Indigenous peoples are quite right to want, indeed to demand, the respect of their fellow citizens, for in the long run it is the only thing that can save them. Amongst the most powerful expressions of this was given in 1886 by an Indian leader of the American Northwest Coast.

We will dance when our laws command us to dance, and we will feast when our hearts desire to feast. Do we ask the white man, 'Do as the Indian does?' It is a strict law that bids us dance. It is a strict law that bids us distribute our property among our friends and neighbours. It is a good law. Let the white man observe his law; we shall observe ours. And now, if you come to forbid us dance, be gone. If not, you will be welcome to us.

O'waxalagalis

Of course the 'white man', however unwelcome, did not leave the Northwest Coast to the Indians. Are the demands of indigenous peoples today likely to fare any better? Before concluding this guide, I look at the main points used to argue for their support, both by themselves and others.

Should they have it?

Our wisdom is not useless. It is the wisdom of the Earth, which is very important for the survival of humanity.

Davi Kopenawa, Yanomami, Brazil

Arguments for supporting tribal and indigenous peoples are broadly divisible into two camps: firstly, the idea that they can help the rest of the world, so harming them risks damaging everyone; and secondly, the anti-racist and anti-colonialist view which holds that, as a matter of ethics and principle, the rights of vulnerable minorities should not be trampled on.

Until fairly recently, the first view was often considered revolutionary, even cranky, but it is now becoming more accepted in mainstream thinking. For example, UNICEF, an organization not normally noted for its radical views, made this pronouncement in 2011: *Over generations, indigenous peoples have developed highly specialized knowledge, livelihood strategies, occupations and cultures, which are closely linked to lands, territories and natural resources. In the context of today's crisis, indigenous knowledge is critical to the search for new solutions, which link human development, human rights, peace and environmental sustainability. Indigenous peoples are in a unique position to contribute to addressing the most pressing environmental and social challenges of our time.*

Who knows what?

This somewhat 'selfish' reason for supporting indigenous peoples requires more detailed explanation. It is frequently cited that they have some unique knowledge from which we could all benefit, particularly concerning the environment. This is undoubtedly true, and it is easy to point to important drugs which have reached the West through research on tribal plant use. I have described how muscle relaxants, derived from Amazonian arrow-poison, revolutionized surgery in the 1940s. Quinine from cinchona bark, discovered by Andean Indians, is also extremely important and has been used to treat malaria in Europe since the seventeenth century. Opiates, which were known to ancient European tribes, are still used as important painkillers. Indigenous peoples from several places were aware of the antibacterial properties of fungi centuries before the West isolated penicillin.

There is no doubt that there is a vast repository of plant use which remains unstudied by scientists; this includes thousands of species used in ways still known only to particular tribes. It is likely that further important medicines remain to be found, which may otherwise be lost if tribes are destroyed, and it is often correctly pointed out that their knowledge has taken centuries to accumulate, and that destroying them is akin to burning libraries of unique books. Tribal people have built up extremely detailed observations of the natural world; they have passed on and refined them for hundreds of generations, and this simply cannot be replicated in a few years research, however computerized it may be.

We have also seen how three of the world's biggest food staples – potatoes, maize, and manioc – which now sustain an enormous swathe of humankind, were unknown outside the Americas until the sixteenth century. They have now saved millions of poor people from starvation throughout the world. It is unlikely that further discoveries of such a revolutionary and far-reaching nature will be made, but important tribal knowledge, for example of how insects interact with plants, or how deliberate plant modifications can produce disease-resistance, remain possible: the yield and nutritional value of our foods may be enhanced by further study of indigenous plant use, and one day this may prove crucial for us all.

Indigenous people's experience and thoughts, as everywhere, is expressed in complex language. As thousands of these languages head rapidly towards extinction, so the millennia of knowledge they codified also stands to be lost forever. Some believe this is the most serious extinction now facing the world.

Another clear benefit of not destroying indigenous peoples is to preserve their role as conservationists. Some extremists who do not want people inside conservation zones reject this idea, and they may have a point: not all indigenous peoples are automatically good at managing their resources. For example, it was thought that the Polynesians who landed in Rapa Nui (Easter Island), about fifteen hundred or a thousand years ago, deforested their island so much that it became virtually uninhabitable (though this is contested). But the history of Greenland, where Inuit survived as the weather grew colder, whilst Viking settlers died out or left, is more indicative of indigenous peoples' advanced abilities to adapt.

A few anthropologists once claimed that if Amazon Indians had chainsaws they would cut their forests down as quickly as anyone, but this has now been proved wrong:

satellite imagery shows that tropical forest is best preserved when it is under indigenous management. Forest destruction, whether in Amazonia, Southeast Asia or Central Africa, is not only harmful locally, polluting rivers and killing animal life, but is also seen as an important catalyst of climate change.

The climate agenda is now pushing the West to look for quick, often expensive, fixes to deforestation. Many do not work. This is especially unfortunate, as the proven solution – ensuring indigenous peoples control as much land as possible – is also by far the most economical. Cynics even argue that its cheapness is precisely why it is not more widely adopted: it is ignored because it neither feeds money to those in the new climate industry, nor provides more cash to governments in tropical countries.

There are other areas where mainstream societies might benefit from tribal knowledge. For example, a generation ago notions of childrearing were influenced by the way some indigenous people maintain bodily contact with their babies much longer than is the norm elsewhere. This may well lead to increased security and confidence for the child, though it is not always practical for many Western parents, and the initial enthusiasm which greeted the idea in the post-hippy 1970s has largely waned.

On the other hand, what *is* gaining momentum in the industrialized West, is the realization that living in a mutually-supportive community is one of the most important factors affecting people's sense of wellbeing and fulfilment, as well as significantly reducing crime. The results of several recent polls indicate that the widespread demise of community life is viewed as increasingly worrying to the general public, and is amongst the most important of all social problems.

There is no doubt that tribal notions valuing reciprocity and sharing are very good for our species as a whole: they are probably the key reasons why it has survived at all, and have much to recommend them over and above any fervour for personal aggrandizement and accumulation. The latter seem increasingly to characterize an industrialized world in which notions of service and self-sacrifice are seen as pointless and old-fashioned.

It is difficult to see this trend continuing without it leading to yet more fragmentation of communities, which are, as tribal peoples remind us, the natural condition for human life. Who knows where this might lead? Already ideas of 'virtual communities' and 'virtual reality' are gaining ground, despite them being only pretend communities and pretend reality. They are undoubtedly valuable tools for some people and in some situations, but surely they can never replace the real thing.

Examining how different tribal societies organize themselves and arrive at decisions, such as the evident lack of leadership prevalent in small communities, can be informing about what aspects of human life are 'hard-wired' into us all, and what derive just from local culture. On close examination, a great deal of what the West thinks is intrinsic to human nature turns out to be simply a result of social conditioning. Had anthropology followed a different path in the twentieth century, perhaps the widespread recognition of this fact could have been its great contribution to the world. As it is, this theory still remains largely in the realm of academia. On the other hand, views that humankind is endlessly striving for 'progress' remain common, perhaps even more so than a generation ago, and the fact that the idea has roots which are both shallow and recent is rarely acknowledged.

In fact, the term, 'Western civilization', needs unpicking. Contrary to what we are taught – Ancient Greek, to Roman, to Renaissance, to Industrial Revolution, and so on – the concept is neither historically linear, nor geographically specific. 'Progress' did not start in 'the West' a few millennia ago, and did not walk steadily forward to the 'modern world'. Consider for example, a contemporary Cretan peasant, whose ancestors built Europe's earliest known 'high civilization' four thousand years ago. Nowadays, he may be closer in technological lifestyle to a modern New Guinea tribesman than either are to a Japanese businessman or Russian oligarch, and who is to judge any of them 'backward'?

Far from being an essential desire of all humanity, what we call 'progress' was born largely from the industrial revolution and colonialism. There are even some who think it has already grown old alongside weary notions of capitalism and communism which have repeatedly failed. All might now be better discarded.

A view which is as theoretical as 'progress', but perhaps of more real substance, derives from the observation that indigenous peoples form the largest sector by far in humankind's diversity and that is, of itself, potentially invaluable for everyone's future in an uncertain world. After all, those who are least affected by the energy crisis are those who need no oil or electricity. The people least threatened by food shortages are those who provide their own. Those who contribute least to any climate change are those who leave little or no 'carbon footprint'. They may also be the most adaptable to changing weather patterns, having experienced them so many times without the benefit of electricity. It is even possible (admittedly, only remotely) that they might escape largely intact from any future worldwide deadly contagion, avoiding infection simply by living distant from cities, or because their different genes provide some unique protection. Who knows? Indigenous people escaping such a nightmare scenario would be paradoxical of course, considering how many have died from imported diseases.

In brief, there is little disadvantage and surely much to be gained from having peoples in the world who have thrived for thousands of generations relying solely on their own resources, and at no one else's expense.

Personally, I believe that the growing gap between an increasingly homogenous – essentially state-controlled and profit-driven – twenty-first century Western existence, and the diverse ways of living practised by tribal peoples, which have served human beings well for so long, reveals the main thing to be gained from them. It is to do with relearning something once obvious to everyone: 'value' and 'price' are not the same; not everything which is valuable is a commodity carrying a price tag.

Tribal peoples retain a vital sense of who we are in relationship to others, the community, and the animals, plants and Earth which surround us. What really is our place in this web? The answer to that may remain elusive, and belong largely in the realms of philosophy and perhaps religion, but even partial and debatable responses can bring their own restoration and healing. A serpent may not really have thrown up the hills and sacred sites of Aboriginals, the moon may not really have bled from an Amazonian arrowshot, the voices heard by dancing Bushmen may not really be those of the ancestors (though in one way, of course, they are – we all carry our ancestors inside us), but such beliefs are really no odder than many held by industrialized peoples. They provide a context and relationship between a people, their environment, and their time, in a way which seems to be naturally fulfilling and wholesome for human beings.

On the other side of the fence, even the faintest glimmers of a natural world are fast disappearing in our dangerous and expanding city slums. That is easy to understand: 'nature' is bound to be shunned in the extreme poor's fight to make a mark in an apparently harsh and selfish world, and in their struggle not to go under. Some anthropologists used to call tribal people's lives, 'nasty, brutish and short', but surely the description resonates more truthfully in the shantytowns of Rio, Nairobi or Mumbai, than in the Amazon, Kalahari or Andaman Islands.

During the time I spent writing this book, the proportion of the planet's population living in cities tipped into a majority for the first time in history. Most people now live in large, often huge, urban conglomerations. This is a new and disturbing evolution which makes all these issues especially urgent and important. Industrialization may have solved many problems faced by humankind, but it also undoubtedly created many others.

Opponents of rights for tribal peoples often assert that it would be impossible nowadays for everyone to live as tribes do – there simply is not enough land. They are right of course, but it is an absurd and empty argument, partly because no sensible person claims that we all should live like this and, at the other end of the spectrum, not everyone can live as the wealthy in the industrialized West do either – there are simply not enough finite resources. Only extremists, however, would suggest that cars, fridges, and overflowing supermarkets be confiscated, like tribal lands, for the good of all.

Old-fashioned romantics?

Many will remain unmoved by these arguments, and will see all this as meaninglessly romantic. Why 'romantic'? Can the anti-apartheid, anti-slavery, or anti-colonialism movements be characterized as 'romantic'? Is it 'romantic' to expose crimes, or seek to bring criminals to justice? Or, if might really *is* right, then is there any meaning at all in 'civilization'? Are ideas about the rule of law and fundamental human rights nothing more than empty conceits to make everyone feel better about the *status quo*? (After all, the phrase, 'human rights', is now being watered down to mean almost anything people think they deserve.)

If everyone had a choice – most do not, of course – between living in the computer age, or creating a rather less technology-dependent, but more fulfilled, life for everyone, many might well opt for the latter. This applies especially to the growing sector amongst us who are alienated, hurt or disturbed, or just cripplingly poor and hungry, and who find no solace whatsoever in our wondrous inventions. Perhaps the muddled romantic and old-fashioned view is not that we might learn from tribes, but rather the idea that 'progress' is a panacea for the growing ills of humankind. Surely, this has been disproven so often that no objective student of history could possibly still give it further credence.

This leads to further consideration of the other assertion in support of tribal peoples, based not on what we might gain, but simply on the morality, justice and law that the industrialized – so-called democratic – nations claim to uphold.

Fundamental rights

There are plenty of people who believe that it is natural, perhaps even inevitable, that vulnerable minorities should give way to more powerful majorities. Put simply, this is tantamount to admitting they disagree with human rights and justice. Following this premise, the mugger making away with an old lady's handbag is justified, and the full-scale invasion of a weak country by a powerful one is in the natural order of things. Likewise, if slavery can support the economies of entire nations, making them once Great (as in Britain), and giving their citizens enormous and enduring advantages, then where is the problem in that? Is it simply 'natural' – just a basic Darwinian law – that those who are stronger should be justified in taking what they like from those who lack the strength to prevent them?

As we have seen, those who want to remove tribal peoples from their lands in order to exploit their resources invariably validate their actions by claiming that these riches are needed by others who are poor or more numerous. Why, for example, should a mineral resource under tribal land not be exploited to help the majority? In reality, those who benefit most are not the needy and the poor, but the directors and shareholders of multinational corporations, development banks and senior government officials. Such arguments are little different from those used to support colonialism, communism or fascism: one group takes what belongs to another, with the excuse that they need, or deserve, it more.

This position admittedly has its own rationality, though it is surely hypocritical to claim it can be held in conjunction with a belief in any law, or in fundamental human rights in general. If governments and corporations actually believed in the rights and laws they write and repeatedly profess, they could not possibly treat indigenous and tribal peoples in the way they do in real life.

The fact that logical arguments, both practical and moral, can be advanced in support of tribal peoples does not of course mean that those who hold an opposing view will be persuaded. I have no illusions that this book will change the attitude of anyone who is convinced of the superiority of an industrialized way of life – or people – over a tribal one. I hope, however, that I have articulated some points which might prove helpful to a growing defence of tribal peoples. I conclude this book with a plea for action, as well as debate.

Conclusion

We recognize that the fight is a long one and that we cannot hope to win it alone. To win, to secure the future, we must join hands with like-minded people and create a strength through unity.

Haudenosaunee, USA

Clashes between indigenous and tribal peoples and their supporters, and those who do not want them around – whether they are governments, extractive industries, conservation zealots, or religious extremists – are not going away; on the contrary, they are becoming more heated and less avoidable.

The battle lines are growing to be as well defined as they were during the colonial era, when Europeans simply wrested tribal land for themselves. The increasing acceptance of multiculturalism, anti-racism, and minority rights occupy one side of the divide; on the other, lie the nationalist and xenophobic backlash that these can provoke. Both sides are infected to some extent with an unquestioned pursuit of profit at any human cost. A new element in this conflict is a growing suspicion that 'civilization', however 'advanced' it becomes, simply might not provide all the answers for a fulfilled life. These are questions which will affect everyone in one way or other.

The attitude of the public towards these issues will play a central role in their future evolution. If the public's perception of tribal peoples is transformed, the way tribes are treated will quickly change. A widespread belief that such peoples are doomed and finished, or its opposite, that they have a right to be here and can play a valuable role for tomorrow's world, will both be self-fulfilling. Tribal peoples will survive if a significant proportion of the public wants them to, and makes their feelings felt. Similarly, such peoples will simply not make it if there is only a tiny movement in their support.

This has been the lesson of all major human rights advances and it applies equally to tribal peoples, however remote they appear from us. Their rights are violated by particular individuals in governments, the armed forces and corporations – people who are, more often than not, schooled in the industrialized West, and who are as subject to the pressures of public opinion as everyone else is. The solution is simple: if these men and women started respecting indigenous lands and peoples, most of the problems would evaporate. There is nothing paternalist in the assertion that tribes now desperately need mainstream society to confront its prejudices and change its views.

The theft of indigenous territory and resources is underpinned by a deeply ingrained prejudice: that such peoples are several rungs 'below' Westerners, or 'behind' them in time. It is even the case that many of those who are actually sympathetic to tribal peoples still view them as backward, fragile societies, left behind by the advanced civilizations which developed from the West's 'discovery' of agriculture. They are thought to be doomed to disappear under an inevitable march of 'progress' because they do not have the capacity to catch up with modernity quickly enough. However commonly accepted these views might be, not a single component in them is true.

The germ of this prejudice has been around for a long time, but it really blossomed with colonialism when it became both the foundation and the excuse for the theft and killing that fuelled European ascendancy. It was no coincidence that, at exactly the same time, Darwin's grasp of species evolution was also applied to human 'races' where it had no relevance at all. This led to the barbarism of not only thinking all other peoples were inferior, but of acting as if they were, with forced segregation or compulsory absorption, and in extreme cases with bombs and concentration camps.

Although many tribal peoples have made different choices to most in industrialized societies – preferring to be mobile rather than settled, opting for hunting or herding rather than agriculture, lacking the ambition to 'improve' by manipulating wealth, and so on – they are no more 'backward' than anyone else. If their lands are not stolen from under their feet, most are not particularly fragile either: they are just as capable of surviving and adapting to new circumstances as any of us.

What is more, a good deal of what we call modernity and 'progress' is simply the enrichment of some of the world's population at the expense of labour and materials taken from others. This is not an inevitable result of history: it is a crime to be measured alongside colonialism and genocide. Such 'progress' has undoubtedly led to healthier, more comfortable, and longer lives for some – but by no means all – in industrialized societies. There is also no doubt that it has enabled enduring and life-enriching genius to flourish in the myriad realms where industrialization excels – though the argument is gaining momentum that, at the same time, it has bred a shallow, albeit insatiable, appetite for ephemeral goods and experiences of little or no real worth, except to those selling them. Despite the undoubted advantages it has brought for some, after a point such 'progress' does not seem to be accompanied, even for them, by any increase in life satisfaction. Surveys designed to measure 'happiness', as well as a huge amount of observation, show beyond doubt that those who live with little 'modernity' are just as capable of living fulfilled lives as the world's richest.

The developed world's achievements surely grew as much out of seeing the advantages in caring for each other, as they did from any hunger to control the weak and take over the world. Those who think that the most fulfilling aspect of life is humanity itself – our thoughtfulness and desire to help each other, our liberty and fraternity – have little difficulty seeing the mistake of emphasizing complex technology above everything else. Our species has not endured through believing in might above all, and there is no sensible reason to suppose it would survive into the distant future if it adopted such an idea universally.

In cases where such a barren philosophy has taken hold, it is a precursor to widespread suffering and eventual social disintegration. History bears this out: wherever the ideology that only a single way of living is correct has prevailed, it has eventually led to the tyranny and suppression that inevitably accompany extreme state control. If the belief continues to flourish worldwide that only 'Western progress' will work, it is likely to lead in the same direction; not only will tribal and indigenous minorities continue to suffer and disappear, but others too will continue paying a high price.

Irrespective of whether or not the self-satisfaction of industrial civilization is deserved, or whether or not its wealth is earned fairly, it clearly does not even work for all of its participants. Crippling poverty can be found just as easily in the industrialized, as the 'developing', world. Many will have seen the homeless in both, hands outstretched in countless cities, hunched at the gates of apartment blocks and offices, and kept well away from the profit-makers by hired heavies brandishing batons and guns.

No one, and no political theory, has so far succeeded in any meaningful way in solving the problems which arise from this, nor figured out how to relieve significantly the suffering caused. This is a far more intractable problem than those faced by tribal peoples, though it is certainly part of the dilemma faced by the wider category of indigenous peoples, particularly those in richer countries such as Australia and North America.

Those who insist that tribal peoples today are 'primitive' or 'Stone Age' are, however unwittingly, shoring up the ideology behind the crimes committed against them; they are helping to prolong the *status quo*. They are also adhering to a philosophy – of eternal 'progress' – that is itself profoundly archaic. When the industrialized world leaves all this behind, and realizes that the acceptance of tribal ways of life does not threaten its own but actually serves to enhance it, then indigenous peoples will not only survive but flourish – at least as well as anyone – into the future.

This does not imply an endorsement of cruel or barbaric practises, whether tribal or industrialized, neither has it anything to do with 'romanticism', 'keeping people as they are', or 'preserving cultures'. Rather, it is a matter of being honest about history, seeking to alleviate the suffering of others, upholding the fundamental principles of justice we claim to hold dear, and accepting that the diversity of humankind, with the knowledge it can bring, is valuable for all.

We must remember in all this that the problems faced by indigenous and tribal peoples will never be solved permanently and completely: whatever the future may bring, there is no reason to believe that the powerful will ever cease posing a threat to the powerless. This is just realism, and it implies that all who care about these crimes ought to say so openly if they want things to change.

If human rights are ever to mean anything more than a rhetorical list of good intentions, then voices – and hands too – will always need to be raised in support of those who are physically weaker – including tribal and indigenous peoples. Oppression continues until the public stands with the oppressed; then it begins to fade.

We all have to make decisions about how we react to the world as we find it. Some – especially those who can – will try and move it a step closer to being the place we would really like to live in and leave behind us. Just as many tribal peoples believe they perpetually re-create the world through their rituals and myths, so we need to be constantly striving for the genesis of an era when suffering is limited to natural – rather than manmade – causes. If these tribal peoples abandon their rituals, they think the globe will be engulfed in pain and chaos; if we stop fighting for justice for minorities, if we simply allow majority rule to prevail unchecked, then – inevitably – it will be.

These are not marginal or even minority issues. Over the next generation they will dictate the kind of world forged by the twenty-first century, which is of course the only thing our descendants – from the still uncontacted Amazon Indian to the billionaire oligarch – will ever stand to inherit.

About the author

Stephen Corry was born in Malaysia in 1951. He won a scholarship to Gresham's School, England, where he excelled in rifle shooting, leaving school at the age of sixteen. In the early 1970s, influenced by travel, European and Asian religions, and listening to Jiddu Krishnamurti and Dwarko Sundrani, he quit the Université de Paris, Jussieu, and volunteered with Survival International. He spent some years visiting tribal peoples in South America, Africa and India. He was asked to become Survival's director in 1984, and led the team which took the not-for-profit from near bankruptcy to becoming the world's principal organization working successfully for tribal peoples' rights. He was the chairman of Free Tibet for many years and remains on its board. He is a climber and ski-tourer. He lives in England's West Country, is married, and has three daughters.